A Theory of Multinational Enterprise

A Theory of
Multinational
Enterprise

Jean-François Hennart

ANN ARBOR THE UNIVERSITY OF MICHIGAN PRESS

338.8
H515t

Published in the United States of America by
The University of Michigan Press and simultaneously
in Rexdale, Canada, by John Wiley & Sons Canada, Limited
Manufactured in the United States of America

1985   1984   1983   1982   4   3   2   1

Library of Congress Cataloging in Publication Data

Hennart, Jean-François, 1947–
    A theory of multinational enterprise.

    Bibliography: p.   85-5707
    Includes index.
    1.   International business enterprises.
I.   Title.
HD2755.5.H46   1982   338.8'8   81-24125
ISBN 0-472-10017-3   AACR2

To Sondra

Preface

What accounts for the fantastic development of multinational corporations since 1945? Why is this phenomenon, previously almost exclusively American, becoming more and more international as Japanese and European multinationals set up subsidiaries on American soil? Is the growth of multinational firms likely to slow down or will it instead accelerate? Policymakers have been turning to economists for answers to these questions, but they have been disappointed: economists have not had an established theory of the multinational firm, and therefore have been unable to explain or predict the development of this new economic institution.

I became increasingly aware of this situation when I started to sift through the literature on foreign direct investment. The ad hoc quality of what had been written on the subject was evident. The further I read, the more I became persuaded that to explain the multinational firm one had first to understand the very nature of the business firm. The conventional wisdom has ascribed foreign direct investment to the internationalization of the world economy; yet the crucial question seems to be not why the firm was selling in foreign markets, but rather why it was choosing to extend its operations overseas, rather than export or license its products. Why was coordination achieved by hierarchical methods in some cases, by market prices and market contracts in others? More than forty years ago, Ronald Coase had attempted to answer that question. He argued that the raison d'être of the firm was its ability to organize some activities more efficiently than market prices, but the relevance of his work to the multinational firm was not fully recognized.

To see why firms had a comparative advantage over markets in organizing some transactions, I started to analyze the nature of the costs involved in market transactions and in hierarchical exchange, and the factors that influenced them. My conviction that I was on the right track was reinforced when I came across a short article in a little-known Canadian anthology. Its author, John McManus, showed how this approach could explain some of the puzzling features of foreign direct investment, such as its uneven distribution across industries, or the investors' insistence on complete control of their subsidiaries. McManus's perceptive analysis provides a firm basis on which to develop a theory of the multinational firm; but, perhaps because of the limited diffusion of his work, his contribution has been largely ignored.

As I started to build a comprehensive theory of the multinational firm on McManus's intuitions, exploring in detail its main implications and testing them with the available empirical evidence, the power and generality of the theory became more and more evident. Here was a theory that provided a sound foundation on which to base policies intended to deal with many of the controversial issues raised by multinational production. In 1977, I presented an early version of the theory in my Ph.D. dissertation defended at the University of Maryland. I found out shortly afterward that others were working along similar avenues of research. Two British economists, Peter J. Buckley and Mark Casson, apparently unaware of McManus's work, had independently developed, in a book entitled *The Future of the Multinational Enterprise,* an analysis that offers some striking parallels to my own. After so many years of false starts, the seeds planted by Coase have eventually begun to germinate. As the very existence of multinational firms is more and more frequently called into question, and the need to understand the role and function of the international corporation widely felt, an increasing number of scholars are beginning to realize that the approach described in the following pages offers a general explanation of the multinational corporation that allows us to understand its characteristics and to predict its development.

I am especially indebted to Mancur Olson for his continued support and for his invaluable comments and criticisms throughout the long time it took me to produce this work. Whatever merit this study has owes much to his incisive critique. Christopher Clague read some of the successive drafts and made many helpful suggestions. Stimulating criticisms were also received from Robin Marris, John McManus, Russell Hardin, and Craig West. At every stage of the writing I derived much benefit from frequent discussions with Penny Davis. I have also profited from useful comments from Ingo Walter and the members of the Workshop in International Business at New York University Graduate School of Business Administration, and from Michael Pelcovits and his students at the University of Maryland. R. A. Cornell, at the International Trade Commission; Augustin Mandeng, at the United Nations; Patricia Walker, at the Bureau of Economic Analysis; and Patricia Gradis provided me with data. But most of all I have had the constant support and encouragement of my wife, Sondra. Besides helping in countless ways, she read the successive manuscripts and mercilessly pointed out flaws in logic or in style. In this long process, much was demanded of her, and much was given. To her I am deeply grateful.

Contents

Tables

CHAPTER 1

Economic Theories of Multinational Enterprise

When a Minnesota farmer buys a tractor from his Ford Motor Company dealer, he probably does not know that its transmission was built by the firm's Belgian employees and its engine cast in Ford's English plant. His Canadian neighbor is probably no more aware that the Massey-Ferguson Industries Ltd. tractor he owns was assembled in the United States with engines shipped from Massey-Ferguson's English subsidiary, transmissions from its French facility, and axles from its Mexican affiliate. To laymen reasonably well informed about recent business trends, there is nothing unique or unusual about these facts; yet to an economist developments like these are puzzling. Of course, the economist expects differences in relative factor endowments between countries to lead to trade and specialization; but he has been taught that exchange will take place between independent parties trading at arm's length on international markets, not between the managers of a firm's subsidiaries striving to implement directives received from headquarters. In the traditional economic model, international trade and specialization are achieved by autonomous traders reacting to market prices. In today's economy, a considerable part of international trade results from decisions by the managers of multinational firms regarding the location of their plants and the tasks allocated to their subsidiaries. The crucial difference between the model and reality is that a considerable volume of trade (perhaps one quarter to one third of the total world trade in manufactures) takes place within the firm and not on international markets. Yet it would seem that markets have a comparative advantage over firms in the coordination of internationally interdependent activities. The presence of separate political jurisdictions poses particular problems for a firm that wants to operate in more than one country. A nation is an area in which a central political power exercises its authority. As a result, economic policy decisions will be enforced equally within the state. Regional income

1

differences and returns to all factors of production will tend to be equalized. Tastes, languages, and currencies will tend to become one within the nation. Clear discontinuities in tastes, incomes, languages, customs, and standards will therefore appear at borders.

Since nation states transform the continuum of differences due to location into a limited number of relatively homogeneous units that differ substantially from one another, operation in a foreign country will usually entail higher costs, everything else being equal, than operation at home.

First, the presence of wider language differences between countries than within a country makes it generally more costly to communicate information internationally than intranationally. Because of the higher cost of transferring information across countries, native entrepreneurs will have an information advantage over their foreign rivals. The local entrepreneur naturally accumulates knowledge about the economic, social, legal, and cultural conditions of his country whereas foreigners must often spend substantial amounts of time and money to acquire the same body of information.[1]

Alien status is also a drawback because it exposes the firm to discriminatory measures by national governments. Discrimination takes various forms: in many countries the tradition of buying from domestic suppliers has been extended to exclude foreign-owned subsidiaries. Access to capital markets, export or import licenses, and special subsidy programs may also be denied to the foreign-owned firm. As Raymond Vernon has put it, "governments are gradually extending and solidifying the principle that local corporations, even though created by domestic law, have rights and privileges that are determined in considerable measure by the identity of their stockholders" (Vernon 1971, p. 244). Foreign firms are also more open than their domestic counterparts to the threat of expropriation or confiscation, and the ability of the parent to repatriate profits from the subsidiary may be seriously limited. Even when foreign subsidiaries are not subject to such discriminatory measures, the fear of attracting xenophobic responses may severely limit the alien firm's freedom of action. The foreign firm will hesitate to lay off workers, to lobby for preferential treatment, to cut prices, to augment profit margins, and so forth.

There are other reasons why operating in a foreign country is costly. One of the principal attributes of national sovereignty is the right to create money. Nation states usually have their own currencies, and the firm that establishes production facilities abroad will normally do business in more than one currency. Since the rate at which one currency is exchanged for another tends to vary over time, multinational firms are subject to exchange risk. For example, if a subsidiary borrows Swiss francs and converts the proceeds into local currency, but the Swiss franc appreciates while the loan is outstanding, the subsidiary will take a loss. A devaluation or a revaluation will also affect the value of the subsidiary's dividends in terms of the parent's currency. These risks are not borne by the firm's purely domestic counterparts.

Because economists are aware of the complex problems that face the foreign direct investor, they have tended to assume that whenever local production is necessary, it will be undertaken by domestic producers, while the interdependence between producers of different countries will be organized by international markets. Thus, while many of his academic colleagues seem to take the multinational corporation for granted, economists realize that multinational enterprises represent a costly method to achieve international trade and specialization.

It has often been argued, for example, that foreign direct investment arises from the desire of firms in capital-rich countries to transfer funds abroad to take advantage of international differences in the rate of return on capital.[2] But if capital can be profitably transferred to other countries, it does not follow that firms should necessarily be the chosen transfer medium. Instead of sending employees to foreign countries to investigate investment prospects, why not leave the control of capital to native entrepreneurs, who have a better knowledge of their country's resources and opportunities than foreigners? Why should firms, whose expertise is in domestic production and marketing, have to struggle with the intricacies of international finance, when international financial markets are specialized institutions that could presumably perform international capital transfers at lower cost? Indeed, up to World War I, most international capital movements were not effected by firms, but consisted in flows of portfolio investment. If foreign direct investment is primarily a movement of capital across national boundaries, how then do we explain the increased dominance of firms as vehicles for such transfers?

Foreign direct investment is also often presented as the method used by domestic firms to exploit their technological advantage in foreign countries. But since manufacture and sale abroad usually require adaptation to local production and market conditions, and since native entrepreneurs presumably possess this knowledge, how do we explain the fact that firms often incur the high fixed costs inherent in foreign operations when they can sell their know-how through licensing agreements? Contrary to what is sometimes as-

4 Multinational Enterprise

sumed, ownership of valuable knowledge by firms cannot be a sufficient condition for foreign direct investment; for if this was the case,
how would we explain the failure of the nineteenth-century British
firms responsible for the Industrial Revolution to exploit their technological lead through foreign direct investment?

One way to assess the validity of these two theories of foreign
direct investment is to look at its industrial structure. There are
great differences in the extent of foreign direct investment across
industries, but these differences do not seem related to an industry's capital intensity; and whereas many foreign subsidiaries are in
research-intensive industries, a substantial number are active in
sectors that are not particularly technologically advanced, such as
mining, farming, food product manufacturing, and distribution.
What factors determine this particular industrial pattern?

In the minds of many, multinational corporations are synony-
mous with large American firms. It is a fact that the majority of
multinational firms are based in the United States, and that the
United States owns a larger share of the world's stock of foreign
direct investment than of world production or exports. Could it be,
as Raymond Vernon has argued, that the specific characteristics of
the American market are responsible for the dominance of American corporations as foreign direct investors? But then how does one
explain the recent emergence of Western European and Japanese
multinationals?

Still another puzzling feature of multinational firms is the policies they have followed concerning the ownership of their subsidiaries. To defuse xenophobic pressures from host governments, a natural strategy would be to share the ownership of the subsidiary with
local citizens. Yet in spite of continuous pressure by host countries,
multinational firms have usually refused to sell even a minority of
their subsidiary's shares to local nationals. Indeed, they have in
some cases gone to great length to buy back the shares held in their
subsidiaries by minority shareholders. Should one assume, as Kindleberger does, that managers of multinational firms have an irrational preference for wholly owned subsidiaries? Or are there valid
reasons for such behavior?

In the following pages, we attempt to provide an answer to
these questions. Following McManus (1972), we consider international investments as one alternative to international markets in
coordinating internationally interdependent activities. We will try to
determine, by identifying the strengths and weaknesses of both
modes of organization and the factors that influence them, why
multinational firms have, in spite of the limitations we have just

discussed, an institutional advantage over markets in organizing certain types of international transactions. We will show how McManus's very general model of the comparative advantage of firms and markets as modes of organization explains the particular industrial structure of direct foreign investment, its historical pattern, its geographical distribution, and the observed differences in the ownership policies of multinational firms, features which, as we will now see, are not satisfactorily explained by all the other major theories of foreign direct investment.

Foreign Direct Investment as Capital Transfer

Until the 1960s, direct foreign investment was considered exclusively a form of international movement of capital. The traditional theory of international factor movements assumed that differences in the relative endowment of capital among countries caused differences in the marginal efficiency of capital, and therefore in the level of interest rates. This led to flows of both portfolio and direct investment capital from capital-rich to capital-poor countries.

The dramatic increase of American direct foreign investment in the postwar period led many economists to examine critically the basis for this viewpoint. Stephen Hymer (1976), for example, pointed out that in a world of perfect competition for goods and factors, it was difficult to see how foreign direct investment could be preferred to portfolio investment. Because it is more costly for foreign investors to operate in a foreign country than it is for residents of that country, portfolio investment, which leaves the control of the assets in the hands of the residents of the capital-importing country, would seem to be a much more efficient way to transfer capital between countries than direct investment.

It is surprising then that the larger part of the capital transfers of developed countries is in the form of direct, and not portfolio, investment. Thus over the 1951–64 period, more than four-fifths of the net private long-term capital exports of developed countries were direct investments (Dunning 1970, p. 26).

The form taken by the private international transfer of capital in the recent period is even more puzzling when put in historical perspective. Until World War I, international capital movements took the form of flows of portfolio capital from a few European countries to the rest of the world. Each year between 1870 and 1913, the United Kingdom invested abroad the equivalent of 4 percent of her national income and 40 percent of her gross capital formation. In the last ten years of that period these figures had increased to 7 and 80 percent, respectively (Dunning 1970, p. 18). In 1913 the stock of British foreign investment was put at £4,000 million. Of that amount, 90 percent was in the form of portfolio bonds, mostly of foreign and imperial railway companies, and in foreign government bonds (Tugendhat 1972, p. 10). Moreover, the greater part of these capital transfers went to the United States, Canada, Australia, and New Zealand, countries where it would have been relatively easy for Englishmen to run a business.[3]

What accounts for the present-day reliance on direct investment when portfolio investment seems to be a much more efficient way to transfer capital internationally? A comparison between the pre– and post–World War I periods underlines the inability of the traditional capital theory to explain recent trends. That theory would predict that most of the direct investment capital exported by capital-rich countries would be directed to countries poorly endowed with financial capital. Yet at the end of 1975 only 26 percent of the stock of foreign direct investment of developed market economies was located in developing countries (United Nations 1978, p. 237). Moreover, there is often a two-way flow of foreign direct investment between developed countries. Thus, in 1978, American capital outflows to Switzerland were $366 million, whereas Swiss capital outflows to the United States amounted to $237 million (table 1). These findings cast some doubt on the ability of orthodox capital theory to explain the foreign direct investment phenomenon.

Foreign Direct Investment as Portfolio Diversification

If these facts contradict the classical theory of capital movements, it may be because that theory ignores the existence of risk. The theory of portfolio choice, as exposed by Markowitz (1959) and Tobin (1958), takes into account the risk aversion of asset holders. It postulates that individuals consider both rate of return and risk of return in choosing their portfolio. The risk attached to the ownership of an asset can be measured by the variance of the rate of return around its mean. Total portfolio risk is then a function of the variance of each asset and of the extent to which the returns to the assets are correlated.[4] An optimal portfolio should therefore maximize return given the variance, or minimize the variance given the rate of return. According to that theory, owners of wealth will hold assets bearing relatively low interest if including such assets in a portfolio causes a reduction in total portfolio risk that more than compensates for lower interest rates (the amount of reduction in total portfolio risk being a function of the degree to which the

TABLE 1   Direct Investment Cross Flows, 1978 (in million U.S. dollars)

Direction of Flow	Direct Investment Position at Year End	Equity and Intercompany Account Flows during Year
In and to the United States from:		
Canada	6,180	449
United Kingdom	7,638	799
Netherlands	10,078	979
Switzerland	2,879	237
Sweden	893	165
Germany	3,654	1,010
From the United States in and to:		
Canada	37,071	−600
United Kingdom	20,416	1,640
Netherlands	4,685	24
Switzerland	7,394	366
Sweden	1,198	51
Germany	12,731	113

Sources: Chung and Fouch 1980; Whichard 1980.

return on the assets in question is independent of the return on the other assets in the portfolio). Within a country, interest rates move more or less in unison. Foreign interest rates, however, are usually less correlated with domestic interest rates than domestic interest rates are among themselves. The inclusion of foreign assets in a portfolio may thus significantly reduce total risk. If foreign interest rates are higher than domestic rates, both higher returns and lower risk will be attained. In the opposite case, the attenuation of risk that comes from owning foreign assets will sometimes be worth the lower return. Thus zero or negative interest rate differentials are compatible with foreign asset holding.

An empirical test of the model was attempted by Levy and Sarnat (1970). They obtained data on mean rates of return on common stock and their standard deviation for twenty-eight countries over the 1951–67 period and calculated the set of efficient portfolios, i.e., the combination of investments in various countries that maximizes the rate of return, given the variance, or minimizes the variance, given the rate of return (table 2). Of the twenty-eight countries included in the calculation, only nine were retained in the optimal investment portfolio, and of these, two countries (the

TABLE 2   Composition of Levy and Sarnat's Optimal Portfolio for
Selected Interest Rates (in percentages)

Country[a]	Interest Rates			
	2%	3%	4%	6%
Austria	3.43%	6.99%	9.03%	12.06%
Denmark	2.06	0.01	. . .	. . .
Japan	14.68	16.71	17.65	20.86
Mexico	4.03	4.32	4.53	. . .
New Zealand	13.16	6.27	2.59	. . .
South Africa	10.37	12.51	13.83	12.86
United Kingdom	0.18	. . .	. . .	. . .
United States	36.57	40.99	42.79	51.06
Venezuela	15.51	11.72	9.57	3.16
Total	100.00	100.00	100.00	100.00
Mean portfolio rate of return	9.5	10.5	11.0	12.5
Portfolio standard deviation	5.72	6.41	6.82	8.39

Source: Levy and Sarnat 1970, p. 672.

a. The remaining nineteen countries of the original twenty-eight studied are not
included in any of the optimal portfolios.

United Kingdom and Denmark) received a negligible proportion of
the portfolio. Investments in the United States and Japan made up
the larger part (50 to 60 percent) of the optimal portfolios. Depending on the interest rate assumed, 40 to 60 percent of the portfolio
was invested in countries whose per capita income is intermediate
between that of the developing and that of the high income countries: Venezuela, South Africa, New Zealand, Mexico, and Japan.
No investments were held in Common Market countries or in Canada. Levy and Sarnat found that despite the high return and low risk
of American stocks, American investors would still benefit from the
international diversification of their portfolio. Their findings show
that interflows of portfolio investment will take place between countries as predicted even if there are zero or negative interest rate
differentials.

Levy and Sarnat considered the case of a portfolio investor
diversifying his assets by buying foreign securities. By analogy, the
same analysis can be applied to a direct investor. The multinational
firm can choose the location of its assets so as to maximize a utility
function positively related to the expected return and negatively
related to the variance of the total return on the firm's assets. Be-

cause variations in profit rates in different countries are not perfectly correlated, American firms, for example, can reduce the overall level of risk of their investments (without lowering their overall
rate of profit) by locating part of their assets in Europe. At the same
time, and for the same reason, European firms may find it desirable
to invest in the United States. Thus such a theory would explain
direct investment cross flows.

To assess the validity of the theory, various authors have tried
to test whether multinational firms allocate their direct investment
expenditures so as to both maximize expected returns and minimize
risk. The results of Prachowny (1972) and Stevens (1969) with
American firms were inconclusive, while Mellors (1973) found that
the portfolio model provided a limited explanation of the geographical spread of British multinationals. Benjamin Cohen also looked at
how stability in the profits and the sales of 200 multinational American firms in twenty-two industries over the 1961–69 period was
affected by four factors: size, the number of five-digit Standard
Industrial Classification (SIC) category products they manufactured
in the United States, the industry to which they belonged, and their
foreign activity, as measured by the number of countries in which
they had a foreign subsidiary in 1967. He found that multinationality
reduced variations in profits more than did domestic product diversification (Cohen 1975, p. 51).

The portfolio theory of foreign direct investment does not,
however, explain why and when direct investment will be preferred
to portfolio investment to achieve diversification. Granted that both
capital flows arise as investors seek to diversify their portfolios,
what will determine their choice between direct and portfolio investment? As Giorgio Ragazzi (1973) argues, this question is clearly
relevant in the light of variations among countries in the relative
importance of each type of capital flows on both sides of their
balance of payments. Consider, for example, the net foreign investment position of the United States. Over the last two decades capital inflows in the United States have covered a large part of American capital outflows. Between 1950 and 1970, American private
investment abroad increased from $19 billion to $120 billion. In the
same period, American liabilities to private foreigners increased
from $13 billion to $70 billion. But while American assets were
mostly in the form of direct investments, most American liabilities
were corporate securities and short-term liabilities. In the 1960s,
foreign direct investments in the United States constituted less than
15 percent of the increase of American liabilities to private foreigners. The contrast between the composition of long-term assets

and liabilities is particularly striking when one considers the American investment position vis-à-vis Western Europe (table 3). Between 1960 and 1970, the United States increased its net direct investment in Europe by $13 billion, while Western Europe's net holdings of American corporate securities and other long-term claims increased by $12 billion (Ragazzi 1973). Thus while the portfolio model of direct investment predicts interflows of capital between Europe and the United States, such a model does not explain the structure of the international investment position of the United States vis-à-vis Western Europe. In other words, how can we account for the preference of American investors for direct investment while Europeans opt for portfolio investment?

A major difference between portfolio and direct investment is the personalities of their authors: direct investment is almost exclusively made by corporations while individuals are restricted to portfolio investment (Ragazzi 1973, p. 476). We have seen that under perfectly competitive conditions, portfolio investment would be a more efficient way to move capital in response to international differences in rates of return (corrected for risk). The substitution of direct for portfolio investment therefore hints at the presence of imperfections in international markets.

Giorgio Ragazzi (1973) focuses on capital markets. He argues that imperfections in the capital market make the rate of return and risks associated with foreign securities substantially different from the rates of return and risks of the issuing foreign companies. According to Ragazzi, if there are no organized markets for securities, as in many less developed countries, there is no possibility of portfo-

TABLE 3   United States Investment Position vis-à-vis Western Europe[a] (in billion U.S. dollars)

	Private U.S. Assets Abroad			U.S. Liabilities to Private Foreigners[b]		
	1960	1970	1973	1960	1970	1973
Direct investment	6.6	24.5	38.2	4.7	9.5	12.5
Securities	2.2	3.1	3.6	7.3	18.0	27.4
Other long-term assets	1.1	2.0	2.7	1.0	4.2	5.0
Total long-term assets	9.9	29.6	44.6	13.0	31.7	44.9
Short-term assets	1.3	3.2	7.3	. . .	13.3	12.7
Grand Total	11.2	32.8	51.9	. . .	44.9	57.6

Sources: Pizer and Cutler 1962; Scholl 1972; Scholl 1974.

a. Excluding government assets and liabilities and official reserve assets.
b. Excluding international and regional organizations.

lio investment, leaving direct investment as the only alternative. Even in countries that have capital markets, lack of updated information on a company's operations and narrowness of the market may make the risks run by minority shareholders much higher than those inherent in the operations of that company. Capital outflows will then occur in the form of direct investment, as individuals anxious to invest funds will buy stock in firms that engage in direct foreign investment. Thus French investors eager to invest funds in the profitable French industries may do it by buying International Business Machines stock on the New York market. Portfolio investment and direct investment are close substitutes here.

Ragazzi shows that such a model may explain interflows of capital between the United States and Europe. He argues that, compared to American security markets, European markets are inefficient. Their small size leads to high fluctuations in stock prices and rates of return.[5] He also notes that auditing of corporations by European authorities is much less thorough, and the quantity and quality of information received by stockholders is lower than in the United States, thus increasing the risk of variations in the rate of return.[6] These inefficiencies, he argues, affect portfolio investors more than direct investors. Since direct investors are typically interested in the medium and long run, short-run fluctuations are not as catastrophic for them as for portfolio investors. Direct investors, being in control of the company, also have immediate access to all relevant information; their risk is thus limited to the risks inherent in the operation of the company. Thus, the relative inefficiency of European capital markets will encourage direct investment from abroad, while in the efficient American financial market there is less advantage to direct over portfolio investment. European individuals who do not command enough resources to acquire control shares in European companies will thus be attracted by the low level of risk of American portfolio shares, while American individuals eager to invest abroad will buy shares in American companies that become control investors in Europe to take advantage of the high European rates of profits. Direct investment and portfolio investments are thus substitutes and both are ways to diversify portfolios.

As predicted by Ragazzi, the rate of return on common stock is slightly higher in Europe than in the United States, but the standard deviation in annual rates is considerably higher in Europe. Some support for the theory is also provided by the fact that the three countries with the most developed stock markets, the United States, the United Kingdom, and the Netherlands, were also the only ones with net direct investment outflows over the 1965–70 period (United Nations 1973, table 9).

There are, however, three main objections to Ragazzi's argument. First, inefficiencies in European capital markets may not necessarily lead to inflows of American foreign direct investment. European firms can issue bonds and equities in the New York market to European and American investors and offer them the high European rates of return without having to transact on inefficient European capital markets. Some European firms have taken advantage of this opportunity. More than half of the sixty-five European multinationals sampled by the United Nations had their stock listed on American exchanges or traded over the counter in the United States in 1975 (United Nations 1978, p. 164).

Shares of American multinationals would still be preferred by European and American investors to shares of European firms if the former offered a better package of investments, i.e., if American multinational firms were able to reduce the variance of their profits by investing in countries whose economies are not highly correlated with each other and with the United States.

In 1966, however, almost half of the sales of American majority-owned subsidiaries were in Canada and in the six Common Market countries (U.S., Department of Commerce 1975a). Yet the economies of these countries were highly integrated, as shown by the high correlation between the average rates of return on common stock of these countries over the 1951–67 period (Levy and Sarnat 1970, p. 674). If reduction of risk was a principal motive, one would expect a different geographical distribution of subsidiaries.

As possible tests of his theory, Ragazzi states that

> . . . to the extent that direct investment is determined by the causes just mentioned, one would expect it to have the following characteristics: (a) the company acquired would, in general, be a "healthy" one, with a higher rate of return, at equal industrial risk, than comparable U.S. companies; (b) the management of the foreign subsidiary would remain substantially autonomous and the participation of the foreign company could be limited to a relatively low share of total capital; (c) the foreign subsidiary would not necessarily have to operate in the same sector as the parent company. [Ragazzi 1973, p. 483]

Although Ragazzi does not explain precisely why condition b would hold, it would appear that he had in mind the following: if the subsidiary is owned for diversification, it is not necessary to obtain 100 percent ownership. Indeed, minority ownership is preferable for three reasons. First, complete ownership of subsidiaries makes their alien status highly visible, and this increases the chances they will become the target of nationalistic attacks. Second, the smaller the participation taken in each venture, the greater the degree of diversification achieved with a given portfolio. Finally, the investing firm should try to keep its investments as liquid as possible, so as to be able to rearrange portfolios in response to changes in profit rates and risk. The larger the percentage of shares owned, all other things being equal, the larger the costs of rearranging portfolios.

In fact, most subsidiaries of multinational enterprises are not minority-owned. Harvard's Multinational Enterprise Project has looked at the ownership structure of the 10,950 manufacturing subsidiaries of the 391 largest multinationals based in the United States, Europe, and other countries. Only 18 percent of the 8,621 subsidiaries for which ownership is known were minority-owned, that is, parent firms owned more than 5 but less than 50 percent of the stock of the subsidiaries, whereas 57 percent were more than 95 percent owned by parent firms (Vernon 1977, p. 34).

We would also expect subsidiaries held for diversification to enjoy a large degree of autonomy: since local managers usually have a better knowledge of local conditions, central direction would seem inefficient. Good management practices would warrant leaving a wide degree of autonomy to foreign subsidiaries. A great deal of qualitative evidence, however, supports the view that foreign subsidiaries are tightly integrated to their parents. Tugendhat asserts that

> the most striking characteristic of the modern multinational company is its central direction. However large it may be, and however many subsidiaries it may have scattered across the globe, all its operations are coordinated from the center. Despite frequent assertions to the contrary, the subsidiaries are not run as separate enterprises each of which has to stand on its own feet. They must all work within a framework established by an overall group plan drawn up at headquarters, and their activities are tightly integrated with each other. [Tugendhat 1972, p. 11]

This point is emphasized by many observers of the multinational corporation and is widely accepted by the managers of international firms. Michael Brooke and H. Lee Remmers, for example, report the following statement by the British managing director of an American-owned subsidiary:

> The manager of a subsidiary must accept that he enjoys a subordinate status, that a subsidiary company is an organ of the parent company,

14   Multinational Enterprise

and that policy is basically formulated and handed down by the parent company. [Brooke and Remmers 1970, p. 8]

These qualitative assessments are supported by some quantitative evidence. One way to assess the degree of interdependence is to look at the procurement and export strategies of the subsidiaries of multinational firms. Subsidiaries that are held as diversification for the parent would likely be independent concerns, obtaining their inputs from local sources and selling their output to local customers. This does not seem to be the case. Thus 73 percent of the total exports to the United States of American foreign affiliates are sent to the parent or its other American affiliates. Moreover, 53 percent of American affiliate exports to third countries are directed to other affiliates of the parent (U.S., Department of Commerce 1975a, p. 198). In 1973, 57.6 percent of the total exports of American manufacturing subsidiaries and branches in the United Kingdom went to the parent and its other affiliates (Dunning 1976, p. 76).

In Canada, as shown in table 4, foreign-owned subsidiaries obtained 78 percent of their imports from parents and affiliates. The increasing division of labor between parents and subsidiaries is also a sign of a high degree of interaction. One of the most striking

TABLE 4   Distribution of Imports of All Reporting Majority-Owned Foreign Subsidiaries in Canada, 1971 (in million Canadian dollars)

	Total Merchandise Imports (1)	Imports from Parents & Affiliates (2)	Column (2) / Column (1) (in percentage)
Mining and primary metals	92	69	75%
Gas and oil	728	658	90
Manufacturing	5,282	4,022	76
Machinery and metal fabricating	[517]	[413]	[80]
Transportation equipment	[3,674]	[2,981]	[81]
Electrical products	[296]	[197]	[67]
Chemical products	[261]	[148]	[57]
Food and beverage	[225]	[89]	[40]
Pulp and paper	[64]	[25]	[39]
Other manufacturing	[245]	[169]	[69]
Wholesale trade	281	237	84
Other nonmanufacturing	73	30	41
Total	6,456	5,016	78%

Source: Canadian Department of Industry, Trade, and Commerce 1974, p. 30, summary table 17.

aspects of that growing specialization is in research and development. The 1966 census of American foreign direct investment indicates that 94 percent of all research and development expenditures by American multinational firms were made in the United States (U.S., Tariff Commission 1973, p. 582).

To the extent that foreign direct investment is, as Ragazzi contends, a substitute for portfolio investment, one would expect foreign subsidiaries to be active in different sectors than those of their parents, since product diversification is likely to reduce variations in the firm's rate of return. Yet the degree of product diversification across countries by multinational firms is very limited. This fact has been noted by Barlow and Wender (1955, p. 159) and is confirmed by looking at American data. Total sales of American majority-owned foreign affiliates in 1966 are both classified by main industry of parent and by main industry of affiliate. By comparing sales of American majority-owned affiliates under both systems of classification, it is possible to estimate the degree to which affiliates manufacture products that are outside their parents' two-digit SIC classification. As shown in table 5, most subsidiaries were in the same industry as their

TABLE 5   Diversification between American Parent Firms and their Majority-Owned Foreign Affiliates, 1966

	Total Sales by Industry of Parent Firms (1)	Total Sales by Industry of Affiliates (2)	Column (2) / Column (1) (in percentage)
All industries	97,783	97,783	100%
Mining and smelting	1,712	3,321	194
Petroleum	27,874	27,457	99
Manufacturing	57,190	47,375	83
Food products	[5,764]	[5,644]	[98]
Chemical products	[9,069]	[7,421]	[82]
Primary and fabri-			
cated metals	[6,480]	[3,904]	[60]
Machinery	[13,517]	[10,902]	[81]
Transportation			
equipment	[12,683]	[11,156]	[88]
Other manufacturing	[9,678]	[8,348]	[86]
Transportation, communi-			
cation, utilities	794	1,366	172
Trade	6,510	14,066	216
Finance and insurance	463	17	4
Other industries	3,239	4,181	129

Source: U.S., Department of Commerce 1975*a*, p. 199, table L-3 and p. 207, table L-11.

parents. Only in mining and smelting, trade, and finance and insurance do figures diverge, but they reflect the presence of vertical investments, not of product diversification.

Proponents of the diversification theory answer these objections by arguing that multinationals need not diversify their holdings to the same extent as individuals. Individual investors can achieve optimal diversification by buying shares of a large number of imperfectly diversified multinationals.

The characteristics of multinational enterprises that we have described earlier seem, however, to make them inferior tools to that end. Jacquillat and Solnik (1978) compared the reduction of risk achieved by buying a portfolio of American and foreign securities with that obtained by acquiring a portfolio of American-based multinationals. Buying shares of American multinationals yielded a 10 percent reduction in risk (i.e., in the standard deviation of the rate of return) over buying a portfolio of American domestic firm shares. A portfolio of securities from domestic and foreign stock markets achieved, however, a 50 to 70 percent decrease in risk over a portfolio of American domestic shares.

These findings do not support the hypothesis that direct foreign investment is a substitute for portfolio investment. And indeed there is considerable evidence that capital transfers are not the most significant feature of foreign direct investments. Recent data indicate that only a small percentage of the affiliates' capital expenditures is financed by their parents. Michael Brooke and H. Lee Remmers (1970) for example, found that local sources (retained earnings, depreciation allowances, local loans and credit, and liquid assets) financed 80 percent of the investment of 115 foreign subsidiaries in Great Britain. Sidney Robbins and Robert Stobaugh (1973) found that, at the end of 1970, American entities held only $78 billion, or 58 percent of the total liabilities and equities of $134 billion of their foreign affiliates (table 6). Over the 1966–72 period, only 13 percent of the funds obtained by a sample of majority-owned American affiliates came from American sources. Half of the funds were internally generated. The rest was obtained from local or third-country sources (Mantel 1975). Another approach is to compare the investment expenditures of American foreign subsidiaries to the net capital inflows they received from their American parents. Capital expenditures by majority-owned foreign affiliates of American companies amounted to $27.5 billion in 1977 and $30.7 billion in 1978. Equity and intercompany account outflows from American parents to all their affiliates were $5.6 billion in 1977 and $4.9 billion in 1978 (table 7).

Parents thus financed a very small fraction of the investment and expenditures of their affiliates, and the transfer of capital does not seem to be central to foreign direct investment.

Other Theories of Foreign Direct Investment

The close links between parent firms and affiliates that we have just underlined have steered many economists toward alternative theories of foreign direct investment. These can be classified in three main categories: the theory of imperialism, the product cycle model, and the market imperfection approach.

TABLE 6 Estimated Balance Sheet of Foreign Direct Investment of American Enterprises, December 31, 1970 (in billion U.S. dollars)

Assets		Liabilities and Equity		
Current	62	U.S. entities' share (book		
Fixed	60	value of U.S. foreign		
		direct investment)		78
		Liabilities to U.S.		
		entities	[21]	
Other	12	Equity owned by		
		U.S. entities	[57]	
		Foreigner's share		56
		Short term liabilities	[34]	
		Long term liabilities	[16]	
		Equity	[6]	
Total assets	134	Total liabilities and		
		equity		134

Source: From *Money in the Multinational Enterprise: A Study in Financial Policy,* by Sidney M. Robbins and Robert B. Stobaugh, table 1-1. © 1973 by Basic Books, Inc. By permission of Basic Books, Inc., Publishers, New York.

TABLE 7 Sources of Financing of American Affiliates (in billion U.S. dollars)

Year	Capital Expenditures by Majority-Owned Foreign Affiliates	Net U.S. Capital Outflows to All Foreign Affiliates
1973	20.5	3.2
1974	25.3	1.3
1975	26.8	6.2
1976	24.7	4.2
1977	27.5	5.6
1978	30.7	4.9
1979	38.4	5.0

Sources: Lowe 1981; Chung 1979; Whichard 1981*a;* Whichard 1981*b.*

Proponents of the theory of imperialism see foreign direct investment as one of the methods used by rich countries to exploit their less-developed neighbors. Firms from developed countries invest abroad because foreign operations bring them monopoly rents. These rents are obtained as direct investors acquire from local authorities discriminatory favors and/or the right to exclude competitors.

The practice of granting monopoly rights in foreign possessions in exchange for taxes is, of course, very old. During the colonial era, the right to operate in the colonies was usually reserved to nationals of the colonial power. In South America, American companies bribed or bullied local governments into granting them exclusive rights to the exploitation of raw materials and other resources. In some instances outrageous terms were obtained and monopoly profits were earned.

There is, however, a considerable amount of evidence that contradicts the hypothesis that political dominance is a prerequisite for foreign direct investment. Even at the height of the colonial era, the greater part of the capital exports of developed countries was not directed to less-developed countries. Only about 8 percent of France's 1914 stock of private foreign direct investment was in her Asian and African colonies. Germany held only about 12 percent of her total stock within her empire. The British invested a mere 3 percent of their private capital exports outside India and their white dominions (Hughes 1970, p. 190). Today only about a fourth of the stock of foreign direct investment from developed countries is invested in developing countries (United Nations 1978, p. 212). Contrary, then, to what imperialistic theories imply, foreign direct investment is not, and has never been, exclusively directed to less developed countries.[7] Even within developing countries, foreign direct investment does not seem to have always been influenced by colonial protection; witness the fact that some of the direct investments of European firms were outside their own colonies (Wilkins 1977).

Even if a link between direct investment and colonial rule can be established, imperialism per se cannot constitute a theory of foreign direct investment. Foreign direct investment implies the extension of managerial control across countries. The granting of special favors to citizens of the colonial (or quasi-colonial) power is compatible with other types of investment, e.g., expatriate or portfolio investment. Indeed the majority of European investments during the nineteenth century were of those two types (Dunning 1970, p. 18). Whenever direct investment took place, it seems to have been caused by the lack of local entrepreneurial capabilities and by the presence of strong interdependence between the resources of the local economy and the needs of the colonial power. The concession of special privileges does not seem to have influenced the form taken by foreign exploitation.

Another approach to foreign direct investment is the product cycle hypothesis. This theory, as developed by Raymond Vernon (1966), considers foreign direct investment as a stage in the penetration of foreign markets. It regards technological innovations as the main determinant of the structure of world trade and of the distribution. of production among countries. The theory notes that the United States, as the country having the largest market and the highest per capita income, is the place where new products are first introduced. Those new products, based on advanced technology, are geared to an affluent society, eager to substitute capital for labor time. A rise in real income in other countries leads those countries to change their consumption patterns and to demand goods that had been originally designed for the American market. The product cycle theory assumes that initial production will be located in the country of innovation, both because the production process uses large quantities of skilled personnel (it is human-capital intensive) and because the new product can only be successfully developed if close contact with the customer is maintained. At that stage demand for the product is typically price inelastic. As the product becomes established in the American market, product features become standardized. American firms then turn to foreign markets, where demand for their product is growing rapidly. Typically, they will first export to foreign markets: but as the foreign and domestic demands for their product grow, these firms will find it both profitable and necessary to manufacture in foreign countries, because the standardization of the product makes its manufacture more suitable to the factor proportions existing in foreign countries and less suitable to American relative input prices, and because the danger of losing sales to local producers increases as overseas markets grow larger.

The product cycle model links foreign investments to a particular type of innovation from a particular country. Vernon argues that the special conditions in the United States—high per capita income, scarce and costly skilled labor, large internal market—tend to bias American innovations toward those that will later be wanted abroad. Since in Vernon's model foreign investment is the usual way to exploit innovations overseas, the unique characteristics of the American market determine the central role of the United States as a home country to multinational companies. Other environments, on the other hand, tend to encourage innovations of a capital- and material-saving nature. These innovations, according to Vernon, have a less promising future. Differences in internal markets thus explain the asymmetry between American and European and Japanese foreign direct investment. Since these differences are not expected to change in the near future, Vernon predicts the continuing dominance of the United States as a foreign direct investor (Vernon 1971, p. 109).

Contrary to Vernon's forecast, the recent period has witnessed a dramatic rise in Japanese and European foreign direct investment. Thus over the 1967–76 period, the book value of Japanese foreign subsidiaries increased twelvefold, that of German subsidiaries sixfold, whereas the book value of American affiliates only grew by 242 percent (United Nations 1978, p. 236). Between 1973 and 1979, American direct investments abroad rose by 190 percent, while foreign direct investments in the United States increased 254 percent (Chung and Fouch 1980; Whichard 1981). There are therefore some indications that the dominant position of the United States as a foreign direct investor is eroding.

In part to take account of these new developments, Vernon has updated his views in *Storm Over the Multinationals* (1977). Vernon concedes that while the United States has a comparative advantage in labor-saving innovations, European and Japanese producers may become dominant in innovations that economize on land and materials. Vernon also emphasizes the oligopolistic nature of the behavior of multinationals. In the intermediate stage of mature oligopoly, location may be more determined by oligopolistic "follow the leader" or "exchange of hostages" strategies than by closeness to markets (as in stage one) or relative cost conditions (as in stage three).

In spite of these refinements, the product cycle model suffers from one basic limitation: it addresses itself to a particular type of foreign direct investments, namely, the production abroad of innovations. The model cannot explain vertical investments, such as raw material ventures, and it cannot therefore provide a unified theory of the multinational firm.

But more importantly, the product cycle model explains the location of manufacturing facilities, but not their ownership. Vernon implicitly assumes that successful innovations always lead to foreign direct investments. But, if his model predicts that foreign production will generally take place, it does not tell us whether it will be undertaken by the innovator or by a foreign firm. Vernon, for example, does not explicitly consider the possibility of imitation. If the cost of copying the technology was low enough, American investors faced with the high costs of operating in a foreign country would be at a disadvantage. Another alternative unexplored by Vernon is that of licensing foreign producers. Because foreigners possess superior knowledge of local conditions, because it is costly to operate plants at a distance, and because it is risky to have assets under foreign jurisdiction, licensing would seem to be an efficient alternative, and is in fact used by American firms. The product cycle thus fails to consider all of the determinants of foreign direct investment. The model does predict the international location of production facilities (i.e., it indicates when local production will be preferred to exports) but not their ownership (whether manufacture of the new products will be undertaken by American subsidiaries or licensed to indigenous firms).

Because it does not consider the costs and benefits of all the possible ways of exploiting innovations abroad, the product cycle model cannot explain why, at other times, many countries have not used foreign direct investment to exploit their technological advantage. Particularly relevant in this respect is the experience of the United Kingdom. In the first half of the nineteenth century, many British firms possessed a technological lead over firms of other countries that can well be compared with the lead over other nations that many American producers enjoy today. During that period many of the new techniques and products that had been developed in England were successfully transferred to Europe and to regions of recent settlement. England also exported during that same period large quantities of capital.

But if it is true that capital and technology moved together, they were transferred independently of each other and their movement was motivated by a separate set of factors. The quasi-totality of capital was exported by buying portfolio shares. Direct foreign investment, involving the control of foreign operations, was of negligible importance. For example, British direct investment in the United States in 1913 is estimated at $700 million, while its portfolio investment in the United States was $3,667 million (Dunning 1971, p. 370).

During that period, the main vehicle for technological transfer was the migration of skilled personnel from England to other countries. But only in rare cases was that migration effected by and within English firms. After the Civil War, J. and P. Coats set up subsidiaries to manufacture cotton thread in the United States. Later Courtaulds and Lever were to be outstanding examples of English direct investment. In many cases skilled English workers were imported to staff the subsidiary. However, most knowledge was not transferred by this method, but in the following three ways. (1) Foreign firms tried to persuade English skilled workers to emigrate and work for them; thus American agents working for American firms visited the United Kingdom to attract skilled workers in the iron, textiles, and glass industries (Dunning 1971, p. 368). (2) Many British technicians that emigrated also became entrepreneurs and started businesses in the foreign country: Job Dixon pioneered machine building and James Jackson was the innovator of steel in France, Thomas Wilson founded cotton factories in Holland, and John Cockerill started an industrial empire in Belgium (Landes 1969, pp. 148–49). Likewise, the first woolen factory with power machinery in the United States was founded by two Englishmen, while Scottish capitalists and superintendents helped establish the American jute industry (Dunning 1971, p. 368). (3) Knowledge was also transferred by the emigration of whole firms. Dunning relates that several British silk companies moved the whole or part of their plants to the United States; sometimes they crated their machinery and moved lock, stock, and barrel with their employees (Dunning 1971, p. 371).

Although it is difficult to show statistically that direct investment played a minor role in the transmission of knowledge, some support for our thesis is given by a study of the migration history of 224 British-born textile workers who died in the United States between 1880 and 1915. From obituaries in trade journals, it is possible to ascertain that 8 of these came to the United States to set up plants for English companies, 26 started mills on their own account, 33 came as superintendents and overseers in American firms, 59 came as operatives, and 29 as children (Dunning 1971, p. 372). Thus only a small minority of the immigrants was transferred by English firms establishing overseas subsidiaries.

From the preceding discussion, we conclude that while the product cycle model describes very well the main elements of the American direct investment experience, it cannot be considered a general model of the foreign direct investment phenomenon.

We have seen earlier that operation abroad is, for a variety of reasons, more costly than operation at home. If multinationals find it profitable to set up foreign subsidiaries, they must have some advantages over native firms that allow them to offset their natural handicap in foreign markets. If markets were perfect, these advantages could be sold to local firms or embodied in products exported to foreign markets. Foreign direct investment implies therefore imperfections in goods and in factor markets.

Robert Aliber suggested in 1970 that imperfections in capital markets were the main cause of foreign direct investment. According to Aliber, direct foreign investments could arise, even if the markets in all other advantages were perfect, if the source-country firm had an advantage in the capital market over host-country firms. Aliber argues that source-country multinationals based in hard currency areas can borrow at a lower rate of interest than host-country firms because portfolio investors overlook the foreign content of source-country multinationals. Source-country firms are thus able to borrow as if their total earnings were in hard currency and can therefore provide their overseas affiliates with cheaper sources of capital than those available to local competitors.

Aliber's theory predicts well the direction of foreign direct investment flows in the postwar period: the American invasion of Europe in the sixties on the strength of the dollar, and the recent surge in German foreign direct investment as the mark gained on the dollar. Nevertheless, Aliber's model does not explain the continued growth of both American and British investments in spite of the weakness of their respective currencies, the presence of simultaneous investment cross flows, nor the existence of foreign direct investments within a currency area (Hood and Young 1979, p. 51). Aliber's model also implies that an investor from a hard currency area can make an immediate profit by taking over a firm in a weak currency area. In that case, one wonders with Buckley and Casson (1976, p. 71) why multinationals would ever set up greenfield ventures in foreign markets. Lastly, Aliber's hypothesis does not square with the fact that affiliates obtain most of their finance from local sources, and that transfer of capital is not a major feature of the foreign direct investment process.

Other authors, such as Hymer (1976) and Kindleberger (1969) have emphasized technology as the major advantage explaining foreign direct investment. Johnson (1970) has argued that knowledge is a public good to the firm, which can be exploited by the subsidiary of an innovating firm at little or no additional cost. The overseas affiliate benefits therefore of a considerable advantage over the native firm that must, to compete, bear the full cost of developing the knowledge.

For Caves (1971), the main advantage that multinationals have over their local competitors in foreign markets is their ability to differentiate products. Knowledge about how to differentiate products is the primary determinant of foreign direct investment because it is "the main advantage for which local production per se increases the rents yielded by a market" (1971, p. 6). This is because product differentiation knowledge cannot be exploited independently of entrepreneurial manpower and because uncertainty about the value of the knowledge in the foreign market will preclude agreement on the terms of the licensing agreement that will capture the full expected value of the surplus available to the licensor.

It seems, however, that knowledge about serving one market is not always an asset in serving another. This is particularly true for differentiated consumer products. Consumer needs are shaped and influenced by a complex array of variables, including the physical environment, the level of economic development, and cultural factors. Marketing strategies also are affected by the stage of the product in the product cycle, the available distribution system, the presence and type of advertising media, and legal restrictions (Buzzell 1968). For that reason, successful production and marketing of new products often requires considerable adaptation to local conditions. Marketing skills acquired by selling a product in the American market cannot always be used as such in another market. The pitfalls of direct transfer can be illustrated by the failure of American firms to sell cake mixes and bowling equipment in France. Even trademarks cannot always be transferred as such to foreign countries.[8]

For these reasons multinational companies usually operate separate marketing campaigns in each national market. As reported by Robert Buzzell,

> the prevailing view is that marketing strategy is a local problem. The best strategy for a company will differ from country to country and the design of the strategy should be left to local management in each country. [Buzzell 1968, p. 103]

The advantages given in successful product differentiation in the home country are thus balanced by the local producer's knowledge of the market. The foreigner has thus no clear advantage.

Since successful product differentiation, and often successful local production, seem to require a detailed knowledge of local conditions, and since the native producers have acquired the knowledge at no cost, licensing and franchising appear to be efficient methods to transfer advantages. And indeed licensing is often used to that end by firms in many industries. Suppliers of differentiated products and services such as the Coca-Cola Company Inc., Holiday Inns Inc., McDonald's Corp., Avis Inc., and Manpower, Inc. franchise foreign firms. A theory of foreign direct investment must therefore go beyond a mere listing of the advantages possessed by multinational firms to an explanation of the factors that determine the choice between sale through markets (licensing, franchising) and transfer within the firm (foreign direct investment).

A New Approach to Foreign Direct Investment

Our brief survey of the various theories advanced to explain foreign direct investment has shown that each fails to account for one or another of the characteristics of international production. Capital flow theories, in either their classical or portfolio variant, do not seem to have much explanatory power; a significant part of foreign direct investment is effected without capital transfer, whereas the tight integration of foreign subsidiaries to their parent firms does not suggest diversification motives. The product cycle model, while it predicts the location of production facilities, does not explicitly consider their ownership. As such it cannot explain the various forms by which technologically advanced countries have exploited their advantage. Caves's theory does not show convincingly how successful product differentiation in the United States is an asset that is valuable abroad and can best be exploited by foreign direct investment.

Thus, although some of the preceding theories have merit and throw some light on the foreign direct investment phenomenon, they do not provide a theoretical framework that takes into account all of the characteristics of foreign direct investment. What is needed is a general theory, capable of explaining the spatial and historical variations in direct foreign investment, as well as accounting for the most distinctive aspects of the phenomenon.

Such a theory was presented in a 1972 article by John McManus. McManus notes that in perfectly competitive markets the reactions of a set of producers to market prices will bring about an efficient allocation of resources, i.e., producers will jointly produce the highest possible output from the available flow of resources, and will thus maximize their joint wealth, given the constraints of perfect competition.

If the traditional model of competitive markets was always the relevant one, markets would organize all interdependences. The relationship between parent and affiliate, however, is usually not market mediated. Parents and affiliates do not maximize independently their profits and transactions between them are not usually conducted at market prices, but rather at prices determined by the parent. A multinational firm is thus an alternative way to coordinate the activities of interdependent agents.

McManus argues that the choice between firms and markets to organize a particular type of interdependence will hinge on the relative costs that are experienced by each institution in constraining individual behavior to make it consistent with joint wealth maximization.

He shows how market prices, market contracts, and firms differ in the way they constrain the behavior of economic agents. The firm replaces prices or contractual constraints by managerial directives, and the more costly it is to organize interdependence through prices or contracts, the greater the advantage to producers of combining their resources within a firm and of subjecting themselves to centralized control. For certain types of exchange, firms will experience lower exchange costs than markets. In these cases, firm organization will be the most efficient method of coordinating the behavior of agents. In spite of the high cost of international operations, interdependent producers in different countries will find it advantageous to form an international firm.

McManus's extremely perceptive analysis provides a firm basis on which to develop a theory of the multinational firm. In the following pages we extend McManus's model in three main directions. First, whereas McManus uses the cost of measuring the flow of services or the stock of assets that is being exchanged as a proxy for transacting costs, we consider also information and bargaining costs. We also expand McManus's static analysis to examine the dynamic aspects of transacting. An attempt is also made to identify the factors that influence the relative efficiency of both modes of organization.

Second, we show in much greater detail how McManus's hypothesis explains the interindustry distribution of international investment. We also demonstrate how the observed differences among international firms in their preference for wholly owned subsidiaries can be explained in terms of the model. Lastly, we identify the factors that determine the relative efficiency of firm and market organization through time and across countries and show how they can account for the historical pattern of foreign direct investment and the differences in the propensity of firms of different countries to own foreign subsidiaries.

The argument is developed in the next five chapters. Chapter 2 presents a general model of the choice between firms and markets as organizational modes. In this chapter, we outline the tasks to be performed by both systems of organization. We show that both firms and markets experience positive costs in fulfilling these tasks, but that because both institutions differ in the method they use to organize activities, they experience, for the same exchange, different levels of organization costs. Each institution will therefore have a comparative advantage in handling a particular type of transaction.

In chapters 3, 4, and 5 we show how the model accounts for the industrial, geographical, and historical patterns of foreign direct investment and for the ownership policies of multinational firms. Foreign direct investment in raw material extraction and in sales subsidiaries is explained by the difficulty of coordinating some long-term exchanges through the market. The important number of foreign subsidiaries that produce technologically advanced products arises, we argue, from the superiority of multinational firms over markets in transferring certain types of knowledge between countries. Since the choice between firm and market organization hinges on the respective costs incurred by both institutions in effecting exchange, we explain the observed historical pattern of foreign direct investment by changes in the relative cost of organizing exchange within firms and across markets. An attempt is also made to explain national variations in the propensity to invest abroad as resulting from systematic differences in the level of organization costs experienced by firms of different nationalities. Finally, we show that the insistence of transnational corporations for the sole ownership of their affiliates is a function of the degree of interdependence between parent and subsidiary. In a concluding chapter, we outline the implications of the model for some of the policy issues raised by multinational firms.

CHAPTER 2

The Model

The following sections develop a model of the institutional choice
between firms and markets. We first show that both markets and
hierarchies are potentially viable devices to organize economic activities. In the real world, there are costs associated with such a task.
These costs will prevent both institutions from achieving Pareto-
optimal results and from internalizing all externalities. But because
markets and hierarchies differ in the method they use to organize
economic activities, they experience, for the same transaction, different levels of external effects. Whether firms or markets are chosen to
organize a particular type of interdependence hinges on the respective costs they experience. An analysis of the choice between firms
and markets requires, therefore, a careful consideration of the methods used by both institutions to organize economic activities.

The model we develop follows the approach pioneered by
Coase in his seminal 1937 article, "The Nature of the Firm," and
developed by McManus (1972, 1975). We also incorporate elements drawn from the property rights paradigm (Demsetz 1964,
1966, 1967; Alchian and Demsetz 1972), Oliver Williamson's writ-
ings on organization (Williamson 1970, 1975), and the market failure literature (Arrow 1974; Coase 1960).

The Agenda of Organization

Firms and markets are two institutions that attempt to organize
economic activities. To understand the role played by these institutions, it is useful to take a close look at the reason for their existence. Social organization is needed because the aggregate result of
each individual maximizing independently his utility is often an inferior social (and individual) outcome. To overcome the divergence
between the interest of the individual and that of society, a certain
number of tasks must be performed. These tasks, which define the
organizational problem, must be fulfilled by any system of organization, be it markets, firms, or governments.

It is often pointed out that people tend to be more aware of their own desires than of those of others and more concerned with their own affairs than with those of their neighbors. As a result, most individuals will do things that may adversely affect others and will fail to perform actions that would be beneficial to their fellow men. Everyday experience tells us that, in the absence of social constraints, economic agents will often engage in socially harmful behavior: they will refuse to cooperate with others, even if such cooperation may be beneficial to them; and they will impose by their behavior losses on others that they would be perfectly willing to avoid if somehow they could be made aware of them and compensated for changing their behavior.

Schelling (1971) illustrates these observations with the example of summer brownouts. If all electricity consumers took pains to reduce by a small fraction their use of electricity, sudden brownouts or prolonged power failures could be avoided. Clearly it is better to cut down a little on air-conditioning than to risk being entirely without electricity for extended periods of time. But unless all consumers can be made to reduce their consumption of electricity, no one will find it in his interest to switch off some of his lights, and, as a result, everyone will be forced to face the potentiality of breakdowns. Because, in the absence of social organization, an individual's perceived interest is often at odds with that of society as a whole, the combined result of each individual's independent action is often an inferior social outcome.

A utility that would attempt to avoid such brownouts would be faced with three problems: first, it would have to inform each homeowner of the impact of his high consumption on the community. It should also extract from each consumer commitments to limit their use of electricity. Considerable bickering would ensue, as everyone would attempt to conceal their preferences in order to shift the burden of reducing consumption onto others. Finally, without a method for enforcing those promises, it is doubtful that any lasting decrease in consumption would be achieved.

Just like our utility, any institution that attempts to organize activities must find a way to perform these three tasks. It must communicate to decision makers the impact of their behavior on others. The institution must curb bargaining, an activity clearly wasteful to society (but rational from an individual's point of view) since the additional benefits that may accrue to one individual as a result of bargaining are necessarily gained at the expense of another. It must devise a method to reward individuals for taking into account the needs and preferences of their neighbors. As will be seen in the next sections, what differentiates firms and markets is the methods they use to accomplish these three organizational tasks.

Organizational Modes

Markets and firms are two institutions devised to solve the organizational problem. They both solve it, however, in different ways. In the following exposition, we stress their fundamental differences, and oppose "pure" types of firms and markets. In particular, we assume that all firms are organized along hierarchical lines. We will have occasion, in the course of the chapter, to refine our analysis and take into account many complications that are not considered at this point.

The goal of this section is to show that both firms and markets would, in the absence of information, enforcement, and bargaining costs, perfectly organize all economic activities. In a world of zero organization costs, the choice between both modes would therefore be purely a matter of subjective preference.

The characteristic of markets is that they rely on decentralized, autonomous adjustment by economic agents. In markets, prices convey information about the social consequences of one's actions. In a perfectly functioning market system an individual does not have to worry about the impact of his actions on society; all he has to know is his own needs. He has only to decide whether his marginal gain in utility is higher or lower than the market price (Arrow 1974, p. 20). Economic agents therefore obtain through prices the information necessary to reach optimum joint decisions.

Markets can theoretically also generate and disseminate the information needed for an efficient intertemporal allocation of resources. For an economy to move efficiently through time it is necessary that every decision maker be able to foresee correctly the future prices that will rule for the goods and services that are relevant to his decisions. Even if there is considerable uncertainty about the future, a system of contingent markets can remove all uncertainties and bring forth an efficient intertemporal allocation of resources. If there are markets in which agents can buy and sell "contingent" goods and services, i.e., if consumers are able to buy today at a given price a good that will be provided at a particular point in the future if, and only if, some defined environmental event occurs, then parties will have a perfect knowledge of all future prices. They will thus be able to reach autonomously a Pareto-efficient intertemporal allocation of resources, in the sense that no one will be able to get a preferred basket of contingent goods without someone being left with a less preferred one (Meade 1970).

The second task that faces an economic system is to monitor behavior and reward performance. In a market system prices automatically meter and reward productive effort. Increasing output by 20 percent at the prevailing market price results in a 20 percent increase in income. Thus, rewards always fall on those responsible for changes in outputs (Alchian and Demsetz 1972, p. 778).

Market competition among buyers and sellers will also reveal the terms of trade, thus eliminating bargaining. If any seller tries to bluff and asks for exorbitant terms, buyers will turn to someone else. Individual investment in strategic bargaining is therefore inefficient (Buchanan and Tullock 1962, pp. 97–103).

In a similar vein, it is possible to show that hierarchies are also theoretically viable systems for organizing economic activities. But whereas markets use decentralized adaptation, hierarchies rely on centralized decision making and enforcement. In a firm, all of the information necessary to make decisions is channeled by agents (employees) to a central party (the boss) that coordinates their activities and retransmits orders for execution.[1] Intertemporal allocation is also achieved by the same technique. Enforcement and bargaining problems are solved by delegating to the boss the right to make decisions for the group and to mete out rewards and punishments.

Organization Costs and External Effects

In the preceding section we have seen that both markets and hierarchies are feasible ways to organize economic activity. In a world of zero organization costs, the problem of the choice between firms and markets would therefore be trivial. The only determining factor would be the preference of economic agents as to the system of organization by which they wish to be ruled.

A cursory look at the real world should convince us, however, that organization costs are always positive. It is costly, both in terms of time and resources, to disseminate information. Indeed, an important part of the labor force of any given country is employed to perform this task. Buyers spend significant time canvasing various sellers. Enforcement costs are also highly significant: the grocery store clerk and the customer simultaneously weigh produce on a state-inspected scale; meat is inspected and graded; employees have to punch time clocks; courts and police officers are needed to enforce contracts and protect property rights. Bargaining is also widespread: a considerable amount of time and resources is invested to obtain better terms of trade or higher salaries.

With positive organization costs, market or firm organization will not lead to Pareto-efficient outcomes.[2] First, while a substantial amount of resources will be spent effecting exchange, only enough will be spent to equate the marginal return on additional expenditure to its cost. For example, it will not pay a trader to keep sampling offers till he finds the highest one. He will stop looking when he believes that the marginal gain from further search will be equal to the cost of further canvasing. Positive information costs will thus prevent the transfer of inputs and outputs to their best use. With positive measurement costs, it will also not be worthwhile to eliminate all measurement errors. There will remain opportunities for cheating. Rewards will not always be commensurate with performance, and output sometimes will exceed, and sometimes fall short, of society's needs.

At the limit, enforcement and bargaining costs will be so high as to exhaust all of the potential gains from exchange. Trading that would take place if there were no organization costs will become unprofitable. If a bargain cannot be struck, an individual will not be able or forced to take into account the effects, positive or negative, of his actions on others. He will tend to produce or consume less than is socially optimal, i.e., the valuation he will put on an extra unit will differ from the total social benefit or cost by the amount of the marginal cost or benefit imposed on others. Since the level of utility he achieves will depend on the level of those activities for which he cannot be forced to pay (or for which he cannot be remunerated), he will be encouraged to create damages—or not to generate gains—on others by varying the level of those activities that are not adequately constrained (McManus 1975). These damages—or foregone gains— have been called external effects.

Since both firms and markets experience positive organization costs, they both will fail to internalize all external effects. The fact that a market system does not always bring forth Pareto-efficient outcomes has been acknowledged in the market failure literature. The innumerable attempts at classification and reclassification that characterize that literature have tended to obscure the fact that market failures arise from the presence of high organization costs (i.e., information, enforcement, and bargaining costs). Market failures are but acute manifestations of positive organization costs, a chronic phenomenon that affects firms, markets, and governments.

Francis Bator (1958), for example, ascribes market failures to the presence of three types of externalities, "ownership" externalities, "technical" externalities, and "public good" externalities. The classical example of an ownership externality is Meade's apple and honey parable. According to Meade, the inability of apple producers to charge beekeepers for the bees' nectar take will result in an inefficient allocation of resources. Technical externalities are said to be present whenever production exhibits increasing returns to scale. In that case, production will not take place at the socially efficient point, that is, at the point where price equals marginal cost. The third type of externality arises in the case of Samuelsonian public goods. Consumption of such a good by an individual leads to no subtraction from any other individual's consumption of that good. Pareto efficiency requires, therefore, that the marginal rates of transformation in production between the public good and all other goods be equal, not to the marginal rate of substitution of each separate consumer, but to the algebraic sum of such marginal rates. If each consumer could be charged an amount corresponding to its marginal rate of substitution, a Pareto-optimal position would be reached. Unfortunately, consumers have no incentive to reveal their preferences because their failure to pay does not jeopardize their ability to consume those goods. As a result, public goods will not be produced in the right amount.

In a world where information, enforcement, and bargaining costs are nil, all these externalities would vanish. Clearly, if apple producers knew at zero cost the nectar take of the bees and could enforce access to the apple blossoms, exchange would lead to a Pareto-efficient result. In a world of perfect knowledge, perfect enforcement, and no bargaining, technical externalities would also disappear: the producer of a good subject to increasing returns to scale could charge each buyer a separate price, enforce nonresale, and therefore produce up to the point where price is equal to marginal cost (Williamson 1975, p. 11). With perfect knowledge of the valuation each consumer puts on the consumption of the public good and perfect enforcement (i.e., costless exclusion of nonpayers) it would be possible to charge each consumer a sum corresponding to the marginal utility derived. An equilibrium level could be attained where total payments would just cover the cost of producing that level of the public good. An optimal amount of the public good would, therefore, be provided.

In the real world, positive organization costs will prevent markets from achieving Pareto-optimal results. But in many cases, markets will not fail completely. It is interesting to note that some purported cases of market failures are in fact handled by markets. Thus, as Steven Cheung (1973) has shown, nectar and pollination services are routinely transacted in the marketplace.[3] Lighthouses can be built, operated, financed, and owned by private individuals, as the early British experience shows (Coase 1974). Market failures are therefore clearly relative, because the same factors, positive organization costs, that are responsible for them also prevent hierarchies from internalizing all external effects.

Hierarchies, just like markets, fail to perfectly constrain individual behavior. Because information gathering and enforcement are expensive, only enough effort will be made in monitoring employee behavior to equate the marginal gain of detection activity with the marginal cost of detection. Employees will thus be able to pursue their own goals at the expense of the organization. They will loaf, indulge in unprofitably high professional standards, and so on. Following McManus (1975), we will call this behavior "on-the-job" consumption. In doing so, employees will be worse off than if, somehow, they could be forced (at zero cost) to maximize the organization's objective function, and this for two reasons: first, employees who consume on-the-job trade such consumption for take-home pay. Consumption of nonpecuniary goods is inferior to the equivalent loss in money income, because money usually allows a greater range of choices (Furubotn and Pejovich 1972, p. 1,152). More importantly, if the employer cannot discover at zero cost the identity of those that indulge in on-the-job consumption, each employee will have an incentive to consume more on the job than he otherwise would find optimal since his income will be reduced whether he shirks or not. The firm's total product, and therefore each employee's salary, will thus be lower than optimal (Alchian and Demsetz 1972).

The Limits of Markets

We have seen that markets and hierarchies are feasible methods of organizing economic activity, but that because exchange costs are positive both systems will not perfectly constrain individual behavior. In firms as well as in markets, there will be opportunities for some to impose uncompensated costs and benefits on others. External effects will thus be present in both institutions. The level of external effects for a given exchange needs not, however, be the same under the two systems, since firms and markets differ in the ways they organize economic activity. If we assume that economic agents will choose whichever method of organization yields them the largest income (pecuniary and nonpecuniary), then each system will be chosen to organize the type of exchange for which it is particularly suited.[4] To explain the respective domains of both institutions, it is necessary to analyze the strengths and weaknesses of each organizational mode (McManus 1975).

Recall that markets rely on prices to communicate information, reward behavior, and curb bargaining. The efficiency of a market system hinges on the ability of prices to perform these three functions. As we will now see, this implies that private property rights be defined and enforced, and that information channels be established.

For markets to organize economic activities, agents must have exclusive property rights to the resources they control. By exclusive property rights we mean that the owner of a good has a limited authority to use an asset, to appropriate the return from this asset, and to change the asset's form and substance, including the right to transfer all rights or some of the rights in the asset at mutually agreeable terms (Furubotn and Pejovich 1974, p. 4). If property rights are not exclusive, then the costs and benefits of changing the physical attributes or the uses of the goods are not borne solely by their owner. There is then an inequality between private and social cost and benefit, and independent action will not lead to joint utility maximization (Alchian and Allen 1969, p. 158). The absence of exclusivity reduces the content of property rights and thus tends to preclude exchange. For example, the value of an automobile is likely to be lower if it can be used by others without permission than if it can be kept easily under the control of the owner. If exclusivity is costly to establish, then transfer will be difficult to effect, and mutually advantageous trades will not take place (Alchian and Allen 1969).

The content of property rights is a function of enforcement possibilities and of legal provisions. If it is not physically possible for owners to detect and to prevent unauthorized use of their resources, the property rights they own are severely diminished. When property rights are exchanged, enforcement costs are the costs of measuring, to the satisfaction of both parties, the bundle of property rights that changes hands. Because it is costly to measure with perfect precision, there will be some range within which exclusive property rights will not be enforceable. Within that range, changes in one activity will not be reciprocated by changes in payment and some of the gains of trade will have to be foregone. Exclusivity of property rights will thus be a function of the technical nature of the commodity or activity in question (McManus 1975, p. 340).

Because states have the monopoly of force in their jurisdiction, they also have the power to arbitrarily affect the delimitation of property rights. The state can restrict property rights that are technologically enforceable and thus prevent the attainment of efficient solutions. For example, although it is physically possible to enforce private property on oyster beds, many states refuse to grant those rights. Oysters then belong to no one until they are harvested, and each waterman has incentives to catch as many as possible before they are taken by others. Wasteful harvesting techniques and over-fishing result. Similarly, governments can ban the transfer of some property rights, as in the case of airwaves. Because transfer is illegal, there is no guarantee that frequencies will go to their most valued uses (Alchian and Allen 1969, p. 247).

If property rights are exclusive, resource owners will be able and motivated to take into consideration the impact of their behavior on society, since they will bear the costs and benefits of their actions. But how will the members of the group communicate their desires and preferences to economic agents? Since markets rely on decentralized decision making, such data must be communicated to all parties. The information transmitted and received must therefore be simple.

As Arrow (1974, p. 20) points out, prices are concentrated information, symbols, and codes that provide traders with the minimum amount of information necessary to maximize the social product. But establishment of prices, like that of any code, requires high setup costs. The real cost of a system of price signals is that of creating information channels and of defining and enforcing codes, such as grading standards, quality controls, and the like. Only when the characteristics of the goods are known to everyone do prices become "sufficient" statistics, i.e., they convey all the information necessary for agents to independently bring forth an efficient social outcome. Thus, the price of a used car by itself does not provide sufficient information unless the bundle of transportation services has been adequately defined. Two observations can be made concerning coding cost: (1) they will differ across goods and services; (2) they will be characterized by high fixed and low variable costs. Coding costs will differ because some goods are easier to measure than others. Goods for which quality characteristics are important, yet difficult to assess, will be more costly to code. Coding also implies setting and enforcing standards, rules to be known and enforced by all parties. The situation is analogous to the learning of a language: once the basic grammar is learned, one can talk with very little effort. Coding thus implies high fixed and low variable costs, and will be profitable only for goods that are frequently traded. The familiar textbook examples of iron, wheat, potatoes, cloth, or gold are all goods that are frequently traded and easily graded. On the other hand, the high cost of disseminating information about heterogeneous goods to economic agents will seriously limit the efficiency of market exchange.

Finally, market exchange will incur high bargaining costs unless the terms of trade are exogenously determined. If parties can affect the terms of trade in their favor, bargaining will become a paying proposition. The smaller the number of potential parties to a transaction, the larger the opportunity for bargaining. Bargaining costs have to be subtracted from each trader's gains from trade, and may even absorb all of these gains thus preventing exchange altogether. The presence of a large number of buyers and sellers is therefore crucial to the elimination of bargaining in market exchange.

While markets are subject to some limitations in organizing some economic activities at a given point in time, they also experience difficulties with intertemporal allocation. Efficient allocation through time requires that agents know the future prices of the commodities that are relevant to their decisions. For contingent markets to generate future prices, producers and consumers have to determine how much they would buy or sell of each contingent good (i.e., of each good at each time-cum-environment point) given a set of prices.

To realize the complexity of such a choice, let us assume with Meade (1970, p. 37) there are only three environmental variables, that every one of these three variables can take three values over each of the next five years. Let us say, for example, that we are uncertain about the rainfall, the fashionable hemline, and technical progress in the textile industry, and that each variable can be high, medium, or low. Then there would be $3^{3 \times 5}$ or over 14 million time paths to consider, and at each point in these time paths one would have to know how much to buy or sell. Thus, even in our simplified example, the sheer multiplicity of time paths to be considered would make contingent markets fail. Furthermore, even if all time-cum-environment points could be compared, it may be impossible for all parties to agree afterward on which state of the environment has taken place, because it is difficult to distinguish these points from one another. In that case it will be impossible to base a firm insurance contract upon the occurrence of some event, and contingent markets will fail.[5] The insurance contracts that underlie contingent prices may also be impossible to draw on account of "moral hazard." For example, a scientist working on a new product may be unable to insure against failure, for such a contract may affect his incentive to succeed in his efforts.

If contingent markets fail, entrepreneurs will not obtain information on future prices. They will have to plan the future as best they can on the basis of their expectations. A set of future prices, as generated by contingent markets, would insure that future plans are consistent. Today's spot prices, however, fail to recognize future interdependences. If interacting parties would candidly reveal their future plans, pooling that information would ensure consistency. But agents will have incentives to distort information for strategic advantage. There is no guarantee that a market system will efficiently allocate resources through time and will generate consistent investment plans.

The lack of future prices will be especially costly in production processes subject to significant time lags between start and completion (Buckley and Casson 1976, p. 36). In that case, it will be difficult to coordinate short-term production schedules. The organization of multistage, capital-intensive production processes also requires a knowledge of future prices. Without such prices, the plans of the parties at each stage will not necessarily be consistent, and the optimal scale of production will not generally be chosen. The more long-lived and specific the capital goods needed in production, the greater the need for long-term future prices will be.

In both cases, the firm will seek to remedy the absence of future markets by entering into contracts to better organize its activities with those of its suppliers or customers. In some cases, however, market contracts will involve high costs, and internal organization will be preferred.

In summary, the relative efficiency of markets in organizing production is a function of the cost of establishing and transferring property rights. That cost varies with the ease with which the stock of assets or the flow of services can be measured. The lower the measurement costs, all else being equal, the more efficient will be market exchange.

Three factors tend to affect the cost of transacting on markets at any given level of measurement costs. One is the exchange volume. If a good is transacted often, its measurement costs can be spread over many trades, and the cost per transaction will be low. Another is the number of potential traders. The greater that number, the lower the costs of effecting market transactions, if everything else is constant. Whatever the costs of measuring the quantity transacted, competition among sellers will lead them to reveal the characteristics of the bundle of goods or services exchanged. A large number of traders will also reduce the costs of enforcing the terms of the bargain: if one seller attempts to cheat, his competitors are likely to alert the buyers so as to obtain his share of the market. Furthermore, the larger the number of parties to the exchange, the smaller the opportunities for bargaining. Finally, the relative efficiency of markets is crucially affected by government intervention. Since governments establish and enforce property rights, they have a considerable influence in determining the scope of market organization.

In a dynamic framework, the efficiency of market allocation depends on the level of uncertainty. The more uncertain the future, the larger the number of contingencies to be considered by market traders, and therefore the greater the likelihood that evaluating these possibilities will overwhelm their information-processing and decision-making capacities.

Contracts

A form of market interaction that reduces market organization costs whenever measurement costs are high is the contract. Contracts are promises, enforceable in court and valid over a specified amount of time.

Effecting exchange through contracts has both advantages and costs. As pointed out by McManus (1972, p. 76) contracts reduce enforcement costs by defining, for the life of the contract, actions that would breach the promise and the compensation to be paid to the damaged party. If it is costly to detect variations in the flow of services being transferred, it will pay traders not to attempt to measure it exactly, but instead to define limits beyond which compensation should be paid. Contracts thus replace the continuous adjustment of market prices by discrete changes in the terms of trade. They leave some opportunity for parties to gain at the expense of one another, but whenever the cost of detecting and being compensated for such cheating is high, parties will find it more advantageous not to attempt to measure precisely the effect of their actions on one another, but simply to specify bounds on their behavior.

Still another reason why contracts may tend to be a cheaper method to constrain some types of interdependences is that, whenever measurement costs are high and the number of traders is small, agreeing to general rules ex ante may be considerably easier than renegotiating after each change in circumstances. At the time contracts are drawn, the parties will not know the precise consequences for themselves of their adoption of contractual rules. They are thus more likely to strike a bargain than if they had to come to an agreement after specific events have taken place (Buchanan and Tullock 1962, pp. 78–79). By agreeing ex ante to a set of general rules to guide their behavior, parties to a contract can therefore significantly reduce bargaining and enforcement costs per transaction. The longer the contract can be made to stick, the larger the amount of savings over a comparable spot market exchange.

Unfortunately, contracts have certain drawbacks. First, they tend to make changes in the allocation of resources costlier to effect than under the price mechanism. In a price system, resources will be reallocated if the total gain from such a change is greater than the total loss. In response to changes in the environment, prices will shift, and the variation in price may lead to a net loss for some individuals. By contrast, contractual rules can only be altered upon termination of the agreement or if losers are compensated. Adaptation to changing circumstances is thus relatively more costly with market contracts than with spot exchange (McManus 1972, p. 77). As a result, while market contracts may be relatively efficient transaction modes whenever the number of parties is limited and/or measurement costs are high, they experience serious disabilities in conditions of uncertainty.

Under such conditions, parties will attempt to share risks. They will try to specify ex ante all the potential events and the rules to be followed in each case. As the degree of uncertainty increases, the number of contractual stipulations to be drawn and agreed upon by the parties—and to be enforced during contract execution—increases. The cost of effecting transactions through contracts thus rises. On the other hand, should parties decide not to agree ahead of time on rules to govern their behavior in specific contingencies and therefore to leave contracts incomplete, adaptation to change would be difficult, and parties would shoulder substantial risks (Williamson 1975).

To alleviate the risks inherent in long-term contracts, it is possible for the parties to reduce contract duration. A reduction in the length of the contract facilitates adaptation to changing circumstances, since the terms of trade can be changed (without compensating the loser) at the expiration of the contract. Shorter contracts also imply lower enforcement costs since nonrenewal is a relatively inexpensive way to enforce contractual terms (Cheung 1969, pp. 37–38).

On the other hand, reducing the length of the contract will negate the very advantages of contracting because it will increase contracting costs per transaction. A series of short-term contracts is more costly than a long-term contract because contractual terms must be redefined and agreed on at each contract renewal stage. More bargaining can also be expected than if the terms of the contract had been defined once and for all. Furthermore, short-term contracting may be deficient if the parties to the contract must make long-term investments. In that case, nonrenewal of the contract would impose large losses on one or both parties (Williamson 1975).

When measurement costs are high and potential parties to the exchange are few, contracts may reduce significantly market transaction costs per transaction. The relative advantages that contracting has over spot exchange decrease as the length of the contract is shortened. In conditions of uncertainty, long-term contracts will become relatively risky and contracting relatively less efficient than when events are more predictable. In the presence of uncertainty, then, as will be argued in the next section, hierarchical organization, that is, exchange within the firm, will be preferred.

Advantages and Limits of Firms

To understand why in some circumstances exchange within the firm has certain advantages over market transactions, it is necessary to recall the points on which they differ.

A firm can be described as a set of contractual relationships by which a group of agents delegates to a central party the power to make decisions on their behalf and to constrain their behavior.

Whenever prices do not adequately reflect social costs and benefits, a system by which each individual takes prices as given and maximizes his pecuniary income will be inefficient. In maximizing their income, agents will use too much of the activities whose price is below social cost and too little of those whose price is greater than the social benefits conferred. In doing so, they will impose external effects on each other and will fail to maximize their joint income.

Because the firm is characterized by a different enforcement and decision-making mechanism, an institutional change to hierarchical organization can, in these cases, reduce some of these external effects and achieve a higher aggregate income for the group.

In a firm, the pecuniary constraints of market prices are replaced by managerial control. Employees are no longer directly rewarded by market prices, but by the extent to which they obey managerial directives. Members of the firm have therefore less incentive to inflict external costs (or to fail to provide external benefits) on each other. Because their income is no longer directly a function of their productive activity, they will be more indifferent as to the allocation of their activities. They are therefore more likely to obey the directives of the central monitor and will agree to alter their behavior so as to internalize the external effects that they impose on one another (McManus 1975, p. 342).

Another difference between firms and markets is in the method used to disseminate information. Hierarchies channel the information possessed by agents to a central party that assimilates all the information dispersed in the system, draws consistent plans, and retransmits directives to members. Such an informational design economizes on the number of channels. In a society consisting of n interdependent parties, market organization requires $\frac{1}{2}(n^2 - n)$ two-way communication channels. If all messages are instead channeled through a central party, only n two-way channels are needed (Williamson 1970, p. 20). Whenever price information needs to be supplemented by complex descriptions, it may be much more efficient to centralize information than to broadcast it to all relevant parties. A system by which every piece of information has to be communicated to everyone would be much more costly than one in which all information is sent to one person and selectively retransmitted to each member of the group. Firms are therefore comparatively efficient when the volume of information to be communicated to interacting parties is large.

Finally, internal organization has major advantages over market contracting whenever disputes arise between parties. In a firm, employees have less incentive to invest in bargaining because internal conflicts can be resolved by fiat. By contrast, conflicts between market traders can involve substantial bargaining and court costs.

The advantages of firms over markets we have just described are especially significant in the context of recurrent, long-term exchanges between a small number of parties under conditions of uncertainty. In such circumstances, exchange within the firm economizes on the limited information-processing and decision-making faculties of the parties. When the transaction is shifted from the market to the firm, market contracts are replaced by managerial directives. If exchange is recurrent and uncertain, making the transaction internal to the firm dispenses with the need to specify ex ante all possible contingencies and to decide on the optimal course of action in each case. Instead, the central monitor can wait until events take place and make adjustments as the future unfolds (Williamson 1975, p. 25). Note that this saving is only significant if trades are recurrent, protracted, and subject to uncertainty. There is no particular advantage of merging over contracting in the case of a one-shot exchange, since the former includes bargaining over the terms of trade, while the latter involves bargaining over asset valuation. If there is no uncertainty, a market contract offers the same characteristics as a merger agreement, since both, once made, will hold indefinitely (Williamson 1975).

In addition, internal organization allows faster adaptation to change because internal trades can be changed without the need to obtain (as in markets) the assent of all the parties to the transaction.

There are no incentives for employees to bargain with other employees about the terms of internal transactions, since these transactions do not affect their income. Thus, should the need arise to respecify the system because of a sudden change in the environment, the central party can quickly realize the need for adaptation and order parties to adapt sequentially. In markets, on the other hand, parties will resist any change that is detrimental to their interests by haggling and distorting information: even if parties cooperate, the time spent to communicate the information necessary to adjust may be such that, by the time partial adaptation is realized, further adjustment is needed (Williamson 1975). The cost of negotiation and the time required to bring the system's parts into adjustment may be such as to prevent the system from ever restabilizing after a shock. Once again, these advantages of internal organization are only felt in the case of long-term trades under changing conditions.

Common ownership also tends to encourage the drawing of consistent plans. For the plans of independent entities to be compatible, expectations of future conditions must be shared. Contingent markets can theoretically reveal future plans, but they are likely to fail in conditions of uncertainty or whenever the number of potential parties is small. In that case internal organization will be advantageous because members of the firm have incentives to pool their knowledge of the future, since they are not rewarded by their individual market-measured product. Common ownership thus encourages the convergence of expectations, an important source of external economies if long-lived fixed investments are necessary (Malmgren 1961).

We have dwelt so far on the advantages that firms offer relative to markets. If those advantages were universal and available without limits, internal organization would have displaced markets altogether. However, the very attributes of firms that make them preferred to markets in organizing some activities seriously limit their efficiency in other cases.

We have already seen how firms replace price constraints by managerial directives. The reduction or elimination of direct pecuniary constraints on behavior weakens the relationship between an individual's pecuniary income and his contribution to the output of the firm. This relaxation of pecuniary constraints on behavior, which is efficient whenever market prices fail to maximize the joint income of the parties, encourages employees to reduce the amount of productive resources they devote to the firm's output since such behavior will have for them no direct pecuniary consequences. As a result the total output generated within the firm will be reduced (McManus 1975).

Opportunities to consume on-the-job will be a function of the cost of preventing such consumption, a cost which will vary according to the type of activities monitored. Firms constrain the shirking of employees by observing and specifying their behavior. The more difficult it is to constrain shirking by managerial directives, the less efficient firms will be relative to markets. In some activities it is relatively easy to evaluate the amount of productive activity that is devoted to the firm's output, because a worker's outward behavior is high correlated with his consumption of leisure. In assembly line processes, for example, it is relatively simple to enforce minimum levels of leisure under the threat of dismissal. In other activities, it is more difficult to specify and enforce general rules of behavior to constrain shirking. In professional and artistic occupations, behavior on the job may be a poor index of performance, and specifying behavior will not elicit a given level of productive activity (Alchian and Demsetz 1972, p. 786). Geographical dispersion also affects the cost of enforcing managerial directives, since physical distance makes observation of input behavior more costly (Olson 1964).

In markets, prices communicate to economic agents the information that they need to enable them to coordinate their actions with those of others. As we have pointed out earlier, whenever prices do not reflect adequately social costs and benefits, a market system will generate external effects and will prevent economic agents from maximizing their joint income. In that case, it may be advantageous to take away from each individual his power to make decisions, and instead ask him to transfer to the boss the information on which his market decisions would have been based. The disadvantage of such a system is that all information has to be transferred to a central party and then retransmitted to the agent.[6] The separation of information collection and decision making that characterizes firms is likely to lead, in some instances, to significant costs. In the course of their activities, economic agents acquire specialized knowledge of what Hayek (1945, p. 521) has called the "particular circumstances of time and place." In a market setting, individuals can be expected to make good use of that idiosyncratic knowledge since using such knowledge will increase the pecuniary rewards they achieve. Dissociating information collection from decision making is likely to lead to some information loss. First, agents have less incentive to become informed, since they will not be directly rewarded for doing so. Furthermore, even if they faithfully report all that they observe, some information is likely to be lost in the transfer. If employees acquire in the course of their activity the greater part of the information they need to maximize group wealth, then centralization of information will be costly, since a significant part of the information dispersed in the system will be wasted in transmission losses. The greater the proportion of the total knowledge necessary to make efficient group decisions that is possessed by the individual, the less efficient centralized systems will be.

The two inefficiencies that are inherent in hierarchical organization, shirking and information loss, rise dramatically with an increase in the number of employees (what we will call the "size" of the firm). We have seen that in firms all of the relevant information is sent to a central party and retransmitted to employees. The limit to such a system is the ability of the monitor to receive, store, and retrieve complex information, make decisions, and retransmit orders for execution. If the volume of messages overloads the capacity of the monitor, the directives issued from headquarters will fail to incorporate the totality of the information that has been sent by employees, and execution of these directives will result in an inefficient outcome for the group. Since the volume of messages received by the monitor is a function of the number of his subordinates, an expansion in the number of employees will seriously increase information losses. Similarly, the ability of the central party to control on-the-job consumption will be reduced as the number of the subordinates he must oversee goes up. The larger the size of the firm, the higher the level of internal organization costs the firm will experience.

If it is assumed that agents will choose to organize a particular set of activities through the organizational mode that maximizes their joint wealth, the choice between firms and markets will hinge on the relative cost of decentralized adjustment by market prices to that of centralized adjustment through managerial directives.

Two factors will tend to influence the relative cost of both modes, if everything else is constant. First is the level of uncertainty: the more uncertain the future, the more efficient a hierarchical organization. Second is the number of interacting parties: the larger the number of agents, all else being equal, the less efficient a hierarchical organization and the more efficient a market exchange.

As the firm increases in size, the level of internal organization costs it will experience will increase. At some point the cost to the firm of organizing internally an additional exchange will be higher than the cost of letting it be organized by the market. That point will set the boundary between firms and markets (Coase 1937).

Variables Affecting Institutional Change:
Internal Organization Costs

In the preceding analysis we have argued that the firm has, in some circumstances, inherent advantages over markets in organizing economic activities. As the number of parties within the firm grows, so do internal organization costs. Here we will refine considerably the model of the firm discussed previously. We consider the impact of changes in the firm's internal property rights and in its information and enforcement structures on the level of internal organization costs it experiences. We conclude that innovations in legal and organizational form, as well as in personnel management, will substantially lower internal organization costs and allow larger equilibrium firm sizes.

Legal Form

One of the reasons we contend that firms are sometimes superior to markets is because managerial control of behavior is socially more efficient than price incentives. The efficiency of firms in that respect hinges, as we will now see, on the particular property right structure that exists within a firm.

In firms, employees delegate to a central party, the boss, the power to constrain their behavior. As Alchian and Demsetz (1972) have pointed out, efficiency requires that the right to monitor the team (i.e., to unilaterally revise the contractual terms of individual employees without having to alter the contract of every other employee), and the right to the total product of the team net of fixed payments to inputs (the residual), be granted to the same person. Only if the boss is given the right to the residual will he have an incentive to act in the interest of all team members. If the right to the residual is granted the monitor, he will be restrained from consuming on-the-job, for if he has full claim to the residual, he will also bear the full burden of relaxing his efforts. If, on the other hand, the monitor does not own full title to the residual, the incentive he has to control shirking by his subordinates is reduced. In that case the opportunity cost of his leisure, i.e., the net earnings foregone by not exercising his duties, will fall, and the monitor will find it advantageous to consume more of his income on-the-job: he will conduct business meetings on the golf links, hire employees solely on the basis of their appearance or personality, and the like. To insure long-term maximization, the monitor should also have the right to sell his right to the residual. If not, he would have incentives, as he advances in age, to reduce to zero the value of the firm.

The coalescing into one bundle of (1) the right to receive the residual, (2) the right to terminate or revise the membership of the team, and (3) the right to sell the above-mentioned rights is the essence of the "classical" capitalist firm (Alchian and Demsetz 1972). Any attenuation of those property rights will tend to reduce the comparative advantage that firms enjoy, ceteris paribus, over markets.

Such attenuation may, however, be inevitable because of the need to obtain capital. When the optimal size of the firm requires the accumulation of capital beyond what a single individual possesses, market transaction costs may prevent an owner-manager from borrowing the requisite amount at fixed terms and instead oblige him to share the residual with lenders.

Theoretically, it should be possible for the firm's manager to raise in the capital market the financial resources he needs. Market transaction costs, however, prevent an entrepreneur from relying completely on borrowing. As Jensen and Meckling (1976) show, if the owner-manager finances the firm with borrowed capital, he will have a strong incentive to engage in activities that are likely to yield very high returns with a low probability of success. If successful, the entrepreneur will appropriate most of the gain, but if unlucky, the stockholders will bear the greater part of the cost. The larger the proportion of borrowed funds in the total capital venture, the greater the incentive the borrower has to engage in such risk-maximizing behavior.[7]

To protect their assets, lenders will therefore specify contractual limitations on the manager's freedom of action. To completely shield the lenders from risk, contractual stipulations would have to be extremely detailed, and therefore costly to draw and to enforce. Because of the cost of writing such contracts, and because of the irreducible opportunity for fraud, borrowing capital will involve substantial costs. If capital markets are efficient, these costs will be borne by the owner-manager. The higher the ratio of borrowed funds to owned funds, the greater the costs of borrowing additional funds (Jensen and Meckling 1976).

One method of avoiding steeply rising borrowing costs as the amount borrowed increases is to give each lender a share in the residual. If the owner-manager has to share the residual with lenders, he will be discouraged from investing in risky projects, for he will share proportionally in any resulting gains or losses. There are two legal forms that provide lenders with a claim to the residual, the partnership and the limited liability company. We argue that the latter experiences lower internal organization costs than the former at any given large firm size.

In partnerships the right to revise membership in the firm and/or to claim the residual is shared by many owners. The weakness of such property right structures is that the residual becomes a public good to the partners. As their number increases, the cost of detecting on-the-job consumption increases, while the effect on the firm's profits of any partner's behavior decreases; as a result, shirking increases. The unanimous consent of partners is required in a partnership for decision to be made. Decision making will become very costly because the detailed information necessary to make decisions has to be communicated to all parties. Furthermore, under the rule of unanimity, each partner has the monopoly of his consent and bargaining becomes a paying proposition (Buchanan and Tullock 1962). The larger the number of partners, the longer it will take to obtain unanimous assent. Because information, monitoring, and bargaining costs increase steeply with an increase in the number of partners, we would expect partnerships to be limited to rather small sizes.

Partnerships have a further disadvantage. Under the partnership form of organization, each partner is liable for all the debts of the partnership. As a result, by becoming a partner in more than one business, an individual increases his liabilities by a multiple of his investment. His risk would therefore increase, rather than decrease, by diversifying his assets (Hicks 1969, p. 80).

The limited liability company is a much more efficient form of organization because it reduces the cost of borrowing capital and that of managing the firm. In limited liability companies, (1) all decision-making and monitoring powers are transferred to one person, the manager—the owners retain decision-making power over a few major decisions that affect the structure of the firm and its dissolution, as well as over the membership of the management group; (2) the liability of owners (stockholders) is now limited to their initial stake; (3) stockholders have the right to sell their shares without approval from the other coowners (Alchian and Demsetz 1972).

The limitation of the liability of owners has two main consequences. First, it allows an investor to reduce his risk by investing in more than one company (Hicks 1969, p. 80). Consequently, it reduces the cost to the firm of obtaining capital. Second, it increases the willingness of owners to delegate decision making to managers, since they are now only liable for their initial stake. The cost of mismanagement to owners (stockholders) is also alleviated by the right granted them to sell their shares without approval from the other co-owners. Should shirking become rampant, or should owners disagree with the decisions made by the board of directors, owners can sell their shares and protect their assets from expected losses (Alchian and Demsetz 1972).

The delegation by owners of the greater part of their monitoring and decision-making rights to managers, if it tends to reduce bargaining and information costs, has also potentially serious consequences. In limited liability companies, ownership is separated from control. In other words, monitors are denied claims in the residual. This should blunt their incentive to control on-the-job consumption by their subordinates. This characteristic of limited liability corporations has been viewed with concern by some authors (Berle and Means 1932).

There are, however, good reasons to believe that the costs due to the separation of ownership and control in modern corporations are not excessive, that the benefits of the joint-stock form of organization more than make up for its costs, and that the limited liability company experiences lower internal organization costs than similarly sized partnerships. As Alchian (1969) persuasively argues, the fantastic growth in equity financing in the United States and elsewhere would be difficult to explain if managers of modern corporations were able to appropriate a large part of their stockholder's wealth (table 8). Why would investors be willing to entrust managers with their money if they thought that their interests were not adequately safeguarded? Furthermore, why would they choose the status of residual claimant if they knew that managers would operate the firm so as to keep distributed profits to a minimum? Clearly, there are many alternative ways in which capital-owners might invest, including single proprietorships, partnerships, real estate, or fixed claims (bonds, notes, or mortgages). It must be that, in spite of the irreducible cost of constraining the behavior of managers, equity shares in limited liability companies are at least as profitable as other types of investment (Jensen and Meckling 1976, pp. 330–31). The empirical evidence thus suggests the existence of constraints on the manager's ability to use stockholder's assets for his own benefit.

Among the possible factors at work to limit managerial discretion, the following two would seem the more effective. First, one would expect potential lenders to discount new share issues by the expected loss (based on the company's past record) due to managerial discretion. Holders of outstanding shares that are dissatisfied with company policies can sell their shares, thus depressing the aggregate market value of the shares below that of the assets behind

TABLE 8   Growth in Equity Financing in the United States, 1960–72

Legal Form	1960	1972	Index (1960=100)
Proprietorships			
Number[a] (in thousands)	9,090	10,173	112
Business receipts[b] ($ billion)	171	276	161
Partnerships			
Number (in thousands)	941	992	105
Total receipts[c] ($ billion)	74	104	140
Corporations			
Number (in thousands)	1,141	1,813	159
Total receipts[c] ($ billion)	849	2,171	256

Source: U.S., Department of Commerce, Bureau of the Census, *Statistical Abstract of the United States: 1975:* (Washington, D.C.: Government Printing Office, 1975) p. 490, table 800.

a. Individually owned businesses and farms.
b. Receipts from sales and services less allowances, rebates, and returns; excludes capital gains or losses, and investment income not associated with the taxpayer's business.
c. Total taxable receipts before deduction of cost of goods sold, cost of operations, and net loss from sales of property other than capital assets. Includes nontaxable interest; excludes all other nontaxable income.

the equity. This, in turn, would increase the chances of takeover, and the subsequent firing of the management team (Marris 1967, p. 19). Furthermore, depressed share prices are likely to raise the firm's cost of borrowing on both the bond and the equity market (Marris 1967, p. 19).

It is also important to realize that managers are paid to maximize stockholder's wealth. Their salary is a function of their performance on their current job and the desire to move to better jobs within and between firms will induce them to maximize stockholder's welfare (Alchian 1969; Fama 1980).

It would therefore appear that the separation of ownership from control that is an inherent defect of limited liability companies does not significantly reduce the advantages enjoyed by this particular legal form over single proprietorships or partnerships for relatively large firm sizes.

Information Structure

We have argued earlier that one of the limiting factors of hierarchical systems is the information-processing capacity of the central monitor. That factor would constrain firms to rather limited sizes were it not for the possibility of adding hierarchical levels; a first line supervisor monitors each group of operators, while the central monitor oversees the supervisors. Thus, the limits to the ability of the boss to run the firm are extended by delegating to subordinates some powers of decision.

Some economists have argued that as the firm expands, the increased number of supervisors relative to operators tends to set limits to the size of the firms. A hierarchically organized firm that combines two previously independent firms would, however, only require one additional level, therefore, one additional employee. Clearly this is a trivial increase in cost. The real limits to firms are due to the problems of transferring information across successive hierarchical levels (Williamson 1970).

Recall that in firms all information is channeled to the monitor who coordinates the behavior of employees and retransmits orders for execution. Clearly, any source of distortion in the process of information transfer will severely affect the firm's efficiency. The observation that serial reproduction of information leads to cumulative distortion was first made by Bartlett. He experimented with the oral transmission of descriptive passages through a chain of serially linked individuals and concluded that

> serial reproduction brings about startling and radical alterations in the material dealt with. Epiteths are changed into their opposites; incidents and events are transposed; names and numbers rarely survive intact for more than a few reproductions; opinions and conclusions are reversed—nearly every possible variation seems as if it can take place, even in a relatively short series. At the same time, the subjects may be very well satisfied with their efforts, believing themselves to have passed on all important features with little or no change, and merely, perhaps, to have omitted unessential matters. [Bartlett 1932, p. 175]

Although Bartlett's findings have great heuristic value in explaining the loss-of-control phenomenon, it should be pointed out that hierarchial organizations rarely rely on pure serial reproduction. Contrary to what we have said before, middle-level supervisors do not usually restrict themselves to reproducing messages upward and downward. Rather they screen and summarize the information coming from lower levels for use by the upper echelons, and operationalize directives received from the top for execution by their subordinates. In the process, middle-level managers exercise critical judgment. The fact that they have an active role in information transfer reduces the load on the central monitor, but, on the other hand, it increases the problem of information distortion. First, data compression and operationalizing by middle-level managers that do not have an overall view of the firm will undoubtedly lead to information loss. Second, managers can use the power to screen and summarize information to their best advantage: they will transmit what superiors want to hear, they will also report what they want their superiors to know. One consequence is that lower levels will have some freedom to pursue personal goals at the expense of the firm. Another is that the flow of information transmitted to upper levels will be systematically biased. As noted by Boulding (1966, p. 8), "almost all organizational structures tend to produce false images in the decision-maker, and the larger and more authoritarian the organization, the better the chance that its decision-makers will operate in purely imaginary worlds."

Williamson (1970) has formalized the argument in a simple model. He considers a hierarchically organized firm with the following characteristics: (1) employees at the lowest hierarchical level do manual work—all other employees are engaged in administrative tasks; (2) output is a constant proportion θ of productive input; (3) productive employees, i.e., those at the lowest hierarchical level, are paid a wage W_o; (4) the ratio between salary at level i (W_i) and salary at level $i + 1$ is β, with $\beta > 1$; (5) the span of control is a constant s ($s > 1$) at every hierarchical level; (6) product and factor prices (P, W_o and W_i) are given; (7) nonwage costs are a constant proportion r of output Q; (8) subordinates only carry out a fraction α ($0 < \alpha < 1$) of the orders given by their superiors and (9) control loss is "strictly cumulative", meaning there is no systematic compensation across hierarchical levels. Let

s = span of control

α = fraction of the work done by a subordinate that contributes to objectives of his superior ($0 < \alpha < 1$); it is thus an internal efficiency parameter

N_i = number of employees at the ith hierarchical level = s^{i-1}

n = number of hierarchical levels (the decision variable)

P = price of output

W_o = wage of production worker

W_i = wage of employees at ith hierarchical level
= $W_o \beta^{n-i}$ ($\beta > 1$)

r = nonwage variable cost per unit output

Q = output
= $\theta(\alpha s)^{n-1}$

R = total revenue
= $P Q$

C = total variable cost

$$= \sum_{i=1}^{n} W_i N_i + rQ$$

Assume that $\theta = 1$. What is the size of the firm (the number of hierarchical levels n) that maximizes net revenue? Net revenue is equal to

$$R - C = PQ - \sum_{i=1}^{n} W_i N_i - rQ$$

Replacing Q by $(\alpha s)^{n-1}$ and W_i by $W_o \beta^{n-i}$ and N_i by s^{i-1}

$$R - C = P(\alpha s)^{n-1} - \sum_{i=1}^{n} W_o \beta^{n-i} s^{i-1} - r(\alpha s)^{n-1}$$

now

$$\sum_{i=1}^{n} W_o \beta^{n-i} s^{i-1} = W_o (\beta^n/s) \sum_{i=1}^{n} (s/\beta)^i$$

where

$$\sum_{i=1}^{n} (s/\beta)^i = [(s/\beta)^{n+1} - (s/\beta)]/[(s/\beta) - 1] \simeq s^{n+1}/[(s - \beta)\beta^n]$$

Thus we have

$$R - C = P (\alpha s)^{n-1} - W_o (s^n/s - \beta) - r(\alpha s)^{n-1}$$

Differentiating this expression with respect to n and setting equal to zero (and letting ln denote natural logarithm), Williamson obtains as the optimal value for n:

$$n^* = 1 + (1/ln\ \alpha) \{ln\ (W_o/P - r) + ln\ (s/s - \beta) + ln\ [ln\ s/ln(\alpha s)]\}$$

α and $W_o/(P - r)$ are between zero and unity. Also $\beta < s$ and $\alpha s > 1$. For the approximation to apply, β must be smaller than s. Williamson argues that the inequality is supported by empirical studies of executive compensation. If $\alpha s < 1$, there would be negative returns to the hiring of additional employees. Since $ln\ \alpha < 0$, the expression in braces must be negative. According to Williamson, this condition is satisfied if the firm is required to earn positive profits. Assuming that the bounds and inequality conditions are satisfied, Williamson draws from his model the conclusion that the optimal value of n is infinite if $\alpha = 1$, i.e., if there is no control loss across hierarchical levels. If α is smaller than one, the cumulative effect of control loss will lead to limited firm sizes. The smaller the value of α, the lower the optimal size of the firm. Williamson shows that this result is not reversed by relaxing the assumption of constant returns to scale, of perfectly competitive product markets and of constant span of control (Williamson 1970, pp. 32–35).

Adding hierarchical levels is not, therefore, a perfect solution to the limited information-processing capacity of the peak coordinator since it increases information distortion, and eventually puts an absolute limit on firm size.

There are, however, two ways to alleviate internal communication costs. The first one is to reduce the number of hierarchical levels and increase the information-processing capacity of the peak coordinator by distributing some of his responsibilities to other managers. The other is to reduce information transmission needs within the system by proper redesign, a process called "decoupling" in the organizational literature (March and Simon 1958, pp. 158–60). One common decoupling procedure is to group richly interacting operators under a supervisor, allowing high intensity interactions to be mediated at a low level, while overall coordination of the weakly interacting supervisors is provided at the top level. This is the basis for dividing the firm into functional departments. The chief executive then tends to specialize in strategic, entrepreneurial decisions, and lower level managers in tactical ones. This form of organization is called by Williamson the unitary (or U-form) firm (Williamson 1970). As the firm increases in size and the main benefits of decoupling have been captured, the firm may attempt to increase information-processing capacity at the top. One way to augment the capacity of the chief executive to provide strategic planning—while maintaining effective control—is to bring heads of functional departments into the peak coordinating process. But because they represent one particular function, the natural posture for functional heads is to become advocates of their respective departments. Because functional chiefs tend to possess more information on their department than the peak coordinator, they will be able to supplant enterprise-wide goals by more partisan ones. The central monitor will not be able to isolate and eliminate such tendencies for three reasons. First, the performance of functional departments is not separable: it is difficult to impute responsibility of successes and failures. Second, it is not comparable. Third, because functional heads have a voice in decision making, they are functionally equal, and it is difficult to discipline equals (Williamson 1970).

Faced with problems of this type, the E.I. Du Pont deNemours company and General Motors Corporation devised in the early 1920s what Alfred Chandler (1961) has called the multidivisional structure. Williamson (1970, chap. 8) has incisively analyzed the characteristics and the efficiency advantages of the multidivision form (M-form) and the following discussion follows his treatment of the topic.

The M-form of organization is characterized by the division of the firm into quasi-firms. Each quasi-firm is responsible for a given product or geographic area and has its own sales, finance, purchasing, and manufacturing divisions; each is therefore self-sufficient. Coordination of the quasi-firms and strategy of the firm as a whole is performed by the central office, assisted by a staff. The staff is independent of any line organization. Its sole task is to monitor the behavior of quasi-firms, to allocate funds to them, and to hire and fire their management. The M-form of organization, therefore, alleviates the problems of limited capacity at the top by creating a staff to help the peak coordinator. Because it is specialized, that staff can better oversee quasi-firm performance. Because it has no line responsibility, the staff can give unbiased advice. Because it is independent from line managers, it has no qualms about firing or disciplining the management of quasi-firms.

The efficiency of M-form organizations depends on the ability to isolate richly interacting parts from weakly interacting ones. An appropriate organizational boundary will encourage intraproduct, while discouraging interproduct, communications. Once this is achieved, quasi-firms will be practically independent of one another. The problem of control can then be alleviated by the elaboration of quantifiable goals (for example, profits). Such criteria, which are commensurable and objective, tend to reduce tremendously the cost of controlling quasi-firms. Because performance is now reflected by profits and spillover cannot be used as an excuse, the M-form increases competition among managers, thus curbing opportunism. Because outsiders can also ascertain the marginal product of managers of M-form firms more easily than they can of functional managers, interfirm competition in the market for managers is also increased.

On-the-job consumption at the higher levels is also reduced by the threat of takeover. The M-form organization reduces significantly the cost of takeovers. Part of that cost results from the need to reorganize the acquiring firm to make room for the new acquisition. The M-form incurs lower costs in that respect, since it has a structure that can add quasi-firms (up to a limit) with little extra cost. The fear of takeover should, therefore, be a stronger deterrent to managerial discretion at the top in firms organized along multidivision lines than in other types of organizations.

For all the preceding reasons, M-form firms should experience lower internal organization costs at any given large size than other types of firms. One would, therefore, expect the equilibrium size of M-form firms to be substantially larger, all else being equal, than that of U-form firms (Williamson 1970, chap. 8).

Another way to increase the capacity of top-level managers to assimilate the information needed to control the firm is through coding. Coding reduces the volume of messages necessary to convey any given quantum of information. Accounting can be seen as a type of coding. By the use of accounting aggregates, information processing capacity at the top is increased. This in turn means that the ability of subordinates to consume on-the-job (to embezzle, to conceal their failures, etc.) is reduced. Internal organization costs should, therefore, decrease with the development and sophistication of accounting methods.

Labor Management

The raison d'être of a firm is to reduce organization costs by increasing the control of a single decision maker over the parties that previously interacted in the market. Coordination is now achieved not by prices but by internal directives. In doing so, the firm trades market transaction costs for internal organization costs. Those costs arise because it is costly to constrain employee behavior, to prevent employees from consuming on-the-job.

To reach that end, both positive and negative reinforcements can be used. The most simple way to curb an employee's undesirable behavior is to dock his pay or to dismiss him altogether. We have argued that the nature of the tasks assigned to employees is such that market-measured output is often a poor index of performance. Control of behavior is usually more efficient, but is often far from perfect. The problem is that to assess performance one must know what is feasible and compare it with what has been done. In some cases that knowledge is very costly to acquire. Negative reinforcements thus will fail to control all aspects of behavior. Because they tend to result in an antagonistic relationship, they usually fail to obtain anything more than short-term compliance on the visible aspects of work performance. Another limitation of negative sanctions is that they are sometimes not credible. Employees often acquire firm-specific skills in the course of their employment. Should the employee leave, he will impose high costs on the firm. The employee thus obtains a strategic advantage that he can use to bargain for higher pecuniary and nonpecuniary rewards (Williamson 1975). The goal of labor management should, therefore, be to get long-term cooperation from workers, and yet curb shirking and reduce bargaining costs.

The method used to achieve these goals is the creation of internal labor markets. First, tasks are made homogeneous and interchangeable. Positions are created with a given workload and a given salary. This reduces the employee's scope for bargaining, since his departure would make little difference—he can now be replaced without the need to reorganize the firm. Internal competition also pushes workers to reveal what is feasible performance, since by doing so they can increase their income. Second, long-term incentives are given to workers. Internal promotion thus ties the interest of the worker with that of the firm. By rewarding behavior with internal promotion, the employer makes compliance and cooperation the principal means for improving an employee's position. Long-term commitments are thus acquired without the need for long-term contracts.

Our analysis has attempted to show that the firm's legal form, the type of organization it has chosen, the methods it uses to convey information, and the kind of incentives chosen to motivate workers all significantly affect its level of internal organization costs. Because of the gains to be derived by curtailing such costs, substantial effort will be expended to that end. The level of internal organization costs will thus vary through time, as legal, organizational, or managerial innovations reduce intrafirm information, enforcement, and bargaining costs, and lead, all else being equal, to larger firm sizes.

Variables Affecting Institutional Change:
Market Transaction Costs

While some technological, legal, and organizational developments tend to reduce internal organization costs and increase the equilibrium size of firms, others have had the opposite effect by increasing the efficiency of market exchange.

We have seen that market exchange presupposes the definition and enforcement of property rights and the existence of grading and other standards. Any technological or legal innovation that reduces those costs increases, all else being equal, the domain of market exchange. Some technological innovations lower the expense of measuring goods and services and therefore increase the efficiency of market exchange relative to that of internal organization. Such was the case, for example, with the development of time-sharing. Before that innovation, a firm that needed computer services had to buy or rent a computer, hire computer experts, and operate their own in-house computer center. The development of time-sharing allowed the firm to buy its computing services on the market. The result is, therefore, an increase in the role played by markets relative to that ascribed to the firm.

Any legal change in the content of property rights will also influence the boundary between firms and markets, since the choice between market versus intrafirm organization hinges on the level of market transaction costs relative to the value of the rights transferred. An attenuation of the right to transfer an asset tends to reduce the value of property rights in that asset, and may lead to a shift from market exchange to internal organization. One instance of this phenomenon is the spate of vertical mergers during and immediately after World War II caused by the establishment of price controls and of government allocation (Stigler 1951). Likewise, rent control tends to make nonmarket modes of allocation preferable to market ones: some large firms that are headquartered in rent-controlled Paris own apartments that they lend to employees as a fringe benefit. Market exchange is then superseded by transfer within the firm.

Since definition and enforcement of property rights are performed by states, and since political decision makers do not always personally benefit from the results of their decisions, they will not necessarily allocate property rights in an efficient manner. Indeed, the historical record shows that governments have often traded inefficient property rights (monopoly privileges, for example) for short-term gains, and in the process have thwarted economic growth (North and Thomas 1973). A particular problem arises whenever transactions take place across national boundaries. Definition and enforcement of property rights then require the cooperation of many states, and free rider problems will arise. It will pay for some states not to abide by international agreements and in the process incite others to do the same. As international transactions grow, these limitations make market exchange a less desirable mode of organization.

Relevance of the Model

In the course of this chapter, the choice of economic organization has been described as being between two institutions, firms and markets. The distinguishing feature of markets is decentralized adaptation by prices, that of firms the replacement of market signals by managerial directives to coordinate and constrain the behavior of resource owners.

Although describing economic organization in terms of polar opposites simplifies the analysis, in the real world one observes a variety of organizational forms. At one extreme is the firm as we have described it. At the other a system where economic activity is organized by market prices. In the majority of cases, activities are organized by a combination of both methods. For example, although it has been argued that the characteristic of firms is the replacement of prices by nonprice criteria to coordinate and reward the behavior of agents, almost all firms make use of the price system in their internal dealings. Some use internal prices to reduce the need for managerial direction and to facilitate the evaluation of divisional performance. Prices are also sometimes used by firms to reward behavior. In some firms part or all of the payment received by workers is transaction specific, i.e., employees are paid on a piecework schedule.

Similarly, what we would define as market transactions often bears little resemblance to the textbook model of buyer and seller trading solely on the basis of market prices. Consider franchising contracts in the fast-food industry: the franchisee has no control over the design of the building, the food he will serve, the inputs he will use, and not even on the price he will charge. The only variable left to him is the intensity of his effort (provided he achieves a certain level of gross sales). His status does not seem to vary greatly from that of an employee.

Do considerations like these reduce the usefulness of the model developed in chapter 2? We think not. There are still important differences between an employee and a franchisee. The former's pay is more independent of his output than the latter. Similarly, internal pricing rules differ from market prices insofar as they are always selectively applied. Thus, in multidivisionalized firms, only certain activities are set up as profit centers and evaluated in function of net revenues; some activities are cost centers and their performance is assessed in least-cost terms. Although the firm makes use of the price system it never applies it across the board to all activities, for by doing so it could recreate the external effects it had sought to internalize. The dichotomy between firms and markets that has been made is therefore valid.

It can also be argued that the distinction is a useful one, since it corresponds to that which is made by law and which is reflected in economic statistics. Thus the size of a firm is usually measured by the number of its employees, not by that of all the parties with which it deals. Similarly, foreign direct investment is defined in terms of control. In other words, a firm is classified as an affiliate or a subsidiary of another firm whenever their relationship is organized through managerial directives rather than through market prices. Therefore, to explain foreign direct investment it is fruitful to reduce the diversity of organizational modes to two polar opposites, hierarchies and markets, and to concentrate on the determinants of the choice between these two methods of organization.

Conclusion

In the course of this chapter we have sought to describe the factors that determine whether a particular exchange will be mediated by a firm or a market. The choice, it has been argued, depends on the characteristics of the activities to be coordinated. At any point in time, markets will be particularly efficient in organizing some activities, while firms will prevail in organizing others. Since there are systematic differences across industries in the cost of measuring inputs and outputs, in the number of potential traders and the degree of uncertainty, one would expect significant interindustry variations in the relative role played by markets, and therefore in the average size of firms. Over time, legal, technological, and managerial innovations will affect the respective spheres of firms and markets. These innovations will shift the relative cost of firm and market organization, and will, therefore, lead to changes in the equilibrium size of firms. Because governments play an important role in the definition and enforcement of property rights, the optimum size of firms will also vary between countries. Whenever states attenuate property rights and/or do not enforce them effectively, intrafirm coordination will be preferred, and the equilibrium size of the firm will rise.

Our model can thus contribute to explain and predict the equilibrium size of firms across industries, between countries, and through time. As such, it is perfectly general. It does not distinguish between expansion of the firm within or across national boundaries. It can, therefore, be used to explain both domestic and international phenomena. In other words, both domestic market structure and foreign direct investment (the extension of firms beyond national jurisdiction) can be understood in terms of our model. If our analysis is correct, the same factors that induce firms to expand into multiplant operations or to integrate backward and forward into specific sectors will also lead them to create overseas subsidiaries in those sectors. In the following chapters, we endeavor to show that this approach can explain the most salient characteristics of the foreign direct investment phenomenon and yield interesting and important predictions.

CHAPTER 3

Vertical Integration

In chapter 2 we described how firms and markets organize economic activities. We identified the strengths and weaknesses of both modes of organization, and the conditions under which intrafirm coordination will be less costly than exchange in the market. Whenever these conditions are present, interdependent parties will find it relatively less expensive to subject themselves to a centralized authority than to coordinate their actions by market prices or market contracts. If we assume that individuals will choose the method of organization that maximizes their utility, they will then decide to organize their interdependence within a firm.

Moving from the domestic to the international plane introduces new elements into the analysis. As shown in chapter 1, international operations are more costly to manage than purely domestic ones because foreigners are handicapped by their ignorance of local conditions, are subject to discriminatory policies by host governments, and have to run the risks that are inherent in conducting business in many currencies. On the other hand, international trade also involves additional costs over purely domestic market transactions: information about bids and offers may be more expensive to obtain; language differences make drawing and enforcing contracts more difficult than if both parties spoke the same tongue; it may also be significantly more costly to obtain redress in foreign than in domestic courts.

Some of these purely international factors may influence the choice between firms and markets as coordination modes. For example, it may be possible to avoid tariffs by substituting an intrafirm transfer for an arm's length transaction. Transfer prices on the goods exchanged between a parent and a foreign subsidiary can be lowered in order to reduce custom duties. (Autonomous traders could theoretically achieve the same result, but the gains from avoiding the tariff would have to be shared between themselves, and opportunities for cheating would be numerous [McManus 1972, p. 88]).

62

Although a complete analysis of foreign direct investment should deal specifically with the additional impact of the international dimension on the comparative efficiency of firms and markets in organizing any given transaction, international variables will generally be ignored in the subsequent discussion. Such effects are extremely difficult to measure. For example, the extent to which intrafirm transactions can reduce tariff barriers is likely to be kept confidential by multinational firms. Introducing such factors into the analysis would be highly speculative. Fortunately, in spite of this limitation of the analysis, transactional considerations of the type presented in chapter 2 go, as will be shown in this and the next chapter, a long way toward explaining the most salient characteristics of foreign direct investment. But before we embark on our analysis of the foreign direct investment phenomenon, it is necessary to dispose of one major objection.

Validity of the Model

The crux of the argument presented in chapter 2 is that a firm will expand internationally whenever organizing a particular transaction within itself is more profitable than allowing it to be handled by the market.

One major objection to this approach is that the respective domain of hierarchical and market organization is not determined by the relative efficiency of each mode of organization, but is subject to a considerable degree of arbitrariness. This arbitrariness, it is argued, is due to the relative freedom enjoyed by the management of modern corporations where ownership is dissociated from control. Because managers of such firms have considerable leeway, they will be prone to behave in ways that do not always maximize stockholder wealth. Since a manager's own salary, power, and prestige is usually highly correlated with the size of the firm, managers of firms with dispersed ownership can be expected to show a preference for growth. Managers are thus likely to expand the firm and integrate activities that would be more efficiently organized through markets, but that yield to them some utility. For example, if foreign operations confer to managers more prestige or amenities than domestic ones, expansion of the firm across national boundaries may be determined by factors quite different than those set forth in our model.

The model argues that, although market transaction costs prevent stockholders of joint-stock companies with dispersed ownership from perfectly constraining managerial behavior, there are reasons to believe that capital markets are efficient and that managers can be made to bear the cost of managerial discretion. If this is true, then managers have incentives to maximize stockholder wealth, and thus are induced to take into account the relative profitability of hierarchical versus market coordination when making expansion plans.

But even if managers benefit from a considerable degree of managerial discretion, our approach can still be shown to be relevant. As long as profits remain a constraint on managers, the analysis developed in the previous chapter will throw light on the respective domains of firm and market organization. If management must earn minimum rates of profits, it can be shown that it will have an interest in expanding the firm into activities that are relatively efficiently organized by hierarchical methods.

The ability of top managers to engage in all types of on-the-job consumption (including expansion of the firm beyond its most profitable size) is a function of their capacity to control slack by their subordinates. If they cannot constrain the behavior of their subalterns, they will not be able to transfer stockholder wealth to themselves. In other words, managers have an interest in reducing shirking by their subordinates, for by doing so they reserve for themselves the benefits of discretion. Should lower-level employees shirk or engage in other types of on-the-job consumption, they will depress profit rates and will severely restrict the ability of top managers to engage in managerial expense: the large degree of slack at lower levels will require efforts by top management to curb such behavior, and to some degree, such efforts may not be successful unless management sets an example. Alternatively, extensive shirking at lower levels will affect the profitability of the firm and may reduce its ability to grow. For these two reasons, we would expect firms to integrate into those activities in which such consumption by subordinates is relatively easy to detect and constrain, and to avoid those activities in which shirking or embezzling by employees would cause severe problems. The latter type of activities would be more readily subcontracted.

Even if managers of modern corporations with dispersed ownership can indulge in a significant amount of discretionary behavior, they will still be induced, when deciding in which directions to expand, to take into account the relative cost of hierarchical versus market organization.

One implication of this hypothesis is that, in spite of the significant degree of managerial discretion enjoyed by managers of many large firms, there should be large variations across industries in the role of markets and hierarchies in organizing production. The number and type of activities that have to be coordinated are likely to differ across industries. In some industries, the cost of coordinating these activities by managerial directives will be lower than in others. These differences should be reflected in the average size of firms: firms that are in industries where consecutive stages in the production process can be more cheaply coordinated by market exchange will be smaller than those in sectors in which hierarchical coordination is the preferred alternative. Sectors in which hierarchical control is relatively less expensive than price incentives will be characterized by larger-sized businesses than those in which coordination by prices is relatively more efficient. Likewise, the expansion of firms in any given industry should follow particular patterns, since firms are likely to expand first in directions that use less of their scarce managerial resources. On the other hand, if the type and number of activities organized by firms is not determined by the relative efficiency of both modes of organization, one should observe no significant differences in the size of firms across industries and no discernable pattern in their growth. Which activities are grouped within a firm and which are subcontracted would be determined by the personal preferences of managers, and the organizational pattern of economic activities would be random.

In fact, transactions do not seem to be randomly distributed between hierarchical and market modes. In some production processes, activities are mostly coordinated by market prices or market contracts and the average size of firms tends to be small. In others, managerial coordination is relatively more efficient and the size of firms is larger. Small firms predominate in construction, agriculture, services, and retail trade, while large firms dominate the transportation, wholesale trade, mining, and manufacturing sectors (table 9).

TABLE 9   Average Employment per Company in the United States, 1967

Industry	Total Number of Companies (in thousands)	Total Employment (in thousands)	Average Employment per Company
All industries	4,410.0	41,921.0	9.5
Mineral industries	20.0	379.5	18.9
Construction	795.5	3,422.8	4.3
Manufacturing	267.0	21,377.0	80.1
Transportation	14.5	144.4	9.9
Wholesale trade	232.8	2,644.1	11.3
Retail trade	1,683.4	9,710.3	5.8
Selected services	1,396.8	4,243.1	3.0

Source: U.S., Department of Commerce 1972, pt. 1, table 3-2.

The residential construction industry, for example, is characterized by small firms coordinating their activities by contract. The residential builder typically employs a small staff of office clerks, salesmen, supervisors, and laborers, and contracts for carpentry, electrical work, painting, and roofing. The small size of firms in construction, as in agriculture and services, seems to be related to the relatively higher costs of coordinating activities by managerial directives than by market prices. In the service sector, much of the work is of a professional or artistic type, a type of work which, as we have seen in chapter 2, is relatively costly to manage. In construction and in agriculture, productive activities take place in dispersed locations, and are therefore costlier to monitor, because of the high cost of observing behavior and directing performance from a distance.[1]

The same interindustry differences in the size of firms are apparent at the international level. The degree to which American firms have engaged in international operations varies significantly across industries. In 1966, for example, the sales of the overseas subsidiaries of American aluminum manufacturers were $1,951 million, or 54 percent of the aluminum industry domestic sales. By contrast, foreign subsidiary sales in the printing and publishing industry amounted to only 2 percent of domestic sales (table 10).

Furthermore, whenever firms expand, they do so in specific directions. The activities they add (through mergers or internal expansion) are not generally random. They are typically related to those undertaken by the expanding firm.

Studies of the structure of American industries tend to support this statement. By and large American firms expand into activities that bear some relationship to those performed by the acquiring firm. To a significant extent, American firms have combined under single ownership activities that are at consecutive states in the production and distribution of a product or service (i.e., they have integrated vertically). Whenever firms have diversified, they have entered product lines that are similar, in a technical and marketing sense, to their existing products. Thus Scherer notes that

> the very notion of diversification—movement into new fields—implies a breaking with past product specialization traditions. Still for most corporations this movement has not been totally unstructured. Much diversification effort has been directed into product lines not greatly different from existing lines. For example, electrical firms have expanded their coverage of the electrical product spectrum; firms like duPont initially specializing in explosives have moved into other chemical products such as plastics, synthetic fibers, paints, and synthetic leather; and dairy products specialists like the Borden Company

TABLE 10   American Domestic and Foreign Subsidiary Sales, 1966

SIC	Industry	Ratio of Foreign Subsidiary Sales to Domestic Sales (percentage)
204	Grain mill products	14.2
208	Beverages	14.0
Rest of 20	Other food products	5.6
26	Paper and allied products	10.3
283	Drugs	39.4
284	Soap and cosmetics	30.2
281	Industrial chemicals	11.4
282	Plastics	24.3
Rest of 28	Other chemicals	14.1
30	Rubber	18.4
33[a]	Primary metals (excl. aluminum, copper, and brass)	1.9
34[b]	Fabricated metals (excl. aluminum, copper, and brass)	6.4
3334;3352;3361	Primary and fabricated aluminum	54.4
3331;3351;3362;3432	Other primary and fabricated metals	4.4
352	Farm machinery	23.4
353;355;356	Industrial machinery	11.8
357	Office and computing machines	41.9
Rest of 35	Other nonelectrical machinery	6.4
361–2	Electrical equipment	10.4
365;366;367	Electronic components, radio, T.V.	6.3
363;364;369	Household appliances and other	25.5
37	Transportation equipment	17.0
22–23	Textiles and apparel	2.1
24–25	Lumber, wood, furniture	5.2
27	Printing and publishing	1.9
32	Stone, clay, glass	8.1
38	Instruments	17.9
19;31;21;39	Ordnance, leather, tobacco, other	3.7
—	All manufacturing	10.4

Sources: Sales by all U.S. foreign affiliates: Unpublished data, U.S., Department of Commerce. Domestic sales: U.S., Tariff Commission, 1973, p. 691, table A-1.

a. Excluding 3331; 3334; 3351; 3352; 3361; 3362.
b. Excluding 3432.

have broadened their coverage of the food products field by adding canned goods and confectionary lines. The trend, however, seems to be toward increasing crossing of two-digit industry group lines. Gort found that product line additions by the 111 firms in his sample were within the diversifying firms' two-digit field of primary interest in 43 percent of all cases during the 1929–1939 period; in 35 percent for the 1939–1950 period; and in only 32 percent for the 1950–1954 period. But even when firms have jumped two-digit industry lines, it has more often than not been into products with some technical or distributional link to existing products. Examples of technically related diversification include Armour's development of soaps and other chemical products using the by-products of its meat-packing operations, and General Electric's entry into the turbojet aircraft engine business, aided by its experience in steam turbine technology. Examples of diversification involving complementarities on the distribution side include the tin can manufacturers' migration into paper container and glass bottle production and the soap manufacturers' development of food product lines distributed through the same retail outlets as their traditional products. "Pure conglomerate" diversification—diversification with no technical or distributional complementarities at all—has been exceptional in the past, although its occurrence evidently increased rapidly during the late 1960s. [Scherer 1970, pp. 68–69]

Adrian Wood (1971), in a recent survey of mergers in American industry, supports Scherer's position. He concludes that (1) most product acquisitions are those of products that are technologically similar to those supplied by the acquiring firm (i.e., the products acquired are classified in the same two-digit SIC group). This is especially clear if one groups the machinery, electrical machinery, fabricated metal products, and instruments sectors into one industry; (2) a significant proportion of other diversification moves are accounted for by the vertical integration between wood products, paper companies, and printing firms, by that of petroleum firms into certain chemicals, that of primary metals into insulated wire, and that of gypsum product firms into paperboard packaging; (3) the remaining 20 percent of extraindustry mergers are accounted for by fifteen conglomerates (Wood 1971, pp. 441–42). Utton (1977) analyzed the diversification trends of the 200 largest manufacturing firms in the United Kingdom and reached similar conclusions.

Finally, if the management of modern corporations had a considerable degree of freedom in determining the size of the firm, we would expect a generalized trend toward increasing firm size. Adding new activities increases the prestige and the pay of top officers, whereas abolishing existing functions within the firm is likely to be strongly opposed by those that are in danger of losing their jobs. The historical record, however, does not show an unambiguous trend toward larger firm size. Increases in the size of the market generally lead to greater specialization, and, in some cases, to smaller firms. Stigler notes, for example, that textile firms used to design and manufacture their own machinery, but that they now rely on specialized manufacturers to perform this task (Stigler 1951). Similarly, the historical record of foreign direct investment shows that firms have sometimes reduced the scale of their foreign operations in the face of changing market conditions. Between 1968 and 1974, the 180 American-based multinationals in Harvard's Multinational Enterprise Project sold or liquidated 717 manufacturing subsidiaries. Of those, 449 were well-established since they were more than five years old (Vernon 1977, p. 100). One recent example of such adaptation to change has been Chrysler Corporation's sale of its European subsidiaries to the French automobile manufacturer, Peugeot.

In summary, it has been alleged that managers of large corporations possess a significant degree of managerial discretion and that this fact seriously reduces the validity of our analysis. We have argued that there are some a priori reasons why efficiency considerations of the type outlined in our model will determine the number and the type of activities performed within firms, and that the empirical evidence does not, in fact, disprove our hypothesis. In the next sections, we will show how transactional considerations explain to a considerable extent the characteristics taken by the international expansion of firms.

The Characteristics of the Foreign Direct Investment Phenomenon

Any theory that seeks to explain foreign direct investment should provide clear and consistent explanations for its four main features: (1) although international companies have a long history, their growth and development has accelerated prodigiously in the postwar period; (2) there are significant international differences in the propensity of firms to establish foreign affiliates; (3) multinational firms have been generally reluctant to share the ownership of their subsidiaries; (4) foreign subsidiaries perform activities closely related to those of their parents and are concentrated in a few industries.

Multinational enterprises are certainly not a new phenomenon. The forerunners of the modern multinationals began to expand across countries in the 1860s. The Singer Sewing Machine Company, for example, built its first overseas factory in Glasgow in 1867, and was the first firm to produce and market its product on a truly international scale. By 1914, multinational companies were active in oil, automobiles, chemicals, and aluminum. But the scale of their operations was small, and their influence limited. In 1914, for example, total employment in American-owned companies in Britain was a mere 12,000 (Tugendhat 1972, p. 17). The growth of multinational companies has, however, accelerated dramatically in the post–World War II period. Thus, the book value of American foreign direct investment went from $7.2 billion in 1946 to $33 billion in 1960, and to $86 billion in 1971. Between 1960 and 1971 the book value of British foreign direct investment rose from $12 to $24 billion, that of Japan from $0.3 to 4.5 billion, and that of Germany from $0.7 to 7.3 billion (United Nations 1973, p. 146).[2] The stock of foreign investment owned by these four countries thus increased 265 percent in eleven years. American firms are responsible for most of this unprecedented expansion of foreign affiliates, but since the late 1960s European and Japanese concerns seem to have developed their international operations at a brisk rate (table 11). The increasing level of foreign direct investment in the United States reflects this growth. In 1950 the foreign stake in the United States amounted to $3.4 billion. By 1959 it had risen to $6.6 billion. By the end of 1979 it had risen to $52.3 billion (Chung and Fouch 1980).

Another way to examine the time pattern of the development of multinational firms is to look at the number of subsidiaries established by American, European, and Japanese multinationals since 1914 (fig. 1). One can clearly see the takeoff of multinational enterprise occurring in the post–World War II period.

As of the early seventies, however, there were still significant differences in the propensity of firms of different countries to establish foreign subsidiaries. These differences were reflected in the asymmetry between the international operations of American and European firms. In 1974, for example, sales by American majority-owned affiliates in the nine Common Market countries amounted to 12 percent of the Common Market's gross domestic product. That same year, sales of all American affiliates of Common Market countries—defined as those American firms in which 10 percent or more of the stock was owned by Common Market countries—were only 5 percent of the United States gross domestic product (table 12).

One characteristic that most multinational firms have in common is their insistence on keeping unambiguous control of their foreign subsidiaries. Fifty-seven percent of the 8,621 subsidiaries of the 391 multinational enterprises in Harvard's Multinational Enterprise Project sample were wholly owned (more than 95 percent owned). Minority-owned subsidiaries (more than 5 but less than 50 percent owned) made up 18 percent of all subsidiaries[3] (Vernon 1977, p. 34).

TABLE 11 Book Value of Foreign Direct Investment, Selected Countries

Year	Book Value of Foreign Direct Investment (in millions of dollars)	Exchange Rate (1 U.S.$=)	Book Value of Foreign Direct Investment in Local Currency (in millions)	Consumer Price Index(1970=100)	Book Value of Foreign Direct Investment in Constant Local Currency (in millions)	Index of Book Value of Foreign Direct Investment in Constant Local Currency (1960=100)
1960						
Japan	289.0	358.3	103,548.7	56.7	182,625.6	100
Germany	758.1	4.171	3,162.0	76.7	4,122.5	100
U.K.	11,988.2	0.3567	4,276.2	67.2	6,363.4	100
U.S.	32,765.0	. . . .	32,765.0	76.3	42,942.3	100
1971						
Japan	4,480.0	314.8	1,410,304.0	106.3	1,326,720.6	726
Germany	7,276.9	3.268	23,780.9	105.3	22,583.9	548
U.K.	24,019.0	0.3918	9,410.6	109.5	8,594.1	135
U.S.	86,001.0	. . . .	86,001.0	104.3	82,455.4	192

Sources: United Nations 1973, p. 146; International Monetary Fund, *International Financial Statistics, 1980 Yearbook,* Washington, D.C.: International Monetary Fund; *Economic Report of the President, 1975,* Washington, D.C.: Government Printing Office, 1975, p. 359.

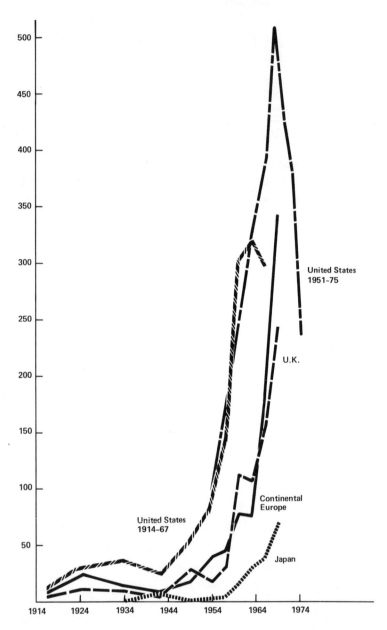

FIGURE 1 Average yearly number of subsidiaries created by American-, British-, continental European-, and Japanese-based multinationals, 1914–75. (*Sources:* For U.S. [1914–67], U.K., continental Europe, and Japan [1914–70]: Vaupel and Curhan 1973, tables 1.17.2–5; for U.S. [1951–75]: Curhan, Davidson, and Suri 1977, table 2.2.4. [Reprinted with permission from *Tracing the Multinationals*, Copyright 1977, Ballinger Publishing Company]).

TABLE 12   Sales by Foreign Subsidiaries as a Proportion of Gross Domestic Product for Europe and the United States, 1974 (in million U.S. dollars)

Sales by U.S. Majority-Owned Subsidiaries in the Common Market[a] (1)	Gross Domestic Product, Common Market[b] (2)	Column 1 / Column 2	Sales of All Common Market Affiliates in U.S.[c,d] (3)	Gross Domestic Product, U.S.[b] (4)	Column 3 / Column 4
138,536	1,153,250	0.12%	69,552	1,407,250	0.05%

a. Data from Chung 1976, p. 31.
b. Data from Statistical Office of the European Communities, *National Accounts: 1960–1975*, p. 6, table A-3.
c. Data from U.S., Department of Commerce, *1976a*, vol. 2, p. 139, table K-5.
d. All affiliates with at least 10 percent Common Market ownership.

There were, however, significant differences in the multinational firm's aversion to joint ventures. American firms had a higher proportion of wholly owned subsidiaries than their European and Japanese rivals. Thirteen percent of the subsidiaries of 180 American-based enterprises were minority-owned, compared to 16 percent for 135 European and British firms, and 80 percent for 61 Japanese multinationals. As shown in table 13, the European average was hiding significant differences: the United Kingdom, Sweden, Switzerland, and the Netherlands had a high proportion of wholly owned subsidiaries comparable to that of American enterprises, while French, German, Italian, and Belgian-Luxemburgian firms seemed to have fewer reservations about joint ventures.

Subsidiaries located in less-developed countries were also more likely to be minority-owned than those in developed countries. This is true even when national differences in the propensity to joint-venture were taken into account. Table 13 shows that, whatever their home base, multinational firms had fewer wholly owned subsidiaries in developing than in industrialized countries.

Finally, direct investments tend to take particular forms and to be concentrated in a few of the many industries found in developed economies. As we have just seen, sales by foreign manufacturing subsidiaries of American firms were 10 percent of domestic sales, but that average obscured wide interindustry differences. Table 10 shows

TABLE 13   Percentage of Wholly Owned Subsidiaries, by Nationality of Parent and Location of Subsidiary, 1971[a]

National Base of Parent Firm	Location of Subsidiary		
	Less-Developed[b] Countries	Developed Countries	All Countries
United States[c]	53	73	66
United Kingdom	. . .	. . .	61
Japan	6	14	6
France	11	36	24
Germany	44	40	42
Italy	33	59	42
Belgium-Luxembourg	21	41	37
Netherlands	33	68	61
Sweden	39	74	64
Switzerland	54	61	59

Sources: Based on Franko 1976, p. 121, table 5.5; Vernon 1977, p. 34, table 4.

a. Wholly owned: owned 95 percent or more.
b. Less-developed: 1970 per capita income less than 1,200 U.S. dollars.
c. U.S. data as of January 1, 1975.

that overseas sales were 54 percent of domestic sales in primary and fabricated aluminum, 42 percent in office machines, 39 percent in drugs, but only 2 percent in printing and publishing and in textiles and apparel, and 5 percent in wood, lumber, and furniture.

The concentration of overseas production in a limited number of industries is also the norm in other countries. Swedenborg (1979, p. 60) reports that 70 percent of the total Swedish foreign investment in manufacturing is concentrated in four industries, metal manufacturing, nonelectrical and electrical machinery, and transportation equipment, a much higher proportion than the share of those industries in Swedish manufacturing output. Foreign direct investment by British firms is large (in proportion to exports) in chemicals, rubber and plastics products, and in paper, printing, and publishing. Surveys of foreign penetration in host countries show that the share of foreign production varies greatly across sectors. In Canada, for example, the proportion of total sales made by foreign-controlled firms varied between zero in breweries and fur goods to 100 percent in batteries and refractories (McManus 1972).

A firm's expansion into a foreign country can take any of the following three forms: horizontal extension (producing the same good elsewhere), vertical integration (adding a stage to the production process that comes before or after the firm's main activity), and conglomerate diversification (adding an activity unrelated to the firm's main activity). Almost all direct investments belong to the first two categories (Caves 1971). A significant part of direct investment takes the form of vertical integration, backward into the production of raw materials and forward into the establishment of sales agencies. In 1972, for example, 43 percent of the sales of American majority-owned foreign affiliates were in trade, petroleum, and mining and smelting (Belli and Maley 1974). Mining and petroleum affiliates of American, British, Japanese, and German parents made up 36, 27, 31, and 7 percent, respectively, of the total estimated book value of all overseas affiliates of those countries in 1970 (United Nations 1973, p. 151).

Multinationals have integrated backward in the extraction of minerals (oil, copper, bauxite, zinc, tin, etc.), or in the production of agricultural commodities (cocoa, tea, rubber, palm oil), have located abroad intermediate production stages (offshore assembly), and have extended their control forward into wholesaling and retailing.

Almost all other subsidiaries produce abroad the same line of goods as is produced at home. A cursory examination of the types of horizontal investment show them to be prevalent in research-intensive industries (machinery, chemicals, transportation equipment, instruments) and in sectors for which goodwill is an important asset (branded consumer goods such as food, drink, and apparel, but especially services such as restaurants, hotels, car rentals, personnel agencies, banks, advertising, and accounting firms).

Empirical tests show that research and advertising intensity are significant determinants of the industrial pattern of foreign direct investments. William Gruber, Dileep Mehta, and Raymond Vernon analyzed the industrial structure of the sales of American subsidiaries and found that they were heavily weighted in favor of research-oriented industries. Gruber, Mehta, and Vernon divided the domestic and overseas sales of four research intensive industries (transportation equipment, electrical machinery, chemicals, and nonelectrical machinery) by the domestic and foreign sales of the other fourteen industries. Sales of these four research intensive industries were 35 percent of all domestic sales, but 70 percent of all subsidiary sales. When normalized by sales in the United States, sales of United States subsidiaries thus appeared heavily concentrated in research-intensive industries (Gruber, Mehta, and Vernon 1967).

Vaupel (1971) compared the research and advertising intensity of large American firms solely engaged on the domestic market with that of large firms having manufacturing subsidiaries in at least six foreign countries. In 1964, domestic firms spent 0.6 percent of sales on research and development, and 1.7 percent on advertising, compared to 2.6 percent and 2.5 percent respectively for their multinational counterparts. Thomas Horst found that the sum of American exports to, and American subsidiary sales in, Canada in each industry was significantly correlated with the American industry research and development expenditures as a percentage of sales (Horst 1972a), whereas Caves (1974) found research and development and advertising intensity to be a significant determinant of foreign firms' shares in Canadian and British manufacturing industries.

Such are some of the characteristics of the phenomenon. In this chapter, we will show how the model developed in chapter 2 accounts for the particular industrial structure of foreign direct investments. But first we must distinguish our explanation of the causes of foreign direct investment from that proposed by Stephen Hymer (1976). Whereas Hymer sees foreign direct investment as motivated by the desire to internalize pecuniary externalities, we argue that internalizing nonpecuniary externalities is a much more prevalent motive for international operations. We will show how our model of the international firm, as an institution internalizing some of the externalities due to international market transactions, can explain the two major types of foreign direct investments: vertical investments in the extraction of raw materials and in sales subsidiaries, and horizontal investments to facilitate the international exchange of knowledge and goodwill.

Two Motives for International Expansion

In the course of chapter 2, we have argued that multinational firms exist to organize internationally interdependent activities. Interdependencies can be of two types. Some arise because one individual's actions can affect another individual's welfare by changing the market prices he faces. Others result from the fact that one individual is affected by another in ways and by means that are not adequately reflected in market prices. In the first case, pecuniary externalities are said to occur; in the second, market exchange leads to nonpecuniary externalities.

The firm can be said to internalize nonpecuniary externalities whenever centralized control achieves a better allocation of goods and services whose marginal cost and benefit is not adequately reflected by market prices. In that case extension of the firm results in a net gain for society.

Pecuniary externalities are found whenever competition leads each producer to disregard the effects of his actions on others. If all interdependent parties could be made to take into account the gains and losses they inflict on other members of the set, the set's total income would be increased. A merger of all the parties within a firm will allow the parties to internalize these pecuniary externalities and to maximize their joint income, provided that entry into the industry is restricted. If interdependent parties are located in different countries, their desire to internalize pecuniary externalities will lead them to constitute an international firm. This is the crux of Stephen Hymer's (1976) theory of foreign direct investment.

The expansion of firms to internalize both pecuniary and nonpecuniary externalities is compatible with the model already presented in this book. Which motive is the most prevalent is a crucial empirical fact, for it will determine the welfare significance of the multinational firm.

One of the implications of Hymer's view of the multinational corporation as internalizing pecuniary externalities is that the development of multinational firms has an adverse impact on the level of competition. Hymer states, for example, that foreign direct investment is "an instrument for restraining competition between firms of different nations" and he argues that "direct foreign investment tends to reduce the number of alternatives facing sellers and to stay the forces of international competition" (Hymer 1970, p. 443).

On a priori grounds, however, Hymer's case is not very persuasive. A firm's foreign expansion can take three forms: the firm can export to the new market, license an existing producer in that market, or produce locally. In the latter case, the firm can either create a new facility or acquire an existing producer.

Whenever the firm builds a new plant, the effect is to increase the number of producers in the local market, and this should increase competition. When foreign firms buy out existing facilities, the number of producers is not increased, and the impact on competition is more ambiguous.

The empirical evidence, though limited, shows that entry into foreign markets has, in most cases, taken the form of creation of new facilities. Reuber and Roseman, in their analysis of the takeover by foreign firms of Canadian companies, found that over the 1945–61 period, the value of the assets of Canadian firms taken over by foreigners was only 12.3 percent of the value of total assets controlled by foreigners in manufacturing in 1962. Corresponding figures for trade were 5.9 percent, 1.7 percent in mining, and only 0.02 percent in finance (Reuber and Roseman 1969). In many cases, entry by foreign producers has substantially increased the level of competition in host country markets. Brash mentions that the entry of Rothmans of Pall Mall, a British firm, and Philip Morris, an American firm, in the Australian market in the mid-1950s broke the monopoly that the British Tobacco's Australian subsidiary had enjoyed in the cigarette market. Likewise, Unilever Australia lost its monopoly in soap and detergents in 1960 when Colgate-Palmolive Company entered the Australian market (Brash 1972, p. 125).

Even when multinational firms have entered foreign markets through takeovers, their entry has tended, in what seems to be the majority of cases, to increase the number of competitors, for foreign acquisition was the only alternative to bankruptcy: entry by foreign firms has thus often prevented a decline in the number of competitors. Reuber and Roseman (1969), for example, found that 43.5 percent of the Canadian mining companies and 18 percent of the Canadian manufacturing concerns acquired by foreign firms were making losses prior to their purchase. The same is true in the United States. In the electrical machinery and computer industries, Plessey Company Ltd.'s acquisition of Alloys Unlimited, Matsushita Electric Industrial Company Ltd.'s acquisition of Motorola Incorporated's television plant, North American Philips Corporation's purchase of the Magnavox Company, that of Amdhal Corporation by Fujitsu Ltd., of

I-O Devices by Ricoh Company Ltd., of Computer Optics by Daini Seikosha Company, and of Computest and Dickson Electronics by Siemens A. G., were all in lieu of bankruptcy (U.S., Department of Commerce 1976*a*, vol. 9, pp. O-28, O-35). Brash found that many Australian firms purchased by foreign concerns were similarly in serious financial difficulties (Brash 1966, pp. 55–56). The same pattern was also noted by Deane in the case of New Zealand (Deane 1970, pp. 121, 137, 356) and by Stonehill in Norway (Stonehill 1965, p. 99).

Foreign direct investment has thus resulted in an increase in the number of competitors. Knickerbocker (1976, pp. 46–47) found that the average number of manufacturing subsidiaries of multinational firms within each industry and country increased from 1.5 in 1930 to 3.3 in 1970. As a result, changes in concentration ratios in Western European and American manufacturing industries are negatively correlated with multinational entry (pp. 77–78). There has been also a marked increase since 1930 in the number of sales subsidiaries and in the volume of multinational exports (pp. 62, 79–88).

But perhaps the main competitive impact of multinational firms is their propensity to enter new industries (pp. 64–76) and their tendency to ignore the "rules of the game" and to be less tolerant of inefficient local traditions than their established local rivals. That behavior is no doubt the main reason for the enmity they have earned from host-country elites (Kindleberger 1969, pp. 76–77).

Thus although the monopoly motive may have played some part in the international extension of firms (by mergers or by creation of new facilities), the bulk of the empirical evidence supports the view that other factors have also been at work. Hymer's thesis therefore provides only a partial explanation of the foreign direct investment phenomenon. In the next chapters, we will show that extension of the firm is principally sought to internalize nonpecuniary externalities. The advantages, in this respect, of firm organization over market transactions, derive (as pointed out in chap. 2) from the different characteristics of both modes of organization.

Backward Vertical Integration

According to the model previously outlined, vertical integration will arise because of the relative inefficiency of markets in coordinating technologically separable production stages. Whenever market prices are less efficient methods of coordination than joint ownership, vertical integration will take place. As shown earlier, spot prices are inefficient methods of coordination in circumstances where there are few parties to the exchange, trades extend over a long period of time, and there is considerable uncertainty. Long-term future markets are needed. In their absence, long-term contracts can, in some cases, be efficient methods of coordination. But they tend to limit the freedom of the parties for the life of the agreement while still exposing them to a substantial amount of risk. Only when common ownership involves high internal organization costs will long-term contracts be a viable alternative. Thus, the smaller the number of parties present, the more durable and specialized the investments necessary at each stage; and the more uncertain market conditions, the more likely vertical integration will be chosen to coordinate successive production stages. If consecutive operations are located in different countries, foreign direct investment will follow.

Vertical foreign investments are of two types: they are either backward investments in raw materials or plantations or forward investments into distribution. Here we analyze backward vertical integration. Forward vertical investments will be discussed later.

Most backward international investments are concentrated in just three industries; oil, copper, and aluminum. Some foreign investments of this type have also been made by other industries, especially by steel and paper manufacturers. Firms in these industries operate in conditions which, according to our model, are favorable to vertical integration. Raw material extraction and processing both involve heavy fixed investments with a long economic life.[4] Crude oil, copper ore, and bauxite are geographically concentrated and do not have alternative uses nor strong substitutes. Market transactions between independent producers and processors would therefore be characterized by small numbers, while the profitability of investment at each stage would be highly dependent on (uncertain) future prices.

Some firms have integrated into the production of perishable agricultural commodities. As pointed out by Buckley and Casson (1976, p. 40), the supply of some of these commodities is likely to be unpredictable, and both supply and demand are inelastic in the short run. Short-term future markets are thus necessary to coordinate production, processing, and distribution. When product quality is difficult to specify and to control, and the number of parties to the exchange is limited, these future markets will fail and internal organization will be preferred.

If foreign direct investment arises from the relative efficiency of hierarchical coordination compared to market exchange, then we would expect firms that integrate into foreign raw material extraction to have followed the same policy at home. In fact there is a striking similarity between domestic and international industry structures. Petroleum refiners have integrated into both domestic and foreign crude oil extraction. Steel works usually own iron mines, either within the country or overseas. Aluminum and copper producers operate domestic as well as foreign mines.

When the optimum scale of production of the supplier and the customer is smaller (relative to the market), the market can support a larger number of efficiently sized firms. In that case buyers and sellers will coordinate their interdependence through spot sales and/ or long-term contracts. Such is the case with bituminous and lignite coal and electric utilities.

Electric utilities typically obtain the coal they burn through long-term contracts. Very few utilities own their captive mines, as shown by the fact that while electric power plants consume 66 percent of the American production of bituminous coal and lignite, 87 percent of the American coal production is sold in the open market (U.S., Department of the Interior 1975, pp. 335, 371). The preponderance of a vertically disintegrated structure in the coal industry is supported by the recent United States Department of Commerce study on foreign direct investments in the United States. The report noted a significant occurrence of loans being extended by foreign firms to American coal producers in exchange for supply contracts, but little direct foreign ownership of coal mines (except of coking coal by foreign steel makers) (U.S., Department of Commerce 1976*a*, vol. 7, p. K-314).

The degree of vertical foreign investments varies therefore across industries as a function of transactional characteristics of the type discussed in chapter 2. In some industries, small number conditions and uncertainty will call for hierarchical organization. In others, a larger number of parties will make market coordination the most efficient alternative.

Forward Vertical Integration

In chapter 2 it was argued that the firm will integrate interdependent activities that are more efficiently organized by managerial directives than by prices or contracts. One particular application of the model is in the choice of distribution channels. Producers and retailers are interdependent in the sense that profits made at one stage depend on activity at another stage. The degree and the characteristics of that interdependence, however, will vary according to the type of products sold.

Retailers and wholesalers of some goods and services can, by their actions, significantly affect the goodwill enjoyed by the manufacturer. On the other hand, there are goods and services for which retailers do not exert any influence on the purchase decisions of consumers. Whenever retailers play an important role in the marketing function, manufacturers will find it desirable to exercise some control over the distribution of their products. If it is costlier to constrain the behavior of retailers through contracts than through managerial directives, manufacturers will establish their own distribution networks. The desire of manufacturers to exert control over the distribution of their products in foreign markets will lead them to create foreign sales subsidiaries. To explain the interindustry distribution of those subsidiaries, we focus on the influence of interproduct differences (1) on the degree of interdependence between manufacturer and distributor and (2) on the most efficient method that will be chosen to constrain that interdependence.

Retailers can influence the sale of products in two major (and interacting) ways. First, the retailer provides some of the attributes of the product such as credit, delivery, repair, and so on.[5] The reputation and image of his store also has impact on the appeal to the consumer of the product he sells. A seller can also exert some influence over the sale of a commodity by providing information about the product and its use, and by his personal advice on the respective merits of competing brands (Porter 1974, pp. 420–21).

As noted by Porter, the ability of the retailer to influence the purchase decision of the consumer depends on the characteristics of the product sold. Some products, such as consumer "convenience" goods, have a relatively low unit price and are bought relatively frequently. Consumers typically do not find it worthwhile to engage in much searching for these goods, and tend to rely on cheap (but relatively less reliable) information to guide their choices. By creating a brand image through advertising, the manufacturer is able to differentiate his product without having to rely on retailers. If a brand image for the product can be established, the retailer has little influence on the consumer's buying decision, and little bargaining power vis-à-vis the manufacturer, since advertising has created a strong consumer demand for the commodity. It is therefore not necessary for the manufacturer or the wholesaler to persuade the retailer to stock the product (Porter 1974, p. 423). If, on the other hand, the manufacturer is unable to differentiate the product through advertising, the retailer becomes powerful, for the manufacturer has to rely on him to help differentiate the product.

Thus, whenever consumer convenience goods can be differentiated through advertising, their sale will not require the joint effort of manufacturers and retailers. Their interdependence will therefore be most efficiently constrained by simple market exchange of the commodities. The distribution of these consumer convenience goods will be characterized by vertically disintegrated marketing channels. On the other hand, the manufacturer selling through convenience outlets who is unable to develop a brand image by advertising will have an incentive to control the distribution of his products by franchising or forward integration into retailing.[6]

In the case of shopping goods, on the other hand, successful product differentiation will require the cooperation of both manufacturers and retailers. Shopping goods are goods that have a high unit price, that are infrequently purchased, and whose purchase can be delayed. Buyers of such goods will typically engage in a substantial amount of search about the attributes of competing brands, and advertising messages will be relatively less effective in influencing purchases. Because the retailer can demonstrate the product and its uses, and because he can give his personal advice to the buyer, he will have a significant influence on the consumer's buying decisions. Ancillary services provided by the retailer, such as repairs and credit, will also constitute an important part of the product's attributes. The retailer of shopping goods will thus generally play an important role in the manufacturer's product differentiation strategy, and both parties will find that they can, by their actions, significantly affect each other's profits (Porter 1974, p. 424). Manufacturers will attempt to persuade retailers to stock and promote their product, and will find that a simple market sale will fail to elicit such behavior. The manufacturer will therefore seek to impose constraints on the behavior of retailers. Depending on the relative levels of internal organization costs and of market contracting costs, contractual agreements (exclusive dealing) or hierarchical methods (factory stores) will be chosen to coordinate manufacturing and distribution.[7]

Contractual agreements between manufacturers and distributors/retailers usually include mutual restrictions on the behavior of parties. A typical contract will contain (1) an agreement by the manufacturer granting the wholesaler/retailer the exclusive right to sell his product in a given territory (exclusive franchising); (2) a promise by the wholesaler/distributor that he will deal only in products supplied or approved by the manufacturer (exclusive dealing).

Exclusive franchising allows a retailer to recoup the large initial expenditures involved in promoting and demonstrating the product. Without such an agreement, the dealer may not be willing to promote the product as much as is needed, and the profits of both manufacturers and retailers will be reduced. Similarly, exclusive dealing guarantees to the manufacturer that the retailer/wholesaler will undertake a more vigorous selling effort for his brand than if he was allowed to sell/distribute many brands of the same product (Thompson 1971, p. 20). Exclusive dealing restricts the ability of the seller to promote some brands to the detriment of others.

An alternative to contractual marketing is vertical integration into distribution. Which of the two methods will be chosen to coordinate manufacturing and distribution will hinge on the relative cost of organizing the behavior of agents through contracts or by managerial directives.

Franchising contracts will be advantageous when coordination of manufacturing and retailing would lead to high management costs. Such would be the case when direction of the retailers through managerial directives would result in a substantial amount of shirking and in poor decision making.[8]

The relative efficiency of franchising will vary according to the particular characteristics of the retailing/wholesaling function. The more heterogeneous the transaction and the smaller the average size of retailing outlets, the greater, we argue, the incentive for franchising. When sales require a detailed knowledge of local conditions and a large degree of adaptation to user needs, central direction will be inefficient (Caves and Murphy 1976). A system by which all the detailed information necessary to direct the behavior of employees has to be obtained from the employee himself is inefficient in this case. Even if employees were perfectly candid (a highly unlikely event since by selective reporting they may be able to indulge in on-the-job consumption), information distortion across hierarchical levels would lead to inferior decision making. Managerial control will also tend to be more difficult to establish the smaller the average size of the retailing outlets, since communication costs will be relatively higher than if there were fewer, but larger-sized, stores. Retailing activities in which a detailed knowledge of local conditions is crucial and which require widely scattered, small-sized outlets will therefore be prime candidates for franchising.

Consider the case of automobile and truck retailing. Maximum profits in automobile sales can be achieved by bargaining, and leaving considerable flexibility in regard to pricing to the seller would seem advantageous. Furthermore, the condition of automobiles being traded in varies widely, and it is difficult to establish clear pricing rules for such vehicles. Control of the inventory is also important in reducing costs, and it requires a detailed knowledge of the local market. It would be difficult for automobile manufacturers to establish rules and regulations to dictate to retailers what inventory they must carry and what prices they must charge. Local managers would enjoy substantial opportunities for fraud because of the difficulty that headquarters would have in obtaining detailed information on local conditions. Because of the difficulty of controlling the behavior of agents through managerial directives, vertical integration into automobile retailing is relatively inefficient (Caves and Murphy 1976, p. 582). It is not surprising, therefore, that 88 percent of all automobile and truck sales in the United States are by franchised dealers (Caves and Murphy 1976, p. 573).

Similarly, manufacturers of beverage syrups like Coca-Cola, Pepsi-Cola, and Seven-Up franchise independent bottlers who then resell to service and institutional accounts. This arrangement dominates the soft drink industry with franchised bottling plants accounting for more than 90 percent of total American sales (Thompson 1971, p. 11). One of the reasons behind this phenomenon may be the difficulty of managing company-owned bottling plants when soft drink wholesaling requires an in-depth knowledge of and close contact with the reselling outlets (Caves and Murphy 1976, p. 582).

Fast-food restaurants also illustrate the determinants of the choice between owning and franchising. Fast-food franchisors typically own outlets in large metropolitan areas and franchise them elsewhere. Monitoring widely dispersed rural outlets would be difficult and would entail considerable travel by supervisors. Franchisors have found that the physical proximity of urban restaurants makes supervision easier. According to Barry M. Rowles, chairman of Kentucky Fried Chicken, "In the metropolitan areas you get a density of store locations that facilitates communication and management, and it gives you distribution and marketing efficiencies," ("Fast Food Franchisors Squeeze Out the Little Guy," *Business Week*, May 31, 1976, p. 48).

The same transactional considerations have determined the method used by multinational corporations to market their products in foreign countries. The use of franchised dealers by automobile companies to distribute their products in foreign markets is general. Ford and General Motors franchise local dealers around the world, and so do Fiat and Volkswagenwerk. American soft drink syrup manufacturers have also exported overseas their domestic marketing methods. For example, 98 percent of Coca-Cola's overseas bottling plants are franchised to local nationals ("The Graying of the Soft Drink Industry," *Business Week,* May 23, 1977).

The disadvantage of selling through franchised dealers are those that are inherent in market contracts. The greater the number of contractual stipulations and the greater the difficulty of defining and enforcing contractual rules, the less advantageous will market contracts be relative to direct ownership. The number of stipulations that will be needed will depend on the ability of the parties to affect the goodwill capital of the trademark. A large degree of uncertainty surrounding the transaction will induce the parties to expand the number of stipulations so as to cover all contingencies. When the contractual stipulations necessary to constrain the behavior of the parties are large, direct ownership will be preferred.

Such is the case with new shopping goods. With such goods, the role of the retailer in promoting and servicing the product is crucial. New products are, by definition, unknown to the public. They are also initially poorly known by wholesalers and retailers. Manufacturers have thus to expend time and effort to demonstrate to distributors the product and its uses, and to persuade them to demonstrate and explain the product to consumers, advise on proper use, and provide repairs. New product characteristics are typically not fixed, and significant alterations can usually be made at reasonable cost. It is therefore in this period that feedback from consumers is crucial.

Market transactions between manufacturers and distributors of these products will often be difficult. The adverse relationship between them is not conducive to efficient information exchange. Since manufacturers will have to instruct distributors in the demonstration and repair of the new product, and since this may involve a substantial commitment of time and resources on the part of both parties, they will insist on long-term distribution contracts. Long-term contracts make adaptation to change difficult, at a time when rapid adjustment to changing market conditions is crucial. In those conditions, unified ownership of manufacturing and distribution may be desirable.

One would therefore expect manufacturers to integrate into distribution whenever they are introducing new, sophisticated products. The more complex the product and the less sophisticated the buyer, the greater the incentive for vertical integration. Firms that have found it necessary to control their own distribution in the home market will similarly create sales subsidiaries overseas. These subsidiaries should be concentrated in sectors that have a strong new-product orientation.

The preceding hypothesis is supported by some empirical evidence. First, industries that are involved in the development of new products have also integrated into the sale and service of these products. This is shown by the fact that the ratio of scientists and engineers employed in sales to total industry employment in nineteen American industries in 1962 was highly correlated with that industry's research and development expenditures as a percentage of industry sales (Gruber, Mehta, and Vernon 1967, table 6).

Second, integration into distribution is a fairly recent phenomenon that was pioneered by the manufacturers of new products in the second half of the nineteenth century. The entrepreneurs who successfully developed and sold these new products first used the only marketing channels known at the time—independent distributors in the home market and licensees overseas. Soon they changed their strategy and took control of distribution and overseas manufacture. An analysis of the reasons for such a shift is particularly instructive, since it involved breaking with custom, and must therefore have been motivated by serious reasons. One particularly well-documented case is that of I. M. Singer and the sewing machine industry. The sewing machine was the first consumer appliance and the first product to be sold on installments. Singer originally sold distribution rights to domestic distributors and licensed overseas production. But soon he found that direct control of domestic and overseas sales was a much more profitable strategy. The reasons for such a shift are summarized by Mira Wilkins.

> The advantages of the salaried-plus-commission agent over the locally financed independent agent were multifold. The independent agent did not pay sufficient attention to the product; he did not bother to instruct the buyer how to use the machine; he did not know how to service it; he failed to demonstrate it effectively; and he did not seek new customers aggressively. Independent agents were not prepared to risk their capital to sell goods on installment nor would they risk carrying large stocks. [Wilkins 1970, p. 43]

Another reason for the change was the difficulty, under a system of independent agents, of adjusting marketing to changes in production or market conditions.

> For example, the company wanted to reduce prices in order to increase sales and meet the competition, and reduce at the same time the percentage discount on machines allowed sales agents. But it found it difficult to do so because of their continued opposition to both measures. [Jack 1957, p. 113]

Discouraged with the agency system, the company decided then to open its own sales offices in the United States and abroad and to staff them with employees (often from among its own top plant machinists).

There is some evidence that many other exporters encountered similar difficulties with their sales agents. S. J. Nicholas (forthcoming) documents the numerous problems experienced by British exporters (such as Ransomes, Sims & Jefferies, Ltd., J. H. Fenner & Company, Cape Asbestos Company, Cadbury, and Andrew Weir & Company) who used agencies to handle their exports. These firms found it difficult to monitor their agents and had to eventually replace them by sales subsidiaries. Two of the most successful pre-1939 British multinationals, Lever Brothers and Brunner Mond, did so in the 1920s as a matter of general policy (Nicholas, forthcoming).[9]

The reasons given by economic historians for direct integration into distribution on both domestic and foreign markets thus are consistent with the predictions of our model. The particular interest of the Singer case is that Singer's strategy could not have been influenced by custom, but represents a rational adaptation to the specific marketing needs of new products. As such, it has great heuristic value to understanding the behavior of manufacturers of a whole class of new, sophisticated products aimed at a large market.

In summary, then, the extent of foreign direct investment in sales subsidiaries is a function of (1) the degree of interdependence between manufacturers and distributors and (2) of the relative efficiency of constraining that interdependence through prices, market contracts, or managerial directives. In industries producing convenience consumer goods, little foreign investment in trade is likely to take place. Penetration of foreign markets is likely to be effected by market sale to foreign importers. The wholesaling or retailing of nonconvenience consumer goods and of some producer goods will sometimes be franchised to independent retailers or, especially in the case of new products, performed in company warehouses and outlets. In the first case the manufacturer will usually establish a local sales subsidiary to franchise local dealers. In the second case, manufacturers will establish larger subsidiaries to directly market their products.

CHAPTER 4

Horizontal Expansion

In the previous chapter we have seen that one of the motives for overseas expansion is the desire to exercise hierarchical control over activities that precede or follow those undertaken by the direct investor. On the basis of the model developed in chapter 2, one would expect horizontal foreign direct investment to result from the same set of factors as those leading to vertical investments, i.e., the existence of strong interdependencies poorly constrained by market prices.

Horizontal subsidiaries (i.e., foreign affiliates that market the same products or services as their parents) can be classified into two nonmutually exclusive categories: (1) those that depend on their parents for knowledge, and (2) those that draw on goodwill created by the parent. In this chapter we contend that the presence of foreign direct investment in both cases is explained by the higher cost of exchanging these two goods on international markets than within firms.

Horizontal Investment and the Exchange of Goodwill

One type of interdependence between producers which is costly to organize through market prices is that which arises from the sharing of goodwill. Whenever foreign producers have as principal customers residents of the home country, the reputation acquired at home by firms producing the same product has a significant market value (positive or negative) on foreign markets. Foreign producers may have as customers residents of the home country either because they cater to a substantial number of tourists, immigrants, or foreign subsidiaries, or because they export their production to the home country. In those cases, using trademarks that are known and appreciated in the home country will increase sales and profits, since it economizes on the customers' search costs. Consumers will be ready to pay a premium since they save on the cost of ascertaining quality and on that of being disappointed. There are therefore circumstances where trademarks used in one country have a positive value in another country. For example, owners of hotels in European resorts frequented by American tourists will increase their sales and profits by using a Holiday Inns Incorporated or a Hilton Hotels Corporation trademark. On the other hand, the quality of the goods or services supplied by anyone using a given trademark affects the profits of all those that use that trademark. A poorly run Hilton anywhere tends to reduce the sales and profits of Hiltons everywhere. All producers using a given trademark are thus interdependent (McManus 1972, p. 82).

Market exchange could theoretically organize that interdependence. The reputation enjoyed by one producer can be shared by others at zero or low marginal cost, provided that each producer using a trademark agrees to compensate all other parties using the same trademark for the gains or losses they incur due to variations in the quality of the good or service he produces. One conceivable solution to that problem would be to establish a market in the quality of the services supplied by those sharing the trademark (McManus 1972, p. 82). Any variation in quality would be compensated by a payment equal to the sum of the marginal losses (or gains) imposed on all producers in the system. But the high cost of detecting variations in quality and their effect on the goodwill capital of the brand will make this mode of organization prohibitively expensive (McManus 1972, p. 82).

A system of contracts, by which producers obtain the right to use a trademark in exchange for a certain payment provided that they keep minimum standards, is usually cheaper to establish. In both cases, however, the associated information, enforcement, and bargaining costs are significant: as we have seen, the quality of the products of one franchise holder will influence the opinion of consumers regarding the products of all the producers sharing that trademark. If contract stipulations are lax, each producer will not bear all the gains and losses that result from his actions, and the goodwill capital of the trademark will be dissipated. Franchising contracts have therefore to stipulate carefully product and service characteristics and to enforce the respect of these standards (McManus 1972, p. 82).

Franchising foreign producers is likely to predominate whenever it is relatively easy to constrain profit-seeking owners from free riding on the goodwill capital of the trademark. The wider the scope for lowering product or service quality and the greater the cost of detecting violations and enforcing contractual terms, the less desirable is franchising relative to outright ownership.

Direct ownership, on the other hand, involves managerial costs. These costs are likely to be high if the business requires close adaptation to local conditions and if it is difficult to satisfactorily constrain behavior through operating rules. The average size of production or service units is also a factor, since it is more difficult to manage a large number of geographically dispersed establishments than a smaller number of larger units.

These general considerations seem to explain the sectors in which foreign direct investment takes place. We have seen that goodwill spillovers are present whenever citizens of one country in which a particular producer has built up goodwill are temporarily or permanently present in a foreign country. The goodwill created in one country thus has a positive value in another country. This fact, however, can lead to different levels of foreign activity: if local producers are franchised, overseas operations may be limited to a small staff of inspectors, accountants, and lawyers. If direct ownership is more profitable, the foreign presence will be substantially greater.

Although little detailed data are available, the characteristics of international operations seem to fit closely the model. Important goodwill spillovers exist (1) in the hotel, restaurant, transportation, personal services, and retailing sectors and (2) in banking, insurance, and business services. Foreign operations in the first type of activities are generally established to cater to the tourist trade. For example, American car rental companies have followed their tourist customers and have established franchised or wholly owned agencies overseas.[1] American firms operate or license hotels (Hilton Hotels Corporation, Sheraton Corporation, Holiday Inns Incorporated, Burger King Corporation and Tastee Freeze International), fast-food outlets (Pizza Hut Incorporated, McDonald's Corporation, Kentucky Fried Chicken) and convenience stores (7-Eleven) throughout the world.

In the second type of sectors, domestic firms have also tracked their customers' overseas operations. Home-country banks have established foreign branches to finance the imports and exports of domestic firms and to provide their overseas subsidiaries with the services they require (Koszul 1970, p. 276). In 1975, 126 American banks operated 751 branches in eighty countries with $166 billion in assets (and an unknown number of subsidiaries with another $25 billion in assets), whereas foreign banks had 184 agencies, branches, subsidiaries, and investment companies in the United States with $64 billion in total assets (U.S., Department of Commerce 1976*a*, vol. 4, p. F-7). Between 1971 and 1976, the number of foreign affiliates[2] of the world's 50 largest banks went from 1,819 to 2,930, an increase of 60 percent (United Nations 1978, p. 215). The American employment agencies, advertising agencies, and accounting and management consulting firms have also expanded overseas to serve American foreign subsidiaries, although most of their clientele is now local. The twenty-one largest American-based advertising firms derived 42 percent of their total billings from foreign sources in 1976, compared to 5 percent for the thirty largest American agencies in 1954 (United Nations 1978, p. 48). Three-fourths of McKinsey and Company's early European clients were American subsidiaries and one-fourth were local firms, but by 1969 the percentages were already reversed ("Europe's Rich Market for Advice: American Preferred," *Fortune*, 1969).

As argued earlier, the size of the foreign stake will vary across activities in direct proportion to the relative efficiency of market versus hierarchical coordination. In some sectors home country firms have franchised local producers either by selling master franchises to local firms which then grant individual unit franchises or by creating a subsidiary to franchise local producers. Foreign operations (as measured by the employment or assets of foreign subsidiaries) are therefore limited in size. Such is the case for fast-food restaurants, employment services, hotels and motels, and convenience stores.

In those sectors, establishing centralized control appears to be more costly than drawing up and enforcing contractual standards. In fast food, for example, it may be difficult to obtain from salaried employees the same outlay of effort as that of independent proprietors. Furthermore, it is relatively easy to restrict the franchisee's ability to affect quality or service. Franchising contracts can require that food supplies be purchased from the franchisor, thus leaving no discretion to the franchisee as to size or quality of portions. By insisting that facilities be designed and built by the franchisor, it is possible to effectively prevent the owner from altering the menu: the outlet can also be designed in such a way as to leave no extra space for anything that was not planned for at the outset by the franchisor (Levitt 1976, p. 86). Pricing initiative can also be denied the franchisee because the franchisor can mention prices in his advertising. The same general factors explain the preponderance (both domestically and internationally) of franchised operations in hotels and motels, employment services, and convenience stores.[3]

In banking, insurance, advertising, and in accounting and management consulting, foreign (and domestic) expansion has taken the form of company-owned establishments. Constraining the behavior of franchisees by contracts would seem more difficult in those lines of business. Furthermore, managerial control is facilitated by the concentration of customers in a few large metropolises.

Transactional considerations of the type discussed in chapter 2 are thus useful in explaining the observed variations in the magnitude of foreign direct investment in the service and trade sectors. In the following pages we will show how the same reasoning can throw some light on horizontal foreign investments in manufacturing.

Horizontal Investment and the Transfer of Knowledge

In chapter 3 we mentioned the existence of a relationship between the generation of innovations and foreign direct investment: industries characterized by high research and development expenditures have also a high ratio of foreign to domestic production; firms that own manufacturing subsidiaries abroad tend to spend more on research and development than their purely domestic counterparts. It seems therefore that companies that develop new products and processes at home find it advantageous, at times, to integrate into the overseas manufacture of these products. The logic of our model implies then that there are circumstances under which the market exchange of knowledge between domestic and foreign firms is so costly that unified ownership is preferable. To understand why this is so, it is useful to consider carefully the nature of the innovation process and the characteristics of knowledge as an economic good.

As will be shown in the next section, innovation, the process by which new products and processes are commercialized, requires a fusion of three different types of knowledge: scientific principles, production engineering, and market conditions. The innovation process can be seen as the synthesis of these three types of information, the end result being a product that can be successfully sold.

In acquiring knowledge, like in other economic endeavors, specialization is generally efficient. One would therefore expect parties to specialize in particular fields and some to sell others the information they possess. Whether exchange and specialization will take place within firms or across markets hinges on the respective costs of transferring knowledge in both institutions.

Knowledge, as an economic good, has certain attributes that make its market exchange costly. It is a commodity the characteristics of which are, by definition, unknown to the buyer. Consequently, knowledge will be costly to exchange in the market, and, as we will show, is more efficiently transferred within firms.

One method that has been devised to decrease market transaction costs in knowledge is to establish limited monopoly rights in the production of the goods embodying that knowledge, namely, to grant and enforce patent rights. This device, however, is subject to serious limitations, which we will later describe in detail. Consequently, although patentable knowledge will usually be more efficiently exchanged by the market, unpatentable know-how will be transmitted within the firm. Both licensing and foreign direct investment will therefore be used to convey know-how to foreign countries. The relative importance of each transfer mode will hinge on the degree to which property rights in knowledge can be established and exchanged.

The Innovation Process

The innovation process starts with the discovery of basic scientific principles and ends with the successful sale of products embodying these principles. It is customarily divided into three stages, invention, development, and final supply.

Inventions are typically unpredictable, requiring more genius and luck than heavy investment of funds. The typical output of the invention stage is a crude model that has required only a modest financial commitment. During the development stage, the invention is redesigned to make it suitable for profitable market sale. Efficient final supply includes the physical manufacture of the product and its distribution, and will necessitate investments in plants and equipment, advertising, and in the building up of distributing and retailing networks.

Popular views of the innovation process tend to emphasize the invention stage and to underestimate the importance of development. The innovation process is often seen as the straightforward embodiment of new science into new products. However, as we will demonstrate, this view is erroneous. The product, as designed by the scientist, often cannot be mass produced, and therefore sold at a profit, without modification. On the other hand, the ideal product from a marketing point of view is often not technically feasible. The creation of a successful product involves therefore a series of compromises: at each step it is necessary to reevaluate the product in both technical and marketing terms. As Donald Schon has put it, "Invention does not move in a straight line. Neither does it simply consist in defining a need and seeking means to fill it or in defining a technique and finding uses for it. In the process of invention need and technique determine one another," (Schon 1967, p. 15).

The innovation process can therefore be described as the synthesis of various types of specialized knowledge. Innovations can result from the application of new technology to cater to traditional needs, as well as from the use of available technology to fulfill previously unmet demands. Because products are designed implicitly or explicitly for a particular set of physical or socioeconomic conditions, transplanting a product designed for one country into another country may be considered an innovation, since it almost always involves adapting the product to local conditions of sale and use. Ward, for example, found that out of ninety-six products introduced in the United States by foreign firms, two-thirds had to be modified to suit the tastes of American consumers (Ward 1973). Our concept of innovation is thus much broader than its usual definition. The success of an innovation hinges on how well science, technology, and consumer needs can be linked. In other words, neither technological expertise, scientific sophistication, or good marketing are guarantees of successful innovative activity. It is, rather, the fusion of these three elements that is crucial.

This view of the innovation process as the synthesis of various types of specialized knowledge is supported by a considerable amount of empirical evidence. Studies of the innovation process emphasize the crucial importance of combining a good understanding of user needs with technical capabilities.

In an extensive study of the characteristics of successful innovations, undertaken by the Science Policy Research Unit of the University of Sussex, twenty-nine successful innovations were matched with twenty-nine unsuccessful ones. Innovations were paired on the basis of the market to which they were addressed. Seventeen pairs were in chemicals and twelve in instruments. The unsuccessful innovation was defined as one that failed to gain for its author a reasonable rate of return on investment. The factors that were determinant in predicting success or failure were: (1) the capacity to understand user needs, (2) marketing effort, (3) the quality of development work, (4) the ability to use outside technology and scientific advice, and (5) the position and prestige of the management team leader. The most important variable differentiating successful innovations from failures was the ability to understand user needs and to educate and persuade consumers (Science Policy Research Unit 1972).

In a similar study confined to innovations that failed, the importance of market orientation was again stressed. The study attempted to discover the reasons for abandonment of fifty-three projects by twenty companies in the electrical, electronic, chemical, and engineering industries. All projects were technically satisfactory, but were shelved because of the size and character of the market. The authors of the study note that a large proportion of the projects should have been shelved earlier, and that indeed some of them should never have been started at all. Fourteen projects were, however, later resurrected and put to commercial use. In those cases the crucial determinant of success was a constant monitoring of market conditions (Science Policy Research Unit 1971).

Similar results were found by Langrish et al. (1972) in their study of the companies that won the United Kingdom's Queen's Award for Technological Innovation. Here again the clear identification of a need to be filled by the product was a major factor in successful innovation.

The importance of demand recognition in the process of innovation is also attested by the fact that a large percentage of successful innovations are based on available technology. Of the 102 technical ideas used by the firms that won the Queen's Award, 24 could be described as originating from common knowledge. The feature that distinguished the innovating company from others was the realization that these ideas might have a particular use. The authors conclude that "it may be that detecting the change in the market circumstances is more important than the production of the idea" (Langrish et al. 1972). Myers reports that two-thirds of the technical information needed was readily available to the innovators in the sample of 567 commercially successful innovations identified in his study of 121 firms in three industries (Myers 1966). Allen's analysis of messages accepted (technical information used) by scientists and engineers in 19 research and development projects shows that only 73 out of 282 items of technical information used were products of analysis and experimentation. All the other messages were based on existing technology (T. Allen 1969, p. 143). We interpret these and the preceding findings as supporting our contention that the ability to link demand to existing or new technology is a binding constraint in the innovation process.

If the creation of new products or their introduction in new markets requires as inputs different types of specialized know-how, one would expect that process to be parceled out to many individuals who would each specialize in a particular field of knowledge.

A central tenet of economics is that specialization often leads to important economies. To master marketing, engineering, or any scientific discipline requires extensive studies and experience. As a result, few persons are able to gain an in-depth knowledge of all the facets of the innovation process. Specialization in one particular field of knowledge is thus efficient.

The argument applies especially well to the introduction of products in new markets. The foreign innovator has accumulated a stock of knowledge about the product and its manufacture, but he is likely to know little about local materials and the characteristics of local demand. A market transaction by which the foreigner and the local producer would exchange knowledge would seem efficient. To understand why such exchange sometimes does not take place, it is necessary to examine the properties of knowledge as an economic good.

Knowledge as an Economic Good

Knowledge is particularly costly to exchange through market channels because the buyer cannot know the characteristics of what he is buying without appropriating it. As a result, interpersonal exchange of knowledge will be difficult unless there is trust between the parties involved. Such a trust relationship is more likely to characterize intrafirm exchange than market exchange, because parties to the exchange within a firm are not rewarded by the quantity of information transferred. The hypothesis that the market exchange of knowledge experiences difficulties due to the lack of trust between the parties is, we will see, strongly supported in the sociological literature. Let us consider these points one at a time.

The market sale of knowledge is subject to high transaction costs because, by definition, the party who buys knowledge does not know prior to sale exactly what he will be purchasing. If the seller were to provide that information in order to persuade the buyer of the value of the commodity, he would, by revealing the information, actually be transferring the knowledge to the prospective buyer. The latter would then be unwilling to pay for what he has already acquired free of charge (Arrow 1962, p. 615). The market sale of knowledge will thus be plagued by high information costs since the seller will be unable to reveal the value of the good to the prospective buyer without at the same time eliminating the need for the transaction altogether.

The high information costs that characterize the market exchange of knowledge seriously reduce its efficiency. Because of the information imbalance between the parties, the buyer will usually engage in a considerable amount of research, trying to determine by various means the nature of the good in which he is interested; consequently, he will be forced to look for secondhand indications regarding the value of the information, perhaps by trying to ascertain the honesty of the seller. If there exists, however, a "trust" relationship between the market traders, the costs of transferring knowledge through market sale are likely to be much lower.

Trust can be seen as a way to economize on search costs. The party who trusts is relieved of the need to engage in research about the seller or the value of what he is selling because he has other assurances that the seller will not default on his promises. These assurances derive from the fact that the seller has no motive for cheating, either by design (he is not entitled to the gains from such action) or because he will be discovered and will not benefit from his dishonesty. When this trust does not exist, the transfer of knowledge will be extremely costly, if not impossible.

The preceding generalizations are supported by the sociological literature on the interpersonal transfer of knowledge, and more particularly by that dealing with the communication of innovations. Students of the communication of innovations have consistently noted the importance of trust in the transfer process. Whereas the press, salesmen, or customers play an important role in alerting individuals to the existence of new products or processes, it is friends and acquaintances (i.e., individuals that do not stand to benefit directly from the information transfer) that are most instrumental in persuading them to adopt the innovation. In a study of the sources of information obtained by farmers regarding new techniques, for example, Bohlen et al., found that sources varied depending on the stage of the adoption process. Bohlen divided the adoption process into five phases: awareness (learning about the existence of a new idea or practice); interest (getting more information about the product); evaluation (working it out mentally); trial (trying the innovation); and adoption (putting the innovation into full-scale use). He interviewed farmers and asked them to rank the sources of information on which they relied when making a decision at each stage. As shown in table 14, farmers learned about a new idea or practice mostly from the mass media. They searched the press to obtain more information. When it came to mental evaluation, trial, and adoption, however, friends and neighbors (mostly other farmers) were consulted. Dealers and salesmen were ranked last in almost all categories (Bohlen et al. 1961). Rogers, an authority in the communication of innovations, studied the effectiveness of "change agents" in persuading Columbian and Brazilian peasants to adopt modern agricultural practices. He found that commercial salesmen were ranked next to last by both groups of farmers. Rogers explains his findings in these terms: "Commercial change agents often carry the albatross of low credibility in the eyes of their clients. The commercial change agent's motives, as perceived by his clients, may be one reason for the low credibility they place on his recommendations" (Rogers and Shoemaker 1971, p. 245). Commu-

TABLE 14 Rank Order of Information Sources by Stage in the Adoption Process

		Stage			
Rank	Awareness[a]	Interest[b]	Evaluation[c]	Trial[d]	Adoption[e]
1	Mass media—radio TV, newspapers, magazines	Mass media	Friends and neighbors	Friends and neighbors	Friends and neighbors
2	Friends and neighbors —mostly other farmers	Friends and neighbors	Agricultural agencies	Agricultural agencies	Agricultural agencies
3	Agricultural agencies— Extension, Vo Ag, and the like	Agricultural agencies	Dealers and salesmen	Dealers and salesmen	Mass media
4	Dealers and salesmen	Dealers and salesmen	Mass media	Mass media	Dealers and salesmen

Source: Bohlen et al. 1961, table 1.

a. Learns about a new idea or practice.
b. Gets more information about it.
c. Tries it out mentally.
d. Limited trial.
e. Accepts it for full-scale use.

nication of information thus seems easier when purchasers know that sellers of know-how are not rewarded in direct proportion to the knowledge they transfer.

This fact constitutes the main reason why transfer of knowledge within the firm is likely to be more efficient than its market exchange. When the information transfer takes place within a firm, all the parties to the exchange are employees. As such they are not rewarded by the market value of the knowledge they sell but by their contribution to the group. Cheating would not be to their best advantage, and knowledge of this fact should facilitate the establishment of trust and reduce the cost of intrafirm information exchange.

The degree of trust in a relationship is also a function of the ability of the parties to detect and punish dishonesty. In markets, dishonest traders will be prosecuted for fraud or acquire a bad reputation that will hurt their future business. The process is not automatic, however, since communication and enforcement costs are positive. Prosecution for fraud is often difficult and expensive. Poor performance will not always lead to a loss of goodwill, since communication costs are substantial, especially if the number of customers and/or the geographic size of the market is large. More importantly, information pooling is difficult because circumstances change, and evaluation of performance is often subjective. Information pooling across markets will also be impaired by the lack of common codes, and sometimes by an adverse relationship between the parties. By contrast, consider the advantages of intrafirm organization. The central party can obtain detailed, continuous information on his employees and, when dissatisfied by their performance, simply discharge them. No transfer of information is necessary, since the evaluator is also the decision maker. Finally, intrafirm codes permit the transfer of a higher volume of information at lower cost. Information pooling within firms will thus be more efficient (Williamson 1975). The greater certitude that cheaters will be discovered facilitates the establishment of trust in intrafirm exchanges.

Another method used to establish trust is repeated face-to-face contact. This contact allows parties to develop personal bonds that tend to increase the psychic costs of dishonesty. This is noted by Paul Strassman in his study of the technology transfer to underdeveloped countries.

> Face to face contact to establish trust appears to be a need throughout the technical transfer network. Lack of full trust invariably means some concealment of information which impairs perception of needs at subsequent stations. Moreover, a sense of insecurity may blur the

transmitter's vision as well, making him incapable of stating his problems, even on paper, and of reaching decisions. To see faces is to see
confusion, satisfaction or antagonism; to gauge whether status is being,
or should be, granted or withheld. The conversational setting from
time to time allows the release of tensions through small talk, jokes
and laughter. The urge to conceal as well as the fear of concealment
weakens. [Strassman 1968, pp. 32–33]

Establishing trust through repeated face-to-face contact involves high fixed costs as it takes time for people to learn to know
one another. This is shown by a study by Pelz and Andrews of 1,300
research scientists and engineers in eleven American research laboratories, in which they found that research and development teams
were most productive after four or five years of working together as
a unit (Pavitt 1971*b*, p. 64). A firm can spread out the high fixed
costs involved in creating a team over a considerable length of time,
since employees typically remain for extended periods with the same
employer. By contrast, the interaction between any particular market buyer and seller is likely to be shorter lived and provides less
opportunities for the establishment of personal bonds between the
parties to the information exchange. A specialized consulting firm,
for example, will typically take many clients, and assignments will
usually come to an end before warm relationships with customers
have time to develop.

Another closely related advantage that firms have over markets in the exchange of information is their ability to choose the
parties to the information exchange in order to increase the confi-
dence that the communicators have in one another. By recruiting
employees that are "homophilous," i.e., that speak the same language, have reached the same educational level, share like cul-
tures, and come from the same socioeconomic background, the
firm can increase the efficiency of the information exchange. This
opportunity has been so widely used by most companies, both
national and multinational, that as a result a profile of the typical
American manager can be drawn with some accuracy. For example, in 1976, 42 percent of the chief executive officers of the 800
largest American firms belonged to the Episcopal and Presbyterian
churches, whereas the percentage of the overall United States
population belonging to these two denominations was only 2.5 percent. Furthermore, the typical manager is male (with the study
showing only 1 woman among the 800) (Burck 1976, p. 175). Since
chief executive officers are promoted from within management,
these statistics would indicate that the subset "managers" tends to

be far more homogeneous than the American population as a whole.[4] The desire of firms to constitute teams of homogeneous employees has led American multinationals to reserve top management posts for American citizens. As a result, American multinationals have often been criticized for their failure to multinationalize their senior management. An enquiry by *Business Week* magazine found discrimination against non-American citizens to be the main reason Europeans leave American subsidiaries in Europe (Tugendhat 1972, chap. 14). Statistics reveal that there are few foreigners in the governing boards of American multinationals. A survey of the 1,029 directors of 187 American multinational companies uncovered only 19 foreigners, of whom 14 were Canadian or British (Vernon 1971, p. 146). Because firms can—and do—constitute teams of homogeneous employees, they are able to increase the efficiency with which knowledge is transferred.

The transfer of knowledge between employees that work together and know each other well should therefore be more efficient than transfer between individuals who are brought together for a specific task but who belong to different organizations and who have separate allegiances. This hypothesis is supported by the findings of many studies in the research management literature. These studies suggest that ideas and suggestions from fellow employees are more likely to be accepted and acted upon than if they come from outsiders (consultants, suppliers, customers, etc.). They also show that whenever outside messages are accepted, they result in poorer performance.

Mansfield et al. studied the relative importance of laboratory personnel, other firm sources, customers, universities, suppliers, etc., as originators of research and development projects and programs. To what extent does research and development result from suggestions made inside the firm? In the sample of 19 industrial laboratories studied, 89 percent of research and development work was initiated by suggestions from internal sources (62 percent from the research and development staff, 20 percent from the marketing staff, 7 percent from other internal sources [Mansfield et al. 1971, p. 37]). These results agree with a study made by Seiler in which he found that in the 117 firms he surveyed, 60 percent of the research and development activity was initiated by suggestions from the research and development staff, 17 percent came from the marketing staff personnel, 9 percent from management sources, and only 8 percent from sources outside the firm (Seiler 1965, p. 133).

Allen looked at the manner in which scientists and engineers obtain the information they need to solve technical problems.

Nineteen projects involving nine general technical problems were considered. Allen identified eight information channels: literature, vendors, customers, external sources, technical staff, company research, analysis and experimentation, and personal experience. "External sources" were paid consultants and unpaid representatives of government agencies. "Technical staff" consisted of engineers and scientists in the laboratory who were not assigned directly to the project being considered. "Company research" was any project performed previously or simultaneously regardless of its source of funding. Allen classified messages received and messages accepted (suggestions adopted) in terms of these eight channels. As a measure of the relative efficiency of the channels, the acceptance ratio, defined as the ratio of messages accepted to messages received, was calculated.

Three channels—technical staff, company research, and external sources—had high acceptance ratios. Vendors and customers received low marks. In an effort to ascertain the quality of the messages accepted, an evaluation of the solutions was obtained from technical monitors in customer agencies. Solutions based on messages emanating from company research were likely to be higher rated, while those obtained from exterior sources were likely to be rated lower. There was no significant difference for those based on information received from the technical staff. A chi-squared test on the comparative performance of external sources, internal sources, and other sources rejected the null hypothesis of no difference in performance. As a third test, the sources used by engineers in generating solutions were considered. Higher and lower performers showed little difference in their use of literature, vendors, and analysis and experimentation, and in their reliance upon personal experience in generating solution alternatives. Poorer performers once again relied more heavily upon external sources, and better performers upon sources within their own laboratory, that is, upon their technical staff and other company research programs (T. Allen 1969, chap. 9). In another study, Allen found that the use of information sources outside the laboratory was inversely related to the technical quality of the proposals (T. Allen 1964). Shilling and Bernard, comparing the extent to which paid consultants are employed by industrial bioscientists with eight measures of laboratory productivity and efficiency also found consistent inverse correlations between the variables (Shilling and Bernard 1964).

Still another support for our hypothesis is the fact that the lag between discovery of a scientific phenomenon and its embodiment in a new product is shorter whenever the information transfer takes place within the firm. In a study of innovations made by the ethical drug industry, Jerome Schnee found that the lag between discovery and innovation of sixty-eight innovations was significantly smaller if the innovator was also the inventor, that is, if the innovation had been produced by the firm that discovered it. Average time lags were 3.1 years if the inventor was also the innovator, 5.7 if it was a university, hospital, or research institute, 6.6 years in the case of other external sources (other domestic firms, individual inventors, or government bodies) and 9.7 years in the case of a foreign firm. The average time lag for all innovations was 5 years. The difference between the mean time lags was significant at the 5 percent level (Mansfield et al. 1971, chap. 8). In another study of significant innovations in the petroleum industry, Enos found that the time lag between invention and innovation was shorter when the innovator was also the discoverer (Enos 1962).

There is, therefore, some empirical evidence that confirms the hypothesis that the market exchange of knowledge is subject to high transaction costs, and that its transfer within the firm is relatively more efficient. One should mention at this point the existence of one legal device, the patent system, the goal of which is to reduce market transaction costs in knowledge.

The Patent System

In the preceding section we have shown how the characteristics of knowledge make its market exchange relatively more costly than its hierarchical transfer. Patents, however, tend to reduce substantially the costs of exchanging knowledge in the market.

Patents grant to the innovator a temporary monopoly of the sale of the good embodying his know-how. Because the seller of knowledge has a monopoly of its use, he can now appropriate the returns from selling the know-how even if he reveals its substance (J. Parker 1974; Kitch 1977). The patent system encourages the seller of knowledge to disclose its content to the buyer, and thus reduces the information costs inherent in market exchange.[5]

By establishing monopoly rights to goods embodying new information, patents facilitate the market transfer of knowledge. This extends the benefits of division of labor and specialization to the production and utilization of know-how, since the knowledge necessary to develop a new product in domestic markets is often different from that required to introduce it in foreign markets. By reducing market transaction costs, patents allow domestic and foreign entrepreneurs to specialize in their respective domains of expertise.

The patent system suffers, however, from a certain number of limitations. Patents reduce the cost of selling knowledge in the market by granting temporary, but exclusive, rights to the manufacture of products embodying that knowledge. The feasibility of such a system hinges on the ability of the innovator to describe adequately the content of his knowledge in the patent application and on the power and willingness of public authorities to establish and enforce monopoly rights to the sale of goods and services embodying the knowledge.

The basic procedure involved in patenting is for the inventor to submit a description of the product or process that he wants to patent to the patent-granting authority of each country in which he intends to obtain monopoly rights. The application is then examined by the patent office to ensure that it meets the conditions for patentability. If granted, the inventor is given the exclusive right, for the life of the patent, to sell the patented product in the patent-granting country.

To obtain patent rights, an inventor must therefore specify exhaustively the characteristics of the knowledge he possesses and submit it to the patent offices of the countries in which he seeks protection. Since a patent grants a monopoly right in a given political jurisdiction, complete patent protection requires simultaneous patenting in every country of the world. Because the language and the format of the application vary across countries, worldwide patent protection is quite expensive to obtain. The cost of acquiring patent rights, though significant, is not, however, the main deterrent to the use of the patent system to exchange knowledge. More important are (1) the cost of embodying the knowledge in the patent, (2) the cost of enforcing patent rights, and (3) the cost of exchanging patent rights.

Recall that patents reduce the high information costs inherent in the transfer of knowledge by revealing it and establishing exclusive property rights in its use. Through such a device, the information can be disclosed—thus facilitating its purchase—and still remain the property of the inventor. The patent is valuable to the buyer because it provides the necessary know-how to manufacture products embodying the knowledge. To reduce market transaction costs, the patent must therefore contain the totality of the information necessary to produce the commodity. If not, a buyer would have difficulty in ascertaining the value of the patent right; the seller, on the other hand, would be unwilling to disclose additional information unless some commitment to buy the patent was made, since otherwise he would be transferring valuable information without receiving payment for it. If the patent does not contain all of the information necessary to produce the patented commodity, the transaction will involve (in part) transfer of unpatented knowledge, and will thus be characterized by high information costs.

There are some a priori reasons why we would expect the information contained in the patent to be incomplete. The first of these reasons has been outlined by Edmund Kitch (1977). A major feature of the patent system is the emphasis on early filing. To obtain a patent on an invention, one must be the first to file an application. The application need not, however, describe an invention that is fully developed or commercially feasible. The only requirement is to disclose an invention that works. These rules encourage filing at an early stage of commercial development, before the discoveries that will, it is hoped, lead to such development have been made.[6] Patent applications often cannot provide the information necessary to a commercial exploitation of an invention because this knowledge is not yet available to the inventor.

There are also more general reasons why the information contained in the patent application may be insufficient. The knowledge embodied into a patent has to be coded by the patent holder and decoded by the prospective buyer. Expressing know-how in printed words and blueprints can be, however, a very inefficient way of transferring know-how. Often only a part of the relevant information can be coded. In many instances the physical objects transferred—blueprints, manuals, and so on—do not contain all of the information that is meant to be transferred. Face-to-face contact is needed to elucidate, complete, and interpret the document. This is especially true for technical knowledge. As has been pointed out by Svennilson,

> it would be far too crude to assume, as often seems to be the case, that there is a common fund of technical knowledge, which is available to anybody to use by applying his individual skill. We must take into account that only a part, and mainly the broad lines, of technical knowledge is codified by non-personal means of intellectual communication or communicated by teaching outside the production process itself. The technical knowledge of persons who have been trained in actual operations has a wider scope especially as regards the application of more broad knowledge. The "common fund," thus, covers only part of the technical knowledge to which individuals or groups of persons apply their personal skill. [Svennilson 1965, p. 407]

Baranson (1969, pp. 28–30) describes industrial technology as consisting of three elements: product design, production techniques, and managerial know-how. Familiarity with the product's design as well as a considerable amount of manufacturing know-how are necessary to duplicate an industrial product. One must know how to operate equipment, machine parts, handle materials, and the like. A third necessary input to any modern manufacturing process is the ability to organize the flow of materials and to meet minimum standards in materials and parts. Product design can be easily transmitted by making blueprints available. Effective transfer of production techniques requires a considerable volume of documentation on machine design, machine speeds and tolerances, and so forth. To impart managerial techniques through written instructions is even more difficult, if not impossible.

Even if the patentee has included in the patent application all that is needed to manufacture the patented product, some information may be lost in the transfer. Problems arise when the sender and the receiver speak different languages. It is easy to underestimate the difficulty of translating. Countries have their own customs and frames of reference, and these are difficult to communicate. Even purely technical information may be difficult to transfer across countries, even between those in which the same language is shared. Thus Kenneth Arrow mentions that when the British supplied the Americans with the plans of a jet engine it took ten months to redraw them to conform to American usage (Arrow 1969, p. 34). Disciplines and industries have also their "languages," and this makes interdisciplinary and interindustry communications difficult.

To the extent that technical considerations make the information contained in the patent insufficient to carry out production, the market transfer of patent rights will be characterized by high information costs. By contrast, whenever the patent states clearly all of the information necessary to produce the product, the appropriability problem is solved. All of the knowledge behind the innovation can then be sold through the sale of monopoly rights, and the problem of transferring knowledge without payment does not arise, provided that patent rights are strictly enforced.

A further limitation of the patent system is due to the fact that it is sometimes costly to enforce monopoly rights in some commodities. Only if the inventor can be assured of an exclusive right to the production and sale of the product embodying his know-how will he consent to disclose it. If he doubts the ability of public authorities to enforce his monopoly right, he will prefer to keep his invention secret and exploit it himself, for by not disclosing it he secures a temporary de facto monopoly for at least as long as it takes for others to market imitations. The efficiency of the patent system as a method of transferring knowledge is thus directly a function of the ability of the patentee to protect his monopoly right.[7]

Since the potential holder has to rely on public authorities to enforce his rights, the relative efficiency of the patent system will hinge on the ability and the willingness of governments to protect patents. To enforce patent rights, one must prevent nonpatentees from using without payment the information contained in the patent. Imitators can appropriate the value of the knowledge by secretly using it, or by making marginal changes to the patented product. In both cases, imitations may be costly to detect and difficult to prove. If the knowledge that is patented cannot be directly incorporated into a tangible process or product, then policing its use will be prohibitively costly. For that reason, such knowledge is not usually patentable (Parker 1974). The cost of enforcing exclusive use of tangible products and processes, though considerably lower than that involved in preventing use of general principles or of theoretical knowledge, is nevertheless significant and is shouldered by the patent holder. States do not usually take action on their behalf; therefore, the cost of defending patent rights falls on the individual. To some extent, "a patent is merely a license to bring a lawsuit" (*Guide* v. *Desperak,* 114 F.Supp. 182, 186 [1956]). Patent infringement suits are extremely costly and time-consuming, and, of course, not always successful. Scherer cites the case of a single lawsuit over petroleum-cracking patents that lasted for fifteen years and cost the parties involved over $3 million in legal fees (Scherer 1970, p. 393).

The efficiency of the patent system in transferring know-how is crucially affected by government policies. Patent law is, by and large, the prerogative of national governments, the constraints imposed by international conventions being of minor significance (Vernon 1977, p. 167). National authorities can therefore unilaterally decide to refuse to issue patents for products that are technically patentable, to fix long or short patent lives, to subject applications to tests of patentability, to define what constitutes patent abuses, and to set up legal remedies for such abuses.

Limits to patent rights are, in fact, substantial. Drugs, for example, are not patentable in at least forty-five countries. Other restricted fields are food products (twenty-one countries), plant varieties and animal breeds (thirteen countries), chemicals (nine countries), and nuclear materials and processes (seven countries) (United Nations Conference on Trade and Development 1975, p. 53). Property rights in knowledge are also limited to what courts deem to be "nonobvious" knowledge. In some countries (including the United States) patent applications are only granted if the invention fulfills the requirements of "patentability."[8] It is always possible that an invention that is genuinely new and that would pass the market test will be declared unpatentable by the patent authorities. Furthermore, the grant of a patent is no proof of its validity. The value of a patent depends on the degree of probability of its validity, and that probability, even in countries that examine patents, is not one. The validity of a patent can always be challenged in court. In the United States, for example, about 60 percent of the patent invalidation lawsuits that have been fought to completion have resulted in invalidation decisions (Scherer 1970, p. 389). Moreover, patent rights are only protected for a finite length of time, which varies among countries from three to twenty years. This may, in some instances, be an insufficient period for the innovator to recoup his investment.

The costs of transferring patent rights are also significant. A patent right is the right to monopolize the sale of a product over a particular area and during a given length of time. A patent holder can either exploit the patent himself or sell his right to independent producers. The choice between the two modes of exploitation will depend on the relative costs of both methods. Here again government policies will have an important impact.

One simple method for patentees to exploit their invention in foreign countries would be to auction off the right to produce their product in a given area. The patent holder has typically little information on foreign input prices and market conditions, and he is therefore ignorant as to the capitalized value of the profit stream that can be obtained by using his invention in a foreign market. By auctioning his right, he forces the bidders to reveal to him the value of the patent; he will be able, therefore, to obtain maximum rents from his invention.

In most cases, however, transferring patent rights through outright market sale will be relatively costlier than instituting a profit-sharing scheme. By paying a lump sum to acquire the right to produce the patented goods, buyers would be committing the bulk of their portfolio in exchange for a stream of profits, the value of which they may be unable to ascertain. The more uncertain the value of the patent, the lower will be their bid price (Caves and Murphy 1976, p. 577). A contractual agreement by which the right to the use of the invention is rented in exchange for a share of the income derived from using it reduces the risk borne by the buyer, but, as we will see, substantially increases market transaction costs.

If the patentee, who has now become the licenser, transfers the right to his invention in exchange for a share of the proceeds, the income he receives will be dependent on the buyer's, or licensee's, actions. By failing to put the patent to its most productive use, the licensee can reduce the total sales and/or profits derived from the venture, and thus the licenser's royalties. Even if both parties cooperate, differences of opinion are likely to arise as to the best course of action. It is theoretically possible for parties to draft a contract that will specify ex ante what is to be done in each case, but, for reasons we outlined in chapter 2, anticipating all contingencies and the adaptation thereto is likely to be extremely costly. Licensing contracts will therefore fail to perfectly constrain the behavior of the parties.

One can expect, for example, licensees to attempt to understate their volume of production in order to minimize royalty payments. Licensees with low production costs may also export part of their production to higher-priced markets. Such an action is detrimental to the licenser because it prevents effective price discrimination across markets. Allowing low-cost licensees to export to high-priced markets will therefore reduce the total profits to be made from the exploitation of the knowledge (Casson 1979, p. 20). Another problem arises whenever the licensee supplies products and services bearing the licenser's trademark. There is then always the danger that the licensee will free ride on the goodwill capital of the licenser by producing lower-quality products. The problem is particularly serious if the licensee exports part of its production. Enforcing quality standards requires continuous supervision over the licensee. In many cases it is extremely difficult to enforce quality standards in the final output without exercising detailed control over all phases of the production process. In the case of diesel engines, for example, Baranson notes,

> the maintenance of international technical standards and specifications for a product is itself a formidable task. In order to maintain international standards, it is necessary to (a) periodically inspect foreign manufacturing affiliates to make sure adequate quality controls are being applied, and (b) sample-test assembled products in the home country plant. For the manufacturer of a diesel engine series, 8 to 10 volumes (3,000 to 4,000 pages) containing materials standards and manufacturing specifications are required. There are approximately 145 technical specifications, engineering information items, testing methods, and engine rebuild standards; 67 special manufacturing methods; 439 materials standards; and 25 salvage procedure standards for damaged parts. [Baranson 1969, pp. 30–31]

Enforcing quality standards through contractual means is likely to be, in many cases, much more costly than doing it by means of hierarchical control: the licenser would then have access to a larger and more effective array of control and reward mechanisms. Lastly, marginal improvements made by the licensee can cause the licensed technology to become obsolete, allowing the licensee to become a powerful competitor (Casson 1979, p. 20).

Licensing agreements usually contain clauses that protect licensers against these risks. Many licensing contracts require the licensee to purchase certain key inputs from the licenser. This helps in enforcing quality standards, and allows the licenser to check the accuracy of the production figures quoted by the licensee. Other common clauses in licensing contracts specify that any improvements made by the licensee will revert to the licenser. This is called grant-back.

Unfortunately for the potential licenser, such clauses have increasingly been declared illegal by host countries. Thus Argentina, Brazil, and India have imposed maximum royalty rates. Territorial restrictions on exports are illegal in Japan, Spain, Argentina, Brazil, and Mexico, and in the countries of the Andean Common Market. Tied purchases are forbidden in many countries, including the European Economic Community, the United States, Australia, and Japan. Grant-back provisions are also forbidden in Japan, Spain, the United States, Argentina, Brazil, and the Andean Common Market (United Nations Conference on Trade and Development 1974).

Government interventions of this type have greatly increased the relative cost of licensing because they have outlawed explicit clauses in licensing contracts. A multinational firm need not, however, draw specific contracts with its majority-owned subsidiaries. Foreign direct investment therefore allows the firm to bypass some of these governmental restrictions and thus obtain a higher return on its proprietary knowledge.

Governments have also, in some cases, restricted the patentee's property right in knowledge by forcing him to license certain producers. In the United States, for example, the courts have compulsorily licensed more than 40,000 patents as a remedy in antitrust cases. Furthermore, whenever compulsory licensing has been ordered, courts have shown a bias toward "cost-oriented royalty standards which permit the patentee to earn little more than a normal return on its development investment, with at best a modest premium for risk bearing" (Scherer 1970, p. 397). There is some evidence that these restrictions have deterred firms from patenting their inventions, and encouraged them to rely on secrecy instead (Scherer 1970, p. 397).

In summary, the relative efficiency of patents as a method to exchange knowledge increases as the ease of incorporating the knowledge into a tangible product or process increases, the cost for the inventor to describe exhaustively the information necessary to utilize the patent decreases, and the degree of uncertainty as to the patent's profitability decreases. Whenever knowledge is difficult to incorporate into a tangible product, or is costly to describe exhaustively, and whenever its value to a licensee is hard to assess, the market exchange of property rights will be characterized by high transacting costs, and internal transfer will be preferred. The extent to which governments establish and enforce property rights will also greatly influence the relative efficiency of market transfer.

Some Implications of the Analysis

An analysis of the transactional characteristics of the transfer of knowledge leads therefore to the following conclusions: (1) a substantial volume of knowledge will be exchanged within the firm; (2) the role played by the firm and by the market in transferring information will vary according to the type of knowledge—patentable knowledge will tend to be exchanged in the market, while unpatentable technology will move within the firm; (3) the preceding considerations apply both domestically and internationally.

It is difficult to compare statistically the volume of knowledge that is transferred within firms and that exchanged in markets. One imperfect method is to measure the value of the royalties and fees paid by the buyer for the use of the technology. However, no such data exists for the intracountry transfer of knowledge, and thus the relative importance of firms and markets in the domestic transfer of knowledge cannot be directly measured. There is, however, a limited amount of data on its international transfer.

The United States Bureau of Economic Analysis compiles statistics on the royalties and fees received by American firms. Although the correspondence between royalty and fee receipts and the transfer of technology is not a perfect one,[9] these statistics suggest that, at least in the case of the United States, the firm is the main vehicle for such transfers. Thus, over the 1956–72 period, net royalties and fees received by American firms from their affiliates (i.e., total receipts minus payments from the parents to the affiliates) amounted to $15.2 billion, while only $5.8 billion were received from unaffiliated foreigners.[10] Seventy-two percent of all royalties and fees were thus received from affiliates. Receipts of royalties and fees from affiliates have also expanded more rapidly—14.8 percent per year compared to 10.6 percent for those of unaffiliated firms

(Teplin 1973). About 40 percent of the British royalty and fee receipts over the 1971–75 period were also obtained from their foreign subsidiaries (United Nations 1978). Some data are also available on American royalty and fee payments over the 1966–75 period. Net payments by affiliates in the United States to their foreign parents amounted to $1,353 million. Gross payments by American firms to unaffiliated foreign parties were $1,336 million. About half of the technology imported by the United States was thus transferred by hierarchical methods (U.S., Department of Commerce 1976*b*).

The Industrial Structure of the Innovation Process

According to our model, firms will specialize in transferring unpatentable know-how, whereas markets will be more active in transferring the patentable variety. This should be reflected in the industrial structure of innovation. We would expect those stages in the innovation process between which nonpatentable knowledge is transferred to be vertically integrated. If the information transferred between stages is patentable, then market exchange between these stages will be possible.

If one analyzes the chain of events that leads from the discovery of general principles to the efficient supply of final products, one reaches the conclusion that there are two points at which interfirm exchange of information is likely to exist—between the invention and the innovation stage, and at the end of the innovation stage. All other stages are likely to be organized through hierarchical processes.

During the invention stage, no significant interpersonal transfer of knowledge is likely to take place. The stock of basic science is freely available in published form to the potential inventor. The invention is usually the fruit of individual effort. Its output, a crude model of a product or process, is often patentable, and can thus be sold to other firms for further development and final supply.

The development stage is characterized by the fusion of many types of specialized knowledge—basic science, engineering, and marketing expertise. Although it could be theoretically possible for a manufacturing firm to buy the relevant knowledge from research laboratories and marketing consultants, we would expect the high market transaction costs that characterize the sale of unpatentable knowledge to lead to vertical integration of development research, manufacturing, and marketing.

During the development stage, the crude model or the basic description that constitutes the invention is gradually modified so it can be produced at reasonable cost and sold in sufficient quantities. Theoretically, the manufacturer could contract with scientists and market analysts. One could present scientists with unmet needs and ask them to develop products filling those needs. Conversely, one could present to marketing experts products embodying a new technique and ask them if they would sell. Unfortunately, neither approach is likely to be successful. There are twists and turns in the development process. The solution of a technical problem has almost always undesirable marketing side effects, and vice versa. At each step it is necessary to reevaluate the product in both technical and marketing terms. Consequently, it is inefficient to contract with both technicians and marketers sequentially. It is impossible to provide beforehand an exhaustive list of the characteristics of a product that will determine its approval or disapproval, just as it is impossible to specify a priori all the technical or performance characteristics of a new product. A successful innovation requires solving both constraints simultaneously. To specify performance and write contracts for both technologists and marketers would be extremely costly, since it is impossible to know beforehand what their contribution will be. As Price and Bass (1969, p. 804) put it, "innovation typically depends on information for which the requirements cannot be anticipated in definitive terms and therefore cannot be programmed in advance." The introduction of "new" products into foreign countries involves the same type of problems. Adaptation to local conditions often requires technical or marketing changes. Tight cooperation between those who know local conditions and those who are familiar with the technical characteristics of the product is necessary. In those conditions, organizing the innovation process through market exchange will often be inefficient.

A firm that wanted to launch new products in its home market or in foreign markets, and that did not have a research and development laboratory and a marketing staff at home or in a foreign subsidiary, would have to contract on the market with a domestic research and development firm and with a domestic or foreign distributor. Such market contracting would be exceedingly costly for two reasons. First, it would be very difficult to specify in advance the responsibilities of the parties. Leaving contracts incomplete would expose contractors to the risk of conflicts, whereas attempting to be too explicit in the face of uncertainty would prevent adaptation to changing circumstances. Second, the unpatented nature of knowledge to be transferred would lead to high information costs of the type described earlier: a potential supplier of information would find it difficult to prove he is competent without revealing the knowledge he possesses.

Without such assurances, however, the buyer would be shouldering substantial risks.

By contrast, the firm seems to be a privileged institution to organize the development process. Within a firm, parties are not rewarded by the information they transfer, and they will be willing, therefore, to reveal the knowledge they possess. An atmosphere of trust is thus more likely to exist, and this will lead to efficient intrafirm information exchange. Redirection of effort in answer to exogenous shocks is also much easier when the parties to the innovation are joined within a firm. Employees are then not rewarded as a function of their specific contribution, and therefore they have no incentives to oppose the changes ordered by their superiors. Bargaining stalemates are attenuated by providing employees with long-term incentives. The firm can thus dispense with the need to specify ex ante all contingencies, and yet avoid the possibility of conflicts. Organization of research and development within a firm should thus result in greater flexibility and efficiency.

The end result of the innovation process is a product and its production function. To the extent to which no further adaptation is needed, all of the information acquired during the development process has now been embedded in the new product. The latter can thus be patented, and the right to its production licensed to other producers. Some market exchange is feasible at this stage.

The preceding considerations have some implications for the industrial structure of the innovation process. Since during the development stage close contact has to be maintained between the research laboratory, the manufacturing operations, and the marketing department, we would expect these three functions to be joined within a firm. On the other hand, invention/development and final supply in separate markets can be efficiently performed by different organizations: easily patentable inventions can be sold or rented to manufacturing firms for development; if new products and processes in one country can be produced in another country without the need for significant adaptation, they can be licensed to foreign producers.

The data that are available on the domestic organization of the innovation process support our argument. Invention and innovation are sometimes performed by different organizations, but the developmental research, manufacturing, and marketing functions are almost always organized within the firm.

Many studies of the innovation process have shown that large manufacturing firms do not produce in-house all the inventions on which their new products are based, but that they buy and develop inventions produced by other firms, by universities, and by independent inventors. Willard Mueller studied the twenty-five most important product and process innovations introduced by the Du Pont Company between 1920 and 1950. He found that only ten of the basic inventions on which these innovations were based were produced in Du Pont's laboratories, the remainder having been purchased from other firms or independent inventors (Mueller 1962). Other studies by Hamberg (1963); Jewkes, Sawers, and Stillerman (1959); and Schmookler (1957) also show that a large proportion of new products are based on inventions that have been developed outside the manufacturing firm (Williamson 1975, p. 186).

The same phenomenon can be observed at the international level. The basic inventions that underlie the synthetic dyestuff industry, for example, were made by British and French inventors, yet it is German and Swiss entrepreneurs that pioneered their commercial production. In the more recent period, American firms have put into commercial use European inventions in, among other things, fluidics, holography, cryogenics, and aerospace engineering (Diebold 1968).

If invention is sometimes carried out outside the innovating firm, development, manufacturing, and marketing are almost always vertically integrated. For American firms, this is shown by the following statistics: first, most of the research performed by American manufacturing firms is of the development type. In 1974, for example, 78 percent of the research funds expended by American manufacturing firms were devoted to development (National Science Foundation 1976). Furthermore, almost all of the industrial research and development utilized by manufacturing firms is performed in company-owned laboratories. In 1973 and 1974, for example, only 2 percent of the company-financed research and development expenditures of American manufacturing firms were contracted out (National Science Foundation 1976). In 1960, only 3 percent of the technical engineers and 5 percent of the natural scientists in American industry were employed by firms providing miscellaneous business services—a category including research and development and commercial testing laboratories (U.S., Department of Commerce 1963).

Similarly, domestic manufacturing firms that invest heavily in research and development own manufacturing facilities abroad. As noted earlier, domestic sales of the four most research intensive American industries (transportation equipment, electrical machinery, chemicals, and nonelectrical machinery) were 35 percent of all domestic sales in manufacturing but the sales of these four sectors' overseas subsidiaries were 70 percent of all American foreign subsidiary sales in manufacturing (Gruber, Mehta, and Vernon 1967). Conversely, American multinational corporations tend to spend relatively more on research and development than their purely domestic counterparts (Vernon 1971). Furthermore, foreign subsidiaries are concentrated in research intensive industries. Seventy-three percent of the total book value of German affiliates in manufacturing, 60 percent of that of American foreign manufacturing affiliates, and 50 percent of the total book value of British foreign manufacturing affiliates are concentrated in the four most research-intensive industries: chemicals, machinery, electrical products, and transportation equipment (United Nations 1973, p. 151). Therefore it appears that, as predicted, the high relative costs of selling some types of knowledge in the market have led firms that innovate to own foreign manufacturing plants.

If our analysis of the transactional characteristics of the innovation process is valid, the correlation between domestic research and development and foreign direct investment should not be a perfect one, for three reasons. First, some of the new products and processes developed by domestic research intensive firms can be exported to foreign markets. The know-how is thus embedded into products that can be sold in the market. Second, there are other motives for foreign direct investment than the high cost of transferring unpatentable knowledge internationally: we have analyzed these motives in chapter 3 and in previous sections of this chapter. Third, foreign direct investment will not always be preferred to licensing. Let us discuss the third point in more detail.

In the preceding discussion we have noted that both foreign direct investment and licensing are methods to transfer knowledge internationally. Whenever inventions require a substantial degree of adaptation to local conditions, foreign direct investment will be preferred to licensing. In that case, successful development of the product requires the cooperation of parties located in both countries. The know-how that is transferred is not patentable, and therefore the information exchange is most efficiently organized intrafirm. When the innovation is applicable with a minimum of local adaptation, licensing may be preferred.

These further implications of the model can be tested against the empirical evidence. Since we have argued that integration into overseas manufacturing will be preferred whenever it is necessary to adapt the foreign product or process to local conditions, one should observe foreign subsidiaries of multinational firms engaging in substantial research and development expenditures; their research and development effort would be mostly centered on development. By contrast, local firms that obtain licenses from foreigners should spend less on research and development. The preceding analysis also implies wide differences between industries in the method chosen for the international transfer of knowledge, since the need for local adaptation of innovations is likely to differ across sectors: the products of some industries are not patentable; in some sectors products require considerable adaptation to local conditions, in others they do not. All these considerations may influence the choice between licensing and foreign direct investment.

There is some evidence that subsidiaries of international firms engage in some research and development, and that those expenditures are mainly devoted to adapting products and processes to local conditions. In 1966, for example, 6 percent of the total research and development budget of American multinational corporations was spent by their foreign affiliates. The percentage of total research and development expenditures performed by the subsidiary varied across industries, from a high of 12 percent in food to a low of zero in textile and apparel (U.S., Tariff Commission 1973, p. 582). There is some evidence that the principal function of the subsidiaries' research and development laboratories was to adapt the parent's products to local demand or manufacturing conditions (Brooke and Remmers 1970, p. 88).

It is interesting to note that foreign subsidiaries tend to devote more to research and development as a percentage of their sales than their domestic counterparts. John Dunning, for example, found that American-controlled firms in Britain had higher research and development-to-sales ratios than British firms in seven out of nine industries (Dunning 1966). Safarian reached the same conclusion in the case of Canada (Safarian 1966, pp. 168–200). Likewise, foreign subsidiaries in the United States were slightly more research and development intensive than all American firms (table 15). It appears then that subsidiaries, far from being passive recipients of their parents' know-how, play an active role in the adaptation of products to local conditions. In other words, both parents and subsidiaries cooperate in the innovation process.

A last implication of our analysis is that the international transfer of technology should take different forms across industries. In some industries the main channel for international technology transfers will be the firm, in others the market. Unfortunately, no data on royalty and fee receipts and payments are collected on an industry basis. The limited amount of empirical evidence that is available, however, suggests wide variations in the pattern of international technology transfers across industries. The 1976 report to Congress on foreign direct investment in the United States, for example,

TABLE 15   Research and Development Intensity of All American Manufacturing Firms and of Foreign Manufacturing Affiliates in the United States, 1974 (in million U.S. dollars)

	All U.S. Firms	Foreign Affiliates
Total company financed research and development expenditures	13,794[a]	574[c]
Sales (net of taxes)	1,060,961[b]	31,301[d]
Research and development as a percent of net sales	1.3	1.8

a. Data from National Science Foundation 1976, p. 25, table B-2.
b. Data from Federal Trade Commission, *Quarterly Financial Reports for Manufacturing, Mining and Trade Corporations* (FT1-18), 2nd quarter 1974 (Sept. 25, 1974), 3rd quarter 1974 (Dec. 26, 1974), 4th quarter 1974 (April 23, 1975).
c. Data from U.S., Department of Commerce 1976a, vol. 2, table N-1, p. 167.
d. Data from *ibid.,* vol. 2, table 2.

analyzes the media for international technology transfers in four industries: (1) pharmaceuticals; (2) electronics, computers, and scientific instruments; (3) nonelectrical machinery; and (4) petrochemicals and their derivatives. The report summarizes the conclusions of a panel of industry representatives and academic experts as to the characteristics of the international transfer of technology in each industry (U.S., Department of Commerce 1976a).

In the pharmaceutical industry, foreign direct investment is, according to the panel, the most common method used to transfer technology across countries. The reasons given by the panel members fit very well into our analysis.

First of all, as a result of increasingly stringent rules relating to the testing of drugs, the time between the initial discovery and, where permitted, patenting of a new therapeutic agent and government approval to market it has greatly increased. Though the period of a product patent extends for 17 years, in the United States as much as two-thirds of the patent life may be consumed by the process of obtaining approval to introduce the therapeutic drug. Under such circumstances, which put a premium on well-managed and efficient drug development and clinical testing programs, individual manufacturers are loathe to license their major innovations to outsiders. The time, cost, and informational penalties of dealing with non-company partners—that is, between a licensor and a licensee—are simply too high for pharmaceutical products, given today's limited patent life.

Furthermore, within any single company, drug innovation is now an international undertaking, calling for careful coordination among investigators located in several or, perhaps, many countries. Accordingly, arm's length relationships with foreign licensees, which makes coordination more difficult, are becoming increasingly incompatible with the requirements for effective drug innovation. As a result, extensive foreign direct investment is practiced by virtually all major drug manufacturers. In other words, licensing is no longer the preferred alternative by which firms can transfer technology.

Another force leading toward foreign direct investment arises from the necessity of pharmaceutical makers to monitor all markets for information relating to the safety of their drugs. Manufacturers need to have access to worldwide product information networks, and they need to be able to pool the experiences of physicians, hospitals, laboratories, and patients everywhere in order to ensure product safety. Licensees may or may not fit in with this worldwide scanning activity; so, rather than take this risk, drug manufacturers prefer to establish their own subsidiaries and data gathering points.

Apart from these important considerations, the increasing complexity of pharmaceutical innovation pushes drug manufacturers toward direct investment in foreign markets. It is simply far easier to transfer complex knowledge within organizations than between organizations. This, too, lessens the acceptability of licensing pharmaceutical products and processes. [U.S., Department of Commerce 1976a, vol. 9, p. O-15]

By contrast, licensing was declared to be the main mode of international technology transfer in the petrochemical industry. According to the members of the panel, "most petrochemical processes are openly licensed and within the industry almost everything is licensed to almost everyone" (p. O-50). Petrochemicals are intermediate goods, derived from petroleum feedstocks, and their production would seem to require little adaptation to local raw materials or market conditions. Transfer of petrochemical technology through licensing would thus appear to be relatively efficient.

In electronics, computers, and scientific instruments, foreign direct investment was thought to play a rather minor role in the international transfer of technology, but was said to be the channel chosen to transfer "the essential soft technology of process engineering, management and marketing" (p. O-27).

In the nonelectrical machinery sector, the panel members distinguished between product, application, and process technologies. While product technology is relatively easy to transfer through licensing,

for this industry, at least, foreign direct investment is often a better way of transferring or acquiring process and application technologies because their successful transplantation is closely linked to local conditions and cultural traditions. [p. O-39]

The conclusions of the panel thus offer some support to the hypothesis developed in this section, which is that the respective roles of firms and markets in the transfer of knowledge (and therefore the extent of foreign direct investment) can be explained by the relative cost of hierarchical versus market exchange.

Conclusion

In this chapter and the one preceding we have attempted to show how an analysis of the transactional properties of firms and markets can throw considerable light on the industrial structure of foreign direct investment. We have shown how the four types of overseas subsidiaries can be explained in terms of such a model. The unity and generality of this approach contrast with the ad hoc character of many of the explanations of foreign direct investment that have been advanced in the literature. In the next chapter, we will attempt to show how the same hypotheses can account for the historical and geographical patterns of foreign direct investment and the ownership policies of multinational firms.

CHAPTER 5

Historical and Geographical Patterns of Foreign Direct Investment

The Historical Pattern of Foreign Direct Investment

Although multinational enterprises have a long history, their growth and development is mostly a recent phenomenon. The forerunners of the modern multinationals began to expand across boundaries in the 1860s, but the scale of their operations was small and their influence limited. As we have noted earlier, the multinational corporation is, for all practical purposes, a postwar institution.

Existing theories of foreign direct investment do not provide satisfactory explanations for this phenomenon. The product cycle theory considers foreign direct investment as the method by which firms exploit their technological advantage. The only explanation consistent with the model would be that there were, prior to the 1950s, no international differences in the technological capabilities of firms. This, of course, is contrary to the historical evidence. During the first eighty years of the nineteenth century, British firms possessed a technological lead over their continental and American (and, a fortiori, Asian and African) counterparts that can well be compared to that enjoyed by some American producers today. Yet English firms of that time failed to exploit their lead through foreign direct investment. We must now ask, why?

During the nineteenth century, the new techniques and products that had been developed by British firms were successfully transferred to Europe and to the regions of recent settlement. The main vehicle for technological transfer was then (as is still probably true today) the international migration of skilled personnel. But only in rare cases was that migration effected within and by English firms: first, skilled English workers were hired by foreign producers to provide training and technical advice. David Landes has estimated that there were at least 2,000 skilled British workers on the

Continent in the first decades of the nineteenth century (Landes 1969, p. 148). At the same time, American agents visited the United Kingdom to try to persuade skilled workers to emigrate and work for them (Dunning 1971, p. 368). Around 1890, there were 15,000 British workers in the United States iron and steel industry, and one-tenth of all the machinists were British immigrants (Berthoff 1953, p. 67). Knowledge was also transferred by the creation of expatriate firms. In many cases the British technicians that emigrated started their own businesses in the foreign country. David Landes reports that

> the best of the British technicians to go abroad were usually entrepreneurs in their own right, or eventually became industrialists with the assistance of continental associates or government subventions. Many of them came to be leaders of their respective trades: one thinks of the Waddingtons (cotton), Job Dixon (machine building), and James Jackson (steel) in France; James Cockerill (machine construction) and William Mulvany (mining) in Germany; Thomas Wilson (cotton) in Holland; Norman Douglas (cotton) and Edward Thomas (iron and engineering), in the Austrian empire; above all, John Cockerill in Belgium, an aggressive, shrewd businessman of supple ethical standards, who took all manufacturing as his province and with the assistance of first the Dutch and then the Belgian governments, made a career of exploiting the innovations of others. [Landes 1969, pp. 148–49]

Likewise, the first American woolen factory using power machinery was started by two Englishmen, while Scottish capitalists and superintendents were pioneers in the New Jersey jute industry (Dunning 1971, p. 368). There were also many expatriate firms in mining, agriculture, and utilities. Once established, these firms severed all connections with the home country, and they eventually became indistinguishable from local firms. Finally, there are some recorded instances of British firms crating their machinery and moving with their employees to foreign countries: such a move took place, for example, in the silk industry in the 1880s when several British companies transferred their operations to the United States (Dunning 1971, p. 371). Foreign direct investment, on the other hand, seems to have played a very limited role in the transfer of knowledge. This is shown by the fact that a small part of the capital exported by England during the nineteenth century took the form of foreign direct investment. In 1913, no more than 10 percent of the total stock of British foreign investments was in direct investments. The limited amount of migration data that are available also shows that most skilled British workers did not emigrate at the request of British firms eager to staff their overseas subsidiaries. As we have noted earlier in chapter 1, a study of the migration history of 224 British-born textile workers who died in the United States between 1880 and 1915 indicated that only 8 of them had come to the United States to establish foreign subsidiaries for British companies (Dunning 1971, p. 372).

If the failure of British firms to exploit their technological advantage through foreign direct investment cannot be explained by the product cycle model, it is consistent with our hypothesis. In chapter 2 we have argued that foreign direct investment will take place whenever market transaction costs exceed internal organization costs, and whenever the latter are sufficiently low to make transfer profitable. If both firms and markets experience high transfer costs, no interpersonal transfer of knowledge will take place: the individual possessing the knowledge will start a business on his own. If market transaction costs are lower than internal organization costs, market channels will be used to transfer technology: knowledgeable individuals will be hired by foreign firms. The fact that these two transfer modes prevailed in the period under study implies that English firms of that time experienced high internal organization costs. If our analysis is correct, then English firms of the early nineteenth century were prevented from investing overseas by the high internal organization costs they experienced. These high costs were due to the primitive stage, in those times, of legal forms, of management techniques, and of communication technology (Olson 1965). Because of high internal organization costs, hierarchical organization played then a smaller role, and markets a larger role in organizing production than in today's advanced economies.[1]

English firms of the Industrial Revolution were small. In 1851, for example, two-thirds of the cotton factories employed less than 50 workers, and the average employment was less than 200 (Landes 1969, p. 120). The largest glassmaker employed 700 workers in 1841 (Pollard 1965, p. 900), the largest potter, 1,000 in 1833 (Pollard 1965, p. 99), and the largest chemical mill 1,000 workers in 1840 (Pollard 1965, p. 97). Multiplant firms seem to have been the exception. By contrast, the largest American firm producing yarn and thread had in 1967 over 50,000 employees, the largest glassmaking firm, over 25,000 employees, and the largest firm in industrial chemicals, over 100,000 employees (U.S., Department of Commerce 1972). Since firms were small, the market played an important role in organizing production. Most of the activities that today are performed within a plant were then undertaken by independent subcontractors. In 1860 Birmingham, then the world center of small arms manufacture,

> the master gun-maker—the entrepreneur—seldom possessed a factory or workshop. . . . Usually he owned merely a warehouse in the gun quarter, and his function was to acquire semi-finished parts and to give these out to specialized craftsmen who undertook the assembly and finishing of the gun. He purchased materials from the barrel-makers, lock-makers, sight stampers, trigger-makers, ramrod-forgers, gun furniture makers. . . . All of these were independent manufacturers executing the orders of several master gun-makers. . . . Once the parts had been purchased from the "material-makers," as they were called, the next task was to hand them out to a long succession of "setters-up," each of whom performed a specific operation in connection with the assembly and finishing of the gun. [G. Allen 1929, p. 116–17]

At the end of the eighteenth century, many of the English manufacturers were characterized by a combination of central workshops for some functions and a large number of semi-independent workers for other processes. In the cotton industry, the tasks of spinning, carding, and printing were performed by employees, while weaving was contracted out to outworker hand weavers. This mixed semidomestic, semifactory framework was still common in the 1820s. In the silk industry, silk-throwing mills coexisted with outworker weavers. The same setup existed in the linen and knitting industries. In the woolen industry, the subcontracting of weaving was the rule until the 1830s. Putting out was also used in nail and file making, apparel making, button making, and other industries (Pollard 1965, pp. 32–37).

Industries in which economies of scale led to large plant size were characterized by internal subcontracting. In mining, the owner contracted with a butty, who in turn subcontracted with a group of workers to have the work done. Internal contracting was also practiced in cotton spinning. Skilled spinners were put in charge of expensive machinery, and they paid and recruited their own child assistants. Domestic weavers commonly employed boy helpers and warpers out of their own earnings. Subcontracting of that type was also current in blast furnaces, in tin mills, in potteries, and so forth.

Sometimes the factory owner was only a subcontractor in the manufacturing process. Thus

> in the largest mechanized woolen mill in existence, that of Benjamin Gott, it was found that as late as 1815 most of the weaving, even on the premises, was done by independent "manufacturer" contractors who were not paid by the firm, but on the contrary paid Gott a

commission for the use of the factory, on the cloth which they made to his order and which he bought from them. [Pollard 1965, p. 43]

Whenever multiplant economies were large, plants were not controlled by one decision maker. Rather each partner managed one establishment. The Carron company had subsidiaries in coal mining and shipping that were managed by partners. David Dale, the Scottish pioneer of cotton spinning, created separate partnerships with separate managers for each of his mills (Pollard 1965, p. 40). In many cases, the partners all belonged to the same family.

In textiles the better-known example included the Horrock brothers, administering between them ten different mills by 1810, the Strutts, who shared the management of their five mills among the three brothers . . . and the Marshalls of Leeds, dividing up control of their father's heritage in the 1830s. [Pollard 1965, p. 266]

These characteristic forms of organization were due to the high cost of organizing production through hierarchical control relative to that of coordinating activities in the market. We have seen that firms replace the constraints of market prices by managerial controls, and that they use centralized decision making whereas markets rely on decentralized adjustment. Firms of that time seem to have had considerable difficulty in supervising workers. Attendance was irregular. In one of the most progressive cotton-spinning firms, turnover rates were about 100 percent per year. In South Wales it is estimated that as late as the 1840s the workers lost one week in five. Factory owners had great difficulty in transforming the behavior of workers. They had to train their workers to a precision and assiduity unknown before and against which they rebelled. The extent of the problem of discipline is attested by the severity of the work rules and of the fines levied to enforce them.

Subcontracting and internal contracting were attractive because they reduced the costs of supervising workers and that of transferring information across hierarchical levels. Subcontracting was a "method of evading management" (Pollard 1965, p. 38), because it shifted to the subcontractor the task of monitoring workers. In mines, for example, the butty, usually working alongside his employees, was better able to supervise them. In their study of the coal industry in the eighteenth century, Ashton and Sykes suggested such an explanation.

. . . it is possible that the difficulty of supervising large numbers of men, burrowing in many small pits, at a time before modern large-scale management had come into being, may be partial explanation of the existence of the collective contract in the Midland and Welsh coalfields. [Ashton and Sykes 1929, p. 111]

Taylor also argues that "The greatest advantage of this system . . . was that it supplied a 'self-acting stimulus,' which dispensed with the necessity of incessant supervision of the managing foreman by the employer" (Taylor 1960, p. 216).

Subcontracting also simplified cost calculations, as the subcontractor was usually paid a fixed price per unit. This advantage was especially great for firms that had to present bids, such as shipbuilders or contractors, where it was necessary to calculate the cost of jobs in advance.

The practice of delegating to partners the management of plants of multiplant firms seems to have been motivated by the unreliability and dishonesty of salaried managers. There was consensus among businessmen of that period that it was impossible to trust a salaried manager. Typical among many is the observation by Sir Robert Peel that, "it is impossible for a mill at any distance to be managed, unless it is under the direction of a partner or a superintendant who has an interest in the success of the business" (Pollard 1965, p. 21). In the paper industry, it was stated in 1813 that "the impossibility of the Proprietor's giving his constant and personal attention must operate greatly to the injury of the concern, or admitting it could be procrured, the expense of others to effect the same must be greater" (Coleman 1958, p. 234). Pollard summarized the contemporary thinking on the subject in this way:

> Up to the end of the eighteenth century the (following) view predominated: management was a function of direct investment by ownership, and if it had to be delegated either because of the absence of the principals or because of the size of the concern, then the business was courting trouble. [Pollard 1965, p. 23]

Naming partners as managers was an answer to the problem, but it led to new difficulties: central direction of the firm was difficult, since all managing partners were de facto equals. Information was dispersed among partners. The informational and decision-making advantages of a hierarchical system of organization, which we have described earlier, were lost. As a result, many of the advantages of multiplant operations could not be secured.

This high level of internal organization costs relative to market transaction costs can be explained by the relative backwardness of contemporary management techniques. As a firm expands, the number of employees eventually exceeds the entrepreneur's span of control. Monitoring and decision-making authority have to be delegated to supervisors and lower-level managers. Today's firms have at their disposition a sophisticated arsenal of accounting techniques to check against abuses by subordinates and to assess speedily and accurately their performance. It is striking to see that accounting as we know it is quite recent. Pollard reviews extensively the accounting aids used by the British entrepreneurs of the Industrial Revolution. He concludes that "the practice of using accounts as direct aids to management was not one of the achievements of the British Industrial Revolution; in a sense, it does not even belong to the later nineteenth century, but to the twentieth" (p. 248).

We have seen that firms relax price constraints and replace them by managerial directives. The efficiency of a firm hinges on its ability to constrain on-the-job consumption and to obtain consummate cooperation, i.e., to persuade workers to use judgment, fill gaps, and take initiative (Williamson 1975, p. 69). Directing workers that are perfunctory cooperators is extremely costly, especially as the production process becomes more complicated, because the consequences of negligence or inattention are then much more serious. Consummate cooperation will be encouraged if the worker can be persuaded that the interest of the firm and his own coincide in the long run. The beneficial effects of an employee's consummate cooperation will often be felt after a significant time lag. Consummate cooperation is thus not a paying proposition if the worker either expects his term of employment to be short or knows that he will not be rewarded for his efforts. Short-term, transaction-specific rewards are not prone to encourage cooperation. Internal promotion, on the other hand, ties the interests of the workers to that of the firm. The creation of "company spirit" is also helpful in establishing an atmosphere of cooperation.

Although little information is available on labor management techniques during the Industrial Revolution, it would appear that they were quite crude. Commenting on the management problems of the three largest firms in England in the first half of the eighteenth century, Pollard notes "they were all troubled by the problems of how to achieve effective controls over their labor, and the tendency for all of them was to involve noneconomic sanctions, either by legal compulsion or discipline, or by dominating the worker's whole lives inside their townships within the framework of long-term 'bindings' " (p. 60).

Later, when long-term contracts were found to be ineffectual in ensuring discipline and hard work, other incentives were used. The most common incentives were corporal punishment, fines, and dismissal. Fines and dismissals were by far the most prevalent. Widespread adoption of payment by result was slow. Even when adopted, payment by result schemes were not very effective. "There were many examples of the usual problems of this type of payment, such as speed-up and rate-cutting, loss of quality, and friction over interpretation and deductions" (p. 190).

These labor management difficulties were due in part to the ideology of the capitalist class "which saw its own rise to wealth and power as due to merit, and the workman's subordinate position as due to his failings" (p. 193). Because of such thinking, little effort was made to obtain the consummate cooperation of workers. Promoting workers to management positions was not considered, and there were no attempts to reduce the antagonism between workers and management by establishing company spirit. As a result, consummate cooperation was generally not the rule, and the cost of supervising workers was high. The same attitude on the part of entrepreneurs led them to attribute poor productivity to the worker's laziness and immorality. While nineteenth century capitalists expended a significant amount of resources to induce workers not to swear and spit, they did not feel the need to instruct workers on the best method to perform a task and to reward them as a function of their productivity. The first concerted effort in that direction was initiated by an American engineer, Frederick Taylor, in the early 1880s. Taylor's method was to analyze the task, to find the best way to perform it, to formulate instructions, and to encourage worker adoption. In the process, Taylor reduced the bargaining power of workers by reducing the information advantage the worker had vis-à-vis the boss, by making the task independent of the worker, and by increasing comparability between workers.

Although the legal framework for limited liability companies was created in the eighteenth century, it is interesting that it is not until the enactment of the Joint Stock Companies Act in 1856 that a legal form was available to separate the ownership from the management of firms. Until that date, "even some of the highest echelons of firms, namely the partners themselves, showed an untidy mixture of ownership, management, subcontract and cooperation" (Pollard 1965, p. 40). The absence of a legal form of organization that separated ownership from control thus subjected English firms of the first half of the nineteenth century to the high internal organization costs inherent in large-sized partnerships.[2]

A final reason why English firms of the early 1800s did not

exploit their advantage through foreign subsidiaries was the high cost of communications. When crossing the Atlantic took twenty-one days, and at a time when telegraph and telephone were not realities, remaining in control of distant subsidiaries would have been almost impossible. The significant improvement in communications that took place after 1850 was surely an important factor in the development of multinational enterprise. By the 1880s, passenger carrying steamships were crossing the Atlantic in five to six days. The first transatlantic telegraphic cable was laid in 1866 and was soon followed by still others. This rather dramatic decline in communication costs made it possible for a firm to obtain fast and reliable information on the performance of subsidiaries and significantly reduced the cost of exercising control over long distances.

From a rapid survey of the evidence, we conclude that internal organization costs were very high in England at the time of the Industrial Revolution. Thus, it would have been utterly impossible for British firms of that time to exert managerial control over widely scattered production facilities. The international transfer of knowledge within firms was then costlier than other transfer modes.

The Geographical Pattern of Foreign Direct Investment

A major characteristic of foreign direct investment is the fact that it originates from a limited number of countries. The most prominent investor is the United States, with an estimated 47 percent of the world's book value of foreign subsidiaries in 1976 (United Nations 1978). The dominant role played by American multinationals is also shown by the fact that whereas American affiliates have a significant share of the European market, European subsidiaries in the United States play a much smaller role in the American economy (see table 12).

How can we account for the difference in the propensity of European and American firms to become multinational? One possible explanation is that ownership of foreign direct investment, like that of any asset, is proportional to a nation's wealth. The United States, with a large share of total world production, should also own a large percentage of the total world book value of foreign affiliates. Statistics show, however, that the United States owns a larger percentage of the stock of foreign direct investment than would be predicted on such a basis: while the United States produced 25 percent of the world's total gross national product, it owned about 47 percent of the total estimated stock of foreign direct investment (World Bank 1978; United Nations 1978). This disproportion is not surprising, however, when one realizes that residents of a country eager to own foreign assets can choose between portfolio or direct investment, and that the distribution of foreign assets between those two types of investment varies systematically across countries. As we have argued previously, foreign direct investment does not arise mainly as a way to internationally diversify portfolios, and we must therefore look elsewhere to understand its characteristics.

Raymond Vernon's previously described product cycle model offers another explanation for the international distribution of the book value of foreign subsidiaries. Vernon sees foreign direct investment as the normal way to exploit overseas the innovations developed at home. For foreign direct investment to take place, two conditions must be met: first, the home market environment must be such as to encourage the development of innovations; second, those innovations must eventually be demanded abroad. According to Vernon, only in the case of the United States are these two requirements fully met. He goes on to argue that while firms of every country can be expected to develop new products that are geared to their particular environment, the special conditions of the United States market—high per capita income, costly labor, large internal size—prompt American firms to develop innovations that cater to the needs of high income consumers and that are labor saving. Such innovations will later be wanted abroad. In other countries, however, market conditions encourage innovations of a material-saving and capital-conserving nature, which, according to Vernon, have a less certain international future (Vernon 1971, p. 109).

Vernon's hypothesis has certain interesting implications. First, if innovations developed in the United States have international market potential, American manufacturers will be induced to allocate more resources to their development than if the newly developed products could only be sold on the American market. If we take research and development expenditures as a rough index of the resources devoted to the production of innovations, then one would expect firms in the United States to invest a significantly larger amount of research and development expenditures per dollar of domesic sales than firms that are located in other countries, where local market conditions discourage the development of new products and processes with international applicability. A comparison of the research effort of American, Western European, and Japanese firms does not, however, confirm the hypothesis.

Keith Pavitt, one of the authors of the comprehensive "gaps in technology" reports written at the Organization for Economic Co-

operation and Development (OECD) in the late 1960s, summarizes
the empirical evidence in these terms:

> With regard to technology, the data on R&D collected by the O.E.C.D.
> have often been misinterpreted. The U.S.A. certainly undertakes con-
> siderably more R&D than Europe, when measured in monetary terms,
> and when including government-financed defense and space research.
> But when such research is excluded, and when corrections are made for
> differences in wage levels and population differences, the European
> R&D effort is not markedly less than that of the U.S.A. Certainly, one
> cannot dismiss the political significance of defense and space research,
> nor its impact on civilian technology in, for example, aircraft, communi-
> cation and electronics. But it is significant that industry in Switzerland
> and the Netherlands—and perhaps also in the U.K. and Germany—
> devotes a greater proportion of its financial resources to R&D than does
> U.S. industry; that these four countries, together with Sweden, all have
> strong competitive positions in world markets in high technology indus-
> tries; and that Switzerland's export pattern is slightly more technology
> intensive than even that of the U.S.A. [Pavitt 1971a, pp. 62–63]

Table 16 shows the research and development financed in industry
as a percentage of net industrial output in thirteen countries in or
about 1967. Clearly American firms did not invest proportionally
more in the production of innovations than their Dutch, Swiss, English, or German rivals.

Second, Vernon's hypothesis implies the continued dominance
of the United States as a foreign direct investor. According to
Vernon,

TABLE 16   Research and Development Financed in Industry

	Percentage of Net Industrial Output	Year
Netherlands	3.2	1967
Switzerland	2.9	1967
United States	2.8	1966
Japan	2.7	1967–68
United Kingdom	2.1	1966–67
West Germany	2.1	1967
Sweden	1.9	1967
France	1.8	1967
Norway	1.1	1967
Italy	1.0	1967
Austria	0.8	1966

Source: Pavitt 1971b.

in the future as in decades past, therefore, the world may have to view the multinational enterprise as an asymmetrical phenomenon in which the American version is thought of as distinctive in scope and in strength. [Vernon 1971, p. 112]

In recent years, however, there has been a dramatic increase in foreign direct investment by non-American companies. Over the 1967–76 period, for example, foreign direct investment by Japanese and German firms grew twelvefold and sixfold, respectively, while American foreign direct investment only increased 242 percent (table 17). Although the absolute increase in the level of foreign direct investment by American firms was larger than the combined investment of Japanese, German, British, and Canadian firms, the relatively higher growth in Japanese and German foreign direct investment suggests an end to the overwhelming dominance of American corporations on the international scene.

There are two weak links in Vernon's model that may account for its limited usefulness in explaining recent trends. First, the categorization of innovations as labor-saving or capital/material-saving is often blurred in practice: many innovations have no apparent factor bias. Moreover, any innovation that reduces cost should be marketable, whatever its factor bias. It is therefore difficult to see why innovations by European and Japanese producers should not have general applicability. Second, Vernon fails to demonstrate why foreign direct investment is the only way by which innovations can be exploited in foreign markets. The same level of innovative effort (as measured by research and development expenditures as a percent-

TABLE 17   Book Value of Foreign Direct Investment, Selected Countries (in billion of U.S. dollars)

	1967	1976	1976 (1967=100)
United States	56.6	137.2	242
United Kingdom	17.5	32.1	183
West Germany	3.0	19.9	663
Switzerland	5.0	18.6	372
France	6.0	11.9	198
Netherlands	2.2	9.8	445
Sweden	1.7	5.0	294
Italy	2.1	2.9	138
Japan	1.5	19.4	1,293
Canada	3.7	11.1	300

Source: United Nations 1978, p. 236.

age of domestic sales, for example) would lead to divergent levels of foreign subsidiary sales (and of foreign direct investment) if countries varied systematically in the method chosen to exploit their innovations abroad. A look at table 18 shows that this is in fact the case. Table 18 compares the share of seven developed countries in world exports and in the world's stock of equity capital. While the United States, Switzerland, and the United Kingdom had a larger share of foreign direct investment than of exports, Canada, Japan, the Netherlands, and Germany relied more on exports than on subsidiary sales to exploit their advantages in foreign markets. The disproportion between the United States's stock of foreign direct investment and that of Western Europe and Japan does not seem to be due to the presence of significant differences in the international marketability of their innovations, but on differences in the method chosen to exploit them in foreign markets.

Richard Caves offers an explanation for these differences, and therefore for the international pattern of foreign direct investment. He argues that the choice between serving a foreign market by export and by direct investment is a function of the cost of home production versus foreign production. Since capital is highly mobile, the choice will be dictated by international differences in efficiency wages: a country with high efficiency wages will be a small importer of direct investment, and (if its comparative advantage lies in differentiated manufactures) a large exporter of equity capital as well (Caves 1971, p. 21).

One way to test the significance of labor costs as a determinant of the choice between exporting and manufacturing overseas is to investigate whether variations in the ratio of exports to subsidiary sales in each industry are a function of the labor intensity of that industry's production process. If labor costs exert a significant influence on foreign direct investment, we would expect the labor intensive industries of high (efficiency) wage countries to have a high ratio of subsidiary sales to exports. On the other hand, in industries where labor costs are a small proportion of total value added, the relative advantages of producing abroad and of paying lower efficiency wages would be smaller. These industries should have a high ratio of exports to subsidiary sales. To test this proposition we calculated the foreign production of American subsidiaries in twenty-seven manufacturing industries (see Appendix and table 19). The foreign production by American subsidiaries in each industry was obtained by subtracting from the 1966 total sales of American foreign subsidiaries their imports from their American corporate parents of products manufactured by the parent (these are largely

TABLE 18 Exports and Foreign Direct Investment, Selected Countries (in billion U.S. dollars)

	1965		1967		1970		1971	
	Exports	% Total	Foreign Direct Investment (book value)	% Total	Export	% Total	Foreign Direct Investment (book value)	% Total
United States	27.5	17	59.5	55.0	43.2	15	86.0	52.0
United Kingdom	13.7	8	17.5	16.2	19.4	7	24.0	14.5
Switzerland	3.0	2	4.2	3.9	5.0	2	6.8	4.1
Germany	17.9	11	3.0	2.8	34.2	12	7.2	4.4
Netherlands	6.4	4	2.2	2.1	11.8	4	3.6	2.2
Canada	8.5	5	3.7	3.4	16.7	6	5.9	3.6
Japan	8.5	5	1.4	1.3	19.3	7	4.5	2.7
World	165.4	100	108.2	100	282.1	100	165.0	100

Sources: Exports: U.S., Department of Commerce 1976*a*, vol. 5, p. G-26. Foreign direct investment (book value): United Nations 1973, p. 139.

TABLE 19 Structure of American Foreign Sales and Labor Intensity

SIC	Industry	Ratio of U.S. World Exports to Local Production by U.S. Subsidiaries (1966)	Labor Intensity Ratio (1968)
204	Grain mill products	0.34	0.263
208	Beverages	0.02	0.307
Rest of 20	Other food products	0.45	0.440
26	Paper and allied products	0.40	0.454
283	Drugs	0.14	0.230
284	Soap and cosmetics	0.05	0.171
281	Industrial chemicals	1.00	0.273
282	Plastics	0.53	0.308
Rest of 28	Other chemicals	0.44	0.335
30	Rubber	0.12	0.479
33[a]	Primary metals (excluding aluminum, copper, brass)	1.07	0.500
34[b]	Fabricated metals (excluding aluminum, copper, brass)	0.45	0.515
3334; 3352; 3361	Primary and fabricated aluminum	0.10	0.450
3331; 3351; 3362; 3432	Other primary and fabricated metals	1.47	0.250

352	Farm machinery	0.86	0.475
353; 355; 356	Industrial machinery	1.46	0.421
357	Office and computing machines	0.27	0.442
Rest of 35	Other nonelectrical machinery	1.42	0.466
361–2	Electrical equipment	1.24	0.504
365; 366; 367	Electronic components, radio, T.V.	0.58	0.536
37	Transportation equipment	0.38	0.510
22–23	Textiles and apparel	0.74	0.541
24–25	Lumber, wood, furniture	0.50	0.524
27	Printing and publishing	0.74	0.498
32	Stone, clay, glass	0.28	0.441
38	Instruments	0.67	0.427
19; 31; 21; 39	Ordnance, leather, tobacco, other	1.43	0.462

Note: For information on sources and computation of ratios, see Appendix, p. 175.

a. Excluding 3331; 3334; 3351; 3352; 3361; 3362.
b. Excluding 3432.

goods sent to the subsidiary for resale). We then correlated the ratio of American exports over American subsidiary production in each industry to that industry's ratio of payroll to value added, a measure of its labor intensity. The correlation coefficient we obtained was a low 0.19.

As another test of the theory, we compared the structure of American manufacturing sales to nine OECD countries in 1974 with the composition of the sales of each of these countries to the United States (table 20). An examination of the table shows wide variations between the cells. Thus the United States supplies Japan, Canada, Sweden, Switzerland, and the Benelux countries by both exports and subsidiary sales, while France, Germany, and the United Kingdom are served primarily by local subsidiaries. Conversely, the Netherlands, the United Kingdom, and Switzerland sell to the American market through local production, while the other six countries rely mostly on exports. If labor costs were a determinant of the structure of foreign sales, a country with high efficiency wages would attract little American subsidiary production, and conversely would find it relatively advantageous to supply the American market through affiliates. On the other hand, a country blessed with low efficiency wages would choose to export to foreign markets, while it would be attractive to American direct investors. One would therefore expect columns (3) and (6) of table 20 to be inversely correlated. As expected, the correlation coefficient has a negative sign, but its value is low (-0.15). Our limited testing thus fails to support the hypothesis that the relative level of labor costs (corrected for productivity differences) is the main explanation for the observed variations in the propensity of firms of various countries to invest abroad.

One possible explanation for the limited influence of labor costs as a determinant of the choice between exporting and foreign subsidiary sales is that while low labor costs abroad encourage foreign production, they do not influence the choice between establishing foreign production facilities and licensing foreign producers. Thus differences in the propensity of American and non-American firms to invest abroad may therefore be due to divergent choices between licensing and foreign direct investment. Some crude indication of that fact is given by an examination of the structure of royalty and fee receipts of the United States, the United Kingdom, and Germany. Between 1971 and 1976, about 80 percent of all royalties and fees received by the United States were from branches and subsidiaries. The corresponding figure for the United Kingdom was 41 percent, and that for Germany only 5 percent (table 21).[3] It thus appears that American firms, whenever the balance of net delivered

TABLE 20 Structure of Foreign Manufacturing Sales, Ten OECD Countries, 1974 (in million U.S. dollars)

Country	Out of United States			Into United States		
	Sales by U.S. Manufacturing Subsidiaries in (1)	U.S. Exports of Manufactured Products to (2)	Col. 1 / Col. 2 (3)	Sales of Manufacturing Subsidiaries of (4)	Exports of Manufactured Products from (5)	Col. 4 / Col. 5 (6)
Canada	30,594	16,504	1.85	5,881	13,007	0.45
Japan	4,532	4,168	1.09	1,311	12,343	0.11
Belgium-Luxembourg	3,101	1,604	1.93	526	1,494	0.35
Netherlands	3,965	1,880	2.11	3,682	948	3.88
France	10,884	2,104	5.17	2,004	2,072	0.97
Germany	16,704	2,746	6.08	2,538	6,308	0.40
United Kingdom	18,247	3,545	5.15	7,660	3,796	2.02
Sweden	1,181	752	1.57	662	803	0.82
Switzerland	1,421	877	1.62	3,753	817	4.59

Sources: For exports (f.o.b.) of manufactured goods (SITC categories 1, 5, 6, 7, and 8): OECD Statistics of Foreign Trade, Series B, (Paris: OECD, 1976). For local sales of U.S. majority-owned manufacturing subsidiaries: Chung, 1976, p. 32. U.S. sales of foreign-owned manufacturing subsidiaries: U.S., Department of Commerce 1976a, vol. 2, p. 139.

TABLE 21   American, British, and West German Royalty and Fee Receipts 1971–76 (in million U.S. dollars)

		United States		United Kingdom		Germany	
		Amount	%	Amount	%	Amount	%
From affiliated	1971	1,927	76	94	40	7	5
firms	1972	2,115	76	112	39	. . .	. . .
	1973	2,513	78	135	39	10	5
	1974	3,070	80	165	41	. . .	. . .
	1975	3,543	82	182	42	17	5
	1976	3,522	81	. . .	. . .	. . .	. . .
From nonaffiliated	1971	618	24	139	60	129	95
firms	1972	655	24	172	61	. . .	. . .
	1973	712	22	207	61	178	95
	1974	751	20	233	59	. . .	. . .
	1975	759	18	247	58	291	95
	1976	844	19	. . .	. . .	. . .	. . .
Total	1971	2,545	100	233	100	136	100
	1972	2,770	100	284	100	. . .	. . .
	1973	3,225	100	342	100	188	100
	1974	3,821	100	398	100	. . .	. . .
	1975	4,302	100	429	100	308	100
	1976	4,366	100	. . .	. . .	. . .	. . .

Source: United Nations 1978, pp. 277–79.

costs favors foreign production, tend to choose foreign direct investment more often than firms from the United Kingdom or Germany. No data on the distribution of royalty and fee receipts of other European countries are available. We have, however, some statistics on transaction in royalties and fees between the United States and Western Europe. Over the 1966–74 period, three-fourths of the royalties and fees received by the United States from Western Europe were from affiliated firms. By contrast, almost two-thirds of the royalties paid by the United States were paid to unaffiliated firms (U.S., Department of Commerce 1976*b*). It appears then that Western European firms have a lower propensity to exploit their know-how through foreign direct investment than their American rivals.

According to our model, whether a particular transaction will be organized within firms or across markets will hinge on the respective levels of market transaction costs and internal organization costs. Differences in the propensity of American and Western European firms to invest abroad could thus arise because the internal organization costs of American firms are lower than those experienced by their European counterparts. For those transactions for which the least costly alternative to American firms is the creation of subsidiaries, European firms, because of higher organization costs, choose licensing.

That internal organization costs can vary systematically across countries has been pointed out by many development economists, and especially by Leibenstein (1966). Like any other type of knowledge, managerial know-how is costly to transfer. The effect of organizational, managerial, or legal innovations on performance is often hard for outsiders to assess. As a result, managerial and organizational innovations spread slowly within countries, and even more slowly internationally. For example, although the multidivision form of organization was developed in the United States in the early 1920s it was not widely imitated until the end of World War II in the United States, and the early 1970s in continental Europe.

The argument that the success of American firms in world (and especially European) markets in the 1960s was due to their superior managerial skills, and the mediocre performance of European firms to their high internal organization costs, was given widespread circulation by the publication of Servan-Schreiber's book, *The American Challenge* (1968). The author ascribed the success of American multinational firms, not to their access to abundant sources of capital, not even to their high investment in research and development, but mostly to their managerial skills.

> There is a good deal of European capital in Europe, but only American firms seem to profit from it. Why? This is the problem, and it cannot be phrased only in economic terms. It involves our capacity for organization: the ability to work under different conditions, to take advantage of an enormous market, to know how to make a profit from it and adapt to its needs. Europe's lag seems to concern *methods of organization* above all. The Americans know how to work in our countries better than we do ourselves.
>
> This is not a matter of "brain power" in the traditional sense of the term, but of organization, education, and training. We have men capable of carrying out research, but we do not have organizations that can develop this research on a large enough scale to succeed in today's world. Our universities are ossified and inadequate, and it is extremely difficult to change them.
>
> Thus the problem is to transform the whole system: business, intellectual talent, education, research. So far our efforts have been misdirected. We have tried to build production centres, but too often they have been only agglomerations of production, financially centralized, but as badly managed as the collection of individual firms that form them. This is no way to build more aggressive, development-conscious organizations. [Servan-Schreiber 1968, p. 134]

Servan-Schreiber's thesis that the poor performance of European firms was not due to their lack of technological skills, but to their inferior management, was echoed by a large number of scholars and management professionals. John Diebold (1968), an American management consultant, also argued that European failings were due to a lack of managerial skills. He emphasized particularly the inability of European firms to put technological innovations into commercial use, mostly because of a predilection for technical sophistication and neglect of market needs. He noted that in many of the most progressive sectors the key discoveries had been made by Europeans, but that they had been put into commercial use by American firms. Americans had had a late start, but had more than made up for it through better management. Theodore Levitt (1968), a professor of business administration at Harvard Business School, expounded the same thesis and illustrated his argument with other examples of European failures. In every case, he attributed the inability of Europeans to translate inventions into commercially viable innovations to their disdain of consumer preferences, their lack of managerial competence, and the deficiency of their entrepreneurial effort. Levitt noted the contempt in which employees engaged into marketing were held by their superiors, the absence of profit planning, market plans, market research, and formal capital budgeting or financial control systems. He commented on the lack of central direction that led manufacturing departments of European firms to behave as independent fiefdoms, operating often at cross-purposes with the marketing staff. Furthermore, the widespread use of double bookkeeping for tax evasion purposes prevented the firm's managers from assessing accurately the overall performance of the firm, the relative profitability of each of its divisions, and the success of its various products.

Parker, the director of the London office of McKinsey & Company, also concurred with Servan-Schreiber and underlined the low degree of professionalism and effectiveness of British management, its neglect of marketing, and its low profit motivation (H. Parker 1967, pp. 38–44; 1968, pp. 10–13). Dubin (1970) emphasized the relative apathy of British managers and their low level of mobility and education.

Hard evidence to support these contentions is difficult to obtain, as international comparisons of profitability are hindered by intercountry differences in accounting procedures and in the possibility of undervaluing profits to avoid taxes. There are, however, a few studies that support the existence of significant efficiency differences between American and British firms.

Channon (1973, pp. 222–25) matched the performance of the

largest British firms to that of their American counterparts. He calculated profits as a percentage of sales, assets, and invested capital, for ninety-three American and British firms in fourteen industry groups. The performance of British corporations, judged by all three measures of profitability, was, in each industry, generally worse than that of their American counterparts. Dunning (1976, p. 84) compared the profit performance of the British subsidiaries of American firms with that of all British firms in the same industry. He found that the average rates of return (defined as net income after depreciation but before taxes, divided by fixed assets plus current assets, minus current liabilities) earned by American subsidiaries were higher in ten of out eleven industries in 1965 and in six out of eleven in 1973.

Channon saw managerial deficiencies as one of the main causes of the poor performance of British firms. His judgment receives confirmation in a provocative book by Granick (1972). Granick studied a sample of French, British, American, and Soviet firms and attempted to evaluate the effectiveness of their management in adapting to changes in the environment. He found that British and French firms were significantly less well managed than American enterprises, although the causes and effects of the lower managerial performance of British and French firms were markedly different.

British firms were overly decentralized. Each was structured as if composed of a number of small, independent units. Top management was weak and unable, or unwilling, to provide guidance and coordination for the firm. Lower- and middle-levels of management, on the other hand, were capable and successful in pursuing their own goals. Suboptimization within the firm was therefore a major problem. According to Granick, the process by which top British managers were recruited and promoted was partly responsible for this problem. British firms choose their managers from among their staff. By opposition to France, and to a lesser degree, the United States, the educational requirements for a British managerial career are very low. Patterns of promotion within the firm are, however, quite different from those followed by American firms.

American managers who are successful in their present job get promoted to different functions and/or to different units within the firm. If they continue to do well, they are rapidly rotated between functions, and between divisions and headquarters. This tends to reduce suboptimization, because, to be transferred, the up-and-coming manager must be acceptable to the other divisions. This forces him to take their point of view into consideration. The rapid transfer of the manager within the firm gives him a better knowledge of the problems and of the needs of each of the firm's units. If a British manager is successful, he will get promoted to more responsibility in the same function and in the same unit. British managers thus tend to spend their entire career within the same function and the same narrowly defined industry. They are likely, therefore, to pursue narrow functional and divisional goals, rather than those of the firm as a whole. Top managers, who have been promoted from divisional or functional heads, are ill equipped to manage the parts of the firm with which they are unfamiliar. They tend, therefore, to be unable and unwilling to exercise effective control over the firm's units. The low prestige and low pay of British managers, relative to those of other professions in Britain and to those enjoyed by their French or American counterparts, has also adversely affected the quality of British managers, the intensity of their efforts, and consequently their ability to effectively manage the firm (Granick 1972, p. 370).

French firms, on the other hand, were highly centralized. Top management was generally well qualified and intent to exercise detailed control over the company. Middle management, however, was unaggressive and ineffective. As a result, decentralization was rare, and loss of control rampant. Granick notes that "four out of the six French companies [studied] seemed, under normal circumstances, to be quite out of control; middle management did not have the authority or incentive to take [sic] decisions, and top management did not receive enough information to make rational decisions" (Granick 1972, p. 358).

French chief executive officers had good reasons to keep all power to themselves. In five of the six firms studied by Granick, middle management could be observed acting in its own self-interest. Granick attributes this phenomenon to the interaction of two variables: the system by which management is recruited, and the French attitude toward job security. In France, top management posts are almost always reserved for the graduates of the few "grandes écoles." This particular method of recruitment has two adverse consequences. First, there is very little variety of backgrounds and points of view among executives. Moreover, because top management posts are filled from the outside, middle-level managers (and especially those who have graduated from the less prestigious grandes écoles) cannot hope to be promoted to top executive positions. Being blocked from promotion, and protected from dismissal by the traditional French reluctance to fire workers (and by legislation making layoffs costly and difficult), these middle-level managers tend to ignore the goals of top management and to exercise a considerable degree of personal preference in the performance of their duties. They find as little incentive to cooperate with other units of the firm as they do to follow their chief executive officer's orders. As a result, Granick found that, in the French firms he studied, all decision making and coordination was centralized at the head office. No wonder then that a majority of these firms were out of control.

One particular aspect of managerial practice on which we have good international comparative data is organizational structure. As we have argued earlier, the way the firm organizes its activities influences its economic performance. As the firm expands into new markets and enters new product fields, the functional form of organization becomes increasingly inadequate. Multidivisional structures can remedy these difficulties by making it possible to better evaluate and control divisional performance and to better plan the long-term strategy of the firm. Both historical and empirical evidence (Chandler 1961; Armour and Teece 1978) support the hypothesis that the multidivisional form of organization is the most efficient structure for large, diversified enterprises.

In the European case, however, there appears to have been a significant lag between diversification and abandonment of inefficient forms of organization. In 1970, 92 percent of the fully diversified American companies among the Fortune 500 had multidivisional structures. The corresponding figure for the largest diversified British, German, and French companies was 70 percent, 63 percent and 52 percent, respectively (Dyas and Thanheiser 1976, pp. 141–51, 269–81; Channon 1973, pp. 52–63).[4]

A small number of these diversified French, German, and British companies were organized along functional lines. Fifteen of the fifty-four largest diversified British firms, eighteen of the forty-one largest French companies, and fifteen of the forty-four largest diversified German firms were organized as holdings. In these holding companies, the control exercised by headquarters on the subunits of the firm was limited and unsystematic: it consisted of the assembly and distribution of earnings and the elaboration of financial reports (Franko 1974, p. 494). Holding companies thus differ from multidivisional firms insofar as they do not make use of the extensive internal controls that are used in the latter to control slack and to coordinate the activities of the subunits. Both Channon and Dyas and Thanheiser found frequent incidences of lack of coordination, duplication of effort, and inefficiency among British, French, and German holdings (Channon 1973, p. 239; Dyas and Thanheiser 1976, p. 295).

A large number of diversified French and German companies were thus still using forms of organization that were relatively inefficient, given their size and the diversity of their product line. Moreover, in many of the companies newly organized into divisions, management had failed to exploit all of the possibilities inherent in the new structure. Channon thus noted that

> despite the widespread adoption of many features of the new structure, British general executives had not wholly emulated their American counterparts in adopting certain characteristic mechanisms associated with the system. In Britain, management was still using some of its traditional techniques in managing the multidivisional firm. Notably there was little use of performance-related rewards or sanctions, except through the indirect link of promotional prospects. The divisional general managers were participating in the formation of central policy in a way that made monitoring and performance measurement difficult. The general officers of many corporations had not yet divorced themselves from the operations of the divisions in order to concentrate on their entrepreneurial role of strategic decision-making. In some corporations transformation to a formal divisional system was incomplete, with parts of the business still run as a holding company or specific functions, especially marketing, still centrally managed. Finally, there was little generation of internal competition between divisions to allow the enterprise to allocate its resources as a small, but highly effective, capital market. [Channon 1973, pp. 239–40]

In many French firms, the new system of management was only formal. Continued use of the collegial management principle in German firms was reducing the effectiveness of the new structure. In Germany as in France, there was a universal reluctance to link the compensation of division managers to their performance. Marketing still had not acquired in both of these countries the status it had in the United States (Dyas and Thanheiser 1976, pp. 123, 127, 137, 255). In short, British, French, and German firms were still lagging significantly behind best American managerial practice.

The same managerial gap was also apparent in the way European firms managed their overseas operations. In 1971, more than a third of the largest continental European multinationals were controlling their foreign subsidiaries in a highly personalized way known as "mother-daughter" organization. Under the mother-daughter form of organization, the foreign subsidiary president reported directly to the parent president. There was little control from the center and a very limited exchange of information. The usual control system was occasional visits by the parent president.

Mother-daughter structures are particularly ill adapted to transnational communication and coordination, since none of the managers have international responsibilities. For this reason, companies that organize their foreign activities in this way tend to experience difficulties in transferring information across markets, in coordinating foreign activities, and in gaining a worldwide perspective. One of the most dramatic examples of the adverse consequences of using mother-daughter structures in an increasingly interdependent world was shown in the case of the European semiconductor industry. Whereas American semiconductors manufacturers were locating the standardized, labor-intensive stage of integrated circuit production in Third World subsidiaries, European producers, hampered by their lack of global vision, kept their plants in Europe. When prices dropped by about 75 percent, European products became uncompetitive, and the producers had to be bailed out by their respective governments (Franko 1976, pp. 131–32). That type of problem is one of the reasons why, although American firms had used mother-daughter structures in the early stages of their foreign expansion, they had abandoned such relationships before they had established their tenth subsidiary. None of the 162 American multinationals studied by Stopford had such structures in 1968 (Franko 1976, p. 188).

In 1971, however, twenty-six of the seventy largest continental European multinationals were controlling their subsidiaries through mother-daughter forms of organization. Yet twelve of these twenty-six firms manufactured in more than ten countries (Franko 1976, p. 188). Here again, the majority of European firms were still clinging to outdated organizational forms. There is also some evidence that those that had adopted supranational structures had not, as of 1972, set up the sophisticated control mechanisms found in their American counterparts (Franko 1976, p. 208).

Although European firms were still, as in the early 1970s, significantly lagging in managerial practice behind American companies, they had undergone considerable organizational change since 1950. Dyas and Thanheiser's study shows that in 1960 only 12 percent of the largest diversified French-owned companies and only 8 percent of the German ones had adopted the multidivisional structure. The corresponding figure for the large diversified American enterprises was 76 percent (Dyas and Thanheiser 1976, pp. 67, 243). Between 1960 and 1970, thirty-five large German-owned firms, thirty-three French companies, and twelve British concerns switched to a multidivisional form of organization (Dyas and Thanheiser 1976, pp. 69, 187; Channon 1973, p. 74). Most of the reorganizations to multidivisional structures have thus taken place since 1960.

The same is true for changes in the way European firms manage their international operations: in 1961, all but nine of the seventy continental European multinational enterprises studied by Franko were having mother-daughter relationships with their subsidiaries. By 1971, only twenty-three of these firms retained this type of relationship and by mid-1974 that number had fallen to thirteen (Franko 1976, pp. 188, 209).

American influence has been paramount in effecting this change. In the case of Germany, Dyas and Thanheiser note

> the scope of transfer of American business culture to Germany was very wide, covering all functional areas of management. The nature of the transfer reached from elements of business philosophy and language, to skills, technology, know-how, and specific methods and procedures. At the level of specific methods, the spread of market-related methods such as market research, selling, promotion, advertising, aftersales service, media research, and so forth, was largely influenced by innovations originating in the U.S. Operations research and systematic approaches to decision-making in general, the routine generation of ideas in brainstorming sessions, and the use of increasingly sophisticated methods of projecting and forecasting in decision-making are also U.S. exports which found widespread use in Germany. [Dyas and Thanheiser 1976, p. 113]

American managerial knowledge was transferred to Europe through a variety of channels that included personal contacts, exchange and sale of public or proprietary information, publications, and education. The 1960s saw increased enrollment of Europeans in American business schools, and the creation in Europe of business schools patterned on the American model. From 1960 to 1975, the number of business schools in Western Europe increased from half a dozen to over two hundred (McNulty 1975). The use of American materials in these schools was widespread.

American consultants also played an important role. In 1969, there were seventy American consulting organizations in Europe doing a thriving business ("Europe's Rich Market for Advice: American Preferred." *Fortune,* 1969). One of these companies, McKinsey & Company, was particularly active in transferring managerial knowledge: that company oversaw the reorganization into divisions of twenty-two British companies, over a dozen German companies, and a large number of French firms (Channon 1973, p. 239; Dyas and Thanheiser 1976, pp. 113, 247).

Foreign direct investments were another powerful factor in spreading American managerial innovations: the example given by

American subsidiaries in Europe was instrumental in persuading European enterprises to reorganize their domestic operations, while the European firms with the largest American operations were the first to abandon mother-daughter structures (Dyas and Thanheiser 1976, p. 112; Franko 1976, p. 198). By the early 1970s, it appeared that European firms had successfully assimilated many of the managerial techniques possessed by their American rivals.

If the managerial gap between American and non-American firms was closing, one would expect the average size of European and Japanese firms to increase over the period. Rowthorn examined the growth of the largest 200 American and non-American corporations between 1957 and 1967. They found that over the ten year period the non-American firms grew at a faster rate than did the American firms. Japanese firms were clear leaders in almost every industry, while continental European firms grew faster than their American rivals in seven out of eight industries (Rowthorn 1971, p. 84). A more recent study also shows that between 1964 and 1974, sales by the 200 largest non-American industrials increased nearly twice as fast as those of the 200 largest American industrials (U.S., Department of Commerce 1976*a*, vol. 5, p. G-34).

The dramatic increase in the size of the largest non-American firms thus suggests a decrease in the level of internal organization costs they experience and, on the basis of our model, should encourage those firms to expand their operations abroad. As predicted, foreign direct investment by European firms has increased dramatically over the recent period. The stock of foreign direct investment owned by Germany increased 176 percent between 1971 and 1974, that of the United Kingdom by 148 percent, whereas the United States increased the book value of its foreign subsidiaries by 143 percent (U.S., Department of Commerce 1976*a*, vol. 5, table 2-2).

In summary, a variety of comparative studies of European and American business enterprises point out the existence of differences in profitability, in managerial practices, and in organizational structures. These differences have been gradually disappearing, as the more effective American methods of management have been adopted by an increasing number of European companies. In the early 1970s, one could still contrast the American and the European method of management. European firms were less efficiently managed and, consequently, were less profitable.

We hypothesized that these differences in internal efficiency are one of the causes of the greater degree of multinationalization of American companies. Although our evidence is somewhat impressionistic, and considerable additional research is necessary before any definitive assessment of the validity of our analysis can be made, its predictions are consistent with the limited amount of empirical evidence that is available.

Ownership Patterns of Multinational Companies

Multinational firms have generally been extremely reluctant to issue share capital in their foreign subsidiaries. This characteristic behavior has been noted by economists, but they have tended to dismiss it as irrational. Kindleberger's treatment of the subject is probably typical.

> The world of affairs abounds in the apparently reasonable suggestion that the overseas investor enter into joint ventures with local interests. Instead of buying 100 percent of a domestic firm, buy half. But the overseas investor asks why he should give half the scarcity value of his advantage away. This reasoning assumes, as I have indicated, that there are barriers to adjusting the price paid for half the enterprise which would enable the foreign investor to capitalize on the scarcity value of his contribution. It may be difficult for the local investor to appreciate the profitability of the prospective enterprise, so that he would be unwilling to make his monetary contribution at an implicit valuation of the foreign contribution which accorded with the foreigner's view. To an economist, as I have said, the problem has an air of irrationality or imperfect knowledge about it. [Kindleberger 1969, pp. 27–28]

The answer given by multinational companies to demands for local participation is to encourage local investors to buy shares in the parent company. Kindleberger finds this answer "hardly satisfactory. . . . The local investor wants a piece of the monopoly profits from the corporation's advantage in the local market, profits which, in the nature of direct investment, are higher than those in the main place of business" (Kindleberger 1969, p. 30).

McManus has shown how this apparently irrational preference for wholly owned subsidiaries can be easily explained by focusing on the fundamental nature of the firm. Multinational corporations are a substitute for international markets as a method of organizing transnational interactions. Their raison d'être is to internalize the external effects that result when producers of one country impose uncompensated losses or benefits on those of another country. For example, rights to the production of innovations developed by American producers are sometimes of value to European manufacturers, since these innovations are likely to appeal to their customers. Yet market exchange of those rights will sometimes fail to organize the mutual dependence, and, as a result, American innovators will disregard the effect on European producers of reducing their research expenditures. By joining both parties within a firm, these external effects are internalized. The parent's know-how will be transferred free of charge to the subsidiary, so that European producers are induced to make use of all the knowledge acquired by the American firm, while the profits from the larger volume of sales will finance a greater research effort. The interdependence between parent and subsidiary is now no longer mediated by market prices, but by hierarchical methods. In other words, European and American firms no longer maximize their separate profits, but instead maximize their joint profit. For if parents and subsidiaries maximized independently their individual profits, there would be no reason for hierarchical organization: the firm could be split in two independent concerns coordinating its interdependence via market prices. If operations at home and abroad are joined within a multinational firm, it is therefore because joint operation is more profitable than separate profit maximization.[5] A claim to a share of the profit of the whole firm will consequently be worth more than a claim to a share of the profit of either the parent or subsidiary (McManus 1972, pp. 90–91).

Empirical studies of the multinational firm confirm these predictions. The management literature tells us that many goods and services exchanged within the firm are not transacted at market prices, even absent tax considerations. Goodwill, and technological, marketing or managerial know-how are usually transferred within the firm free of charge or at prices that bear no relationship to the contribution of the transfer to the profits of the receiving unit (Delapierre and Michalet 1976, pp. 259, 262).

If joint operation is more profitable than separate profit maximization, then multinationals should be eager to acquire foreign firms at a price higher than that which purely domestic firms are willing to pay, a fact that has been consistently noted by observers. The preceding considerations also explain why, as we have seen in chapter 3, foreign takeovers sometimes involve the acquisition and rehabilitation of particularly unprofitable foreign companies, or why multinational firms will go to considerable expense to buy back shares from their minority shareholders.[6]

Since parents will find it more profitable to maximize the firm's overall profits rather than those of each subsidiary, sharing the ownership of their subsidiary will reduce the value of the firm, because it will prevent the firm from exploiting totally the interdependence between parent and subsidiary. As Stephen Hymer has pointed out (1972), the firm will hesitate to transfer resources in optimal amounts from a parent to a jointly owned subsidiary because it will end up sharing the profits from such a transfer with its foreign partners, while shouldering any losses in the home country alone. For that reason, one should expect parents to generally oppose the buying of shares of the subsidiary by host country residents; furthermore, host country residents will tend not to want to buy shares of the subsidiary. They will find it more profitable to buy shares of the parent, and thus partake of the higher profits that arise from integrated operations.

A corollary of our analysis is that the intensity of preference for complete ownership will vary with the extent to which parents and subsidiaries are interdependent in ways that cannot be mediated by international markets. According to the model, tight control will be prevalent when there is a strong degree of interdependence between the firm's constituting units *and* that interdependence is more efficiently organized by hierarchical than by market processes. In the opposite case, the advantages procured by joint ventures (access to raw materials or markets, rapid acquisition of additional resources such as capital and trade connections) outweigh the disadvantage of losing control, and multinational firms will find it profitable to invite local partners into the subsidiary.

As seen earlier, there are three main cases in which interdependences between the members of the corporate system are poorly organized by markets: (1) units of the multinational network are trading in intermediate products that have few alternative uses or substitutes and that are characterized by heavy fixed investments with a long economic life; (2) they are continually exchanging important flows of nonpatentable know-how and/or goodwill; and (3) distribution of the parent's products requires the joint effort of manufacturer and distributor, and control through contractual means is costly.

In other words, we would expect sales and extractive subsidiaries to be wholly owned, and innovating firms to show a marked preference for wholly owned subsidiaries, especially if they are committed to the continuous improvement of products and processes. On the other hand, multinationals will be more prone to joint-venture subsidiaries that produce different products than the parent, that rely on different trade names, that are mainly oriented to local markets, and that are not involved in the exchange of knowledge with other units of the firm.

The ownership patterns of multinational firms, such as they have been analyzed and described in the literature, confirm our hypothesis. John Stopford and Louis Wells (1972), in their extensive study of the ownership patterns of American multinationals, have identified four strategies that lead to a high proportion of wholly owned subsidiaries: (1) the development of new products ahead of competitors; (2) the desire to control sources of raw materials; (3) the use of marketing techniques for product differentiation; and (4) the rationalization of production to reduce manufacturing costs (Stopford and Wells 1972, p. 107).

Development of New Products Ahead of Competitors: According to Stopford and Wells, firms that spend heavily in the United States on research and development have a marked preference for the majority control of their subsidiaries. Seventy-eight percent of the subsidiaries of the American multinationals that spent 5 percent or more of their sales on research and development were wholly owned, compared to 56 percent for firms that spent less than 1.1 percent of sales on research and development (Stopford and Wells 1972, p. 120).[7]

One of the reasons given by the managers of high technology firms for their reluctance to accept minority partners is the difficulty of obtaining a fair return for the technology contributed by the parent to the joint venture. In their eyes, "minority shareholders just get a free ride." (Moore 1969 in Stopford and Wells 1972, p. 120). This is not surprising, given the difficulty of assessing ex ante the value of the technology and the high transaction costs involved in its sale. Another reason given for avoiding joint ventures is the fear that minority partners in joint ventures might use the innovator's proprietary technology to compete with him or might disclose trade secrets to third parties.

The need for complete control is especially strong whenever technical and marketing information are being continually transferred between parent and subsidiary. If the subsidiary is in a highly competitive environment, such as the United States, the firm has to continually improve its products and processes if it is to stay in business. Close communication with the parent and speed of response are essential for survival. If, on the other hand, the need for communication between parent and subsidiary is limited, joint ventures will be more readily accepted. Such is the case when the subsidiary is established to introduce process or product innovations in protected markets (Franko 1976, p. 198). Continental firms thus show a much stronger aversion to joint ventures with their American subsidiaries than with their other subsidiaries: two-thirds of their American subsidiaries are wholly owned, compared to an overall average of only 46 percent (Franko 1976, p. 182).

The Desire to Control Sources of Raw Materials: Firms that have integrated backward into raw materials extraction and forward into sales subsidiaries have also insisted on unqualified control of their subsidiaries. Only 28 percent of the extractive subsidiaries of American multinationals were joint ventures (Stopford and Wells 1972, p. 117). A high proportion of these few joint ventures were organized between two or more vertically integrated competitors. In the developed countries, one of the partners was usually a firm from the country where the extraction was taking place, but in the less developed countries the partners to the joint ventures were usually foreign firms.[8]

Such joint ventures arise from the same motives that lead to vertical integration, namely, the desire to avoid bargaining stalemates between supplier and customer of intermediate products, and the need for close coordination of long-term plans. Whenever the scale of operations is larger than that warranted by the demands of one company, joint ventures between international competitors are established, with the shares held by each parent proportional to the fraction of the output purchased from the joint venture. Arrangements of this sort are not likely to lead to conflicts of interest between the partners to the joint venture, since the associates all share the same information about actual and future demand levels. Where divergences exist, they will generally manifest themselves at the negotiation stage (Stopford and Wells 1972, p. 117). Joint ventures with nonintegrated concerns, however, involve the possibility of divergences of interest between the parties and, except when forced by host-country governments, have been generally avoided by resource-based multinationals.

The same firms that have found it necessary to control their extractive subsidiaries have, however, a high proportion of their manufacturing activities into joint ventures. They have done so in order to obtain assured markets for their production and have entered into joint ventures with local purchasers of their products. Some joint ventures also arise from the need to integrate upstream: a local company that controls inputs needed by a foreign firm can sometimes insist on a share of the foreigner's manufacturing operations. The relationship between parent and subsidiary in these joint ventures is very close to a market exchange. One author points out that these arrangements "are merely glorified supplier-customer relationships, and it is difficult to distinguish between a joint-venture and a simple long-term contract" (Uyterhoven 1963 in Stopford and Wells 1972, p. 137). Consequently, complete control is not necessary from the multinational's point of view: all that is needed is enough control to insure that the parent's materials are used (Stopford and Wells 1972, p. 132–38).

The Use of Marketing Techniques to Differentiate Products: Stopford and Wells have also noted the preference toward wholly owned subsidiaries of firms that rely on a strategy of product differentiation through advertising. Ninety-four percent of the subsidiaries of American parents that spent 10 percent or more of their sales on advertising in the United States were wholly owned, compared to 63 percent for firms that spent less than 10 percent (Stopford and Wells p. 109). Firms that spend heavily on advertising are typically selling mature products (such as food, beverages, drugs, detergents, and cosmetics) in a large number of countries. These products are likely to be simultaneously at the same stage of their life cycle in different markets. Substantial cost savings can therefore be obtained by using standardized marketing techniques. Mature products are also likely to be less specific to any particular market, and thus are more often traded. A firm that seeks to differentiate mature products through advertising will be motivated to integrate the marketing policies of its varied subsidiaries to reduce cost and to make uniform the quality and the image of the firm's trade names.

Joint venture partners are likely to oppose such moves. Unless they receive adequate compensation, they can be expected to counter policies that will maximize the goodwill of the firm as a whole, but not necessarily that of the subsidiary. Because the exchange of goodwill is subject to high transaction costs, we would expect such interdependencies to lead to conflicts between the parent and its joint ventures. In fact, the literature on joint ventures shows that differences of opinion over the level of advertising expense and the content of marketing programs provide the greatest source of conflict between multinational enterprises and their local partners (Stopford and Wells 1972, p. 121). Multinational parents that follow a policy of product differentiation through advertising have consequently avoided joint ventures by establishing wholly owned subsidiaries or buying back the shares of their minority shareholders, a behavior that is fully consistent with our model.

The Rationalization of Production to Reduce Manufacturing Costs: Firms that sell a limited product line of mature products worldwide have reacted to increased competition by consolidating production in a limited number of large-scale plants in order to reduce costs. Ford Motor Company, for example, sells the same models in all European countries and ships components between its various subsidiaries. Firms that have followed such a policy have also found it necessary to keep a tight control over their subsidiaries. As Stopford and Wells have pointed out (1972, p. 114–17), a division of labor between subsidiaries implies a decision as to which subsidiary can best manufacture each product, the level of transfer prices, and the allocation of markets among subsidiaries. Each of the firm's units will want to expand production, manufacture the most profitable products, and export to third markets. Rationalization of production implies, however, that some subsidiaries will have to lay off workers, agree to produce less, or stop exporting. An independent decision by each subsidiary would most likely lead to suboptimization, so centralized control is necessary.[9] Joint venture partners will usually frustrate the firm's rationalization moves, since their interests do not coincide with that of the firm as a whole. For that reason, American, European, and Japanese firms that want to rationalize production find it necessary to avoid local participation in their subsidiaries (Stopford and Wells 1972, p. 113; Franko 1976, p. 208; Yoshino 1976, p. 146).

On the other hand, firms with a more diversified product line have shown a much greater tolerance for joint ventures. Nineteen and a half percent of the foreign subsidiaries of American multinationals that manufactured abroad in at least four SIC three-digit industries were minority-owned, compared to only 8.7 percent for multinationals active in only one industry (Stopford and Wells 1972, p. 126). The greater preference of diversified firms for joint ventures can be explained in the following terms. The failure of any particular product is less crucial to diversified firms than to multinationals that specialize in a limited product line. Goodwill spillovers are smaller, and so is the need to control intersubsidiary variation in price and quality. A lapse in the quality of one product produced in one country affects mostly the reputation of the product, not that of the firm. Opportunities for production and marketing rationalization are quite limited in firms that are diversified, since each product has typically a small market share in any given country. The large number of product lines in diversified firms also suggests that the technological dependence of subsidiaries on their parent is a one-time affair. The fact that joint ventures are often used to manufacture overseas products that are outside the major industry of the parent provides further support to our thesis, since the degree of interdependence between parent and subsidiary is then quite limited (Stopford and Wells 1972, p. 130).

The degree of interpenetration between national markets is also a factor in shaping the ownership policies of multinational firms.

Subsidiaries that are in markets that are isolated by differences in income, tastes, and standards, and by tariff and nontariff barriers, can follow independent policies with limited impact on the rest of the system. The interpenetration of markets, on the other hand, makes unified marketing and pricing policies necessary; decisions must be made as to which subsidiary will export to any particular market. Joint venture partners are then likely to seriously limit the firm's freedom of action.

There is some evidence that multinationals insist on complete control of their export-oriented subsidiaries. Franko notes that the very few subsidiaries of continental European firms in less-developed countries that are exporting a significant share of their output are either wholly owned or are joint ventures with other foreign enterprises (Franko 1976, p. 126). Similarly, Stopford and Wells did not find a single joint venture among American offshore subsidiaries that assembled goods for export (Stopford and Wells 1972, p. 166). Data collected by Curhan, Davidson, and Suri on the exports of American subsidiaries as a percentage of their total sales and on their ownership status support Franko's and Stopford and Wells's findings. Twelve percent of the wholly owned subsidiaries exported more than half of their production, compared to 8 percent for minority-held subsidiaries (Curhan, Davidson, and Suri 1977, p. 386).

We have seen earlier that manufacturers have found it necessary to establish sales subsidiaries in foreign countries whenever local distributors could have an important beneficial or detrimental impact on the sales of their products. In that case, there is a strong interdependence between the parent and the local distributor, as the policies followed by the local agent will strongly affect the parent's profitability, and vice versa. Another implication of the theory is therefore that multinational firms will be reluctant to share the ownership of their sales subsidiaries with local distributors, for such an association would lead to the very problems that integration into sales had sought to circumvent. One would expect to find very few joint ventures among sales subsidiaries. Here again, the data are consistent with our predictions: 80 percent of the sales subsidiaries of non-American-based systems and 88 percent of those of American-based multinationals were wholly owned in 1968 (Vaupel and Curhan 1973, table 10.1).

Our survey of the empirical data on the ownership pattern of subsidiaries shows that, as predicted by our model, wholly owned subsidiaries will be chosen whenever interdependencies between the members of the corporate system are both strong and more efficiently organized by hierarchical than by market processes. Can the same line of argument explain the significant national differences that we have noted in chapter 3? As shown in table 13, Japanese, French, German, Italian, and Belgian firms had, in the early 1970s, a much greater preference for joint ventures than their American, Swedish, Swiss, British, and Dutch competitors.

At the outset, one must distinguish between two types of joint ventures: those undertaken by a group of international competitors and those associating local entrepreneurs to the venture. The first type of joint venture is that undertaken between two or more international competitors. French and Belgian firms were particularly involved in this type of joint venture. In 37 percent of the cases, the principal partner in French manufacturing joint ventures was another foreign, private firm. Comparable figures for Belgium and Japan were 39 and 28 percent, respectively. Switzerland, Sweden, the Netherlands, and the United States had a much lower propensity to enter joint ventures with rivals, perhaps because of the lower tolerance of their governments for anticompetitive actions by their national firms (Franko 1976, p. 117). The predilection of French, Belgian, and Japanese firms for this type of joint venture explains in part the high proportion of joint venture among their affiliates.

The second type of joint ventures are those that associate the foreign firm with local partners, either private firms or governments. In addition to the factors inherent in a firm's activity that we have analyzed in the preceding paragraphs, the policies of host governments have also influenced the choice between this last type of joint venture and wholly owned subsidiaries.

Most of the countries that have instituted systematic programs to force multinational firms to share the ownership of their subsidiaries with local nationals have been less-developed countries. Countries with the most explicit policies in this regard have obtained for their nationals a higher degree of participation in the foreign affiliates (Stopford and Wells 1972, p. 151). As a result, joint ventures are relatively more common in developing than in industrialized countries: 29.3 percent of the subsidiaries established in less-developed countries by 391 multinationals were minority-held, compared to 11.3 percent for those located in developed countries (Vernon 1977, p. 34). Japan, France, and Italy have a higher proportion of their affiliates in less-developed countries than the United States, the United Kingdom, and the other European countries (Franko 1976, table 5-2, p. 108), and this explains in part why a higher percentage of Japanese, French, and Italian affiliates were joint ventures. Table 13 shows, however, that this factor provides only a partial explanation, since the percentage of subsidiaries of German, French, Japanese, and Belgian firms located in less-developed countries that were wholly owned was still lower than that for multinationals from the other countries.

We have seen earlier that the strategies followed by firms influence their policy toward joint ventures. Firms that follow strategies of continuous development of new products, of product differentiation by advertising, of rationalization of production, or of vertical integration, tend to avoid joint ventures. Few European and Japanese firms have followed these strategies, and this also explains their greater tolerance of joint ventures.

In the preceding pages we have shown that firms that are selling a limited product line worldwide can reduce costs by concentrating production in a few large specialized plants and by shipping components between their subsidiaries. Such firms can also attain substantial economies of scale by the use of standardized marketing techniques in different national markets. The successful achievement of such policies requires, however, tight control over all subsidiaries. As a result, firms that sell a limited number of related products throughout the world are less likely to engage into joint ventures than multinationals with a more diverse product line.

Few European and Japanese firms have followed these strategies of regional specialization of production. The four largest Japanese multinationals are trading companies. These giant import-export houses have traditionally handled the products of a large number of Japanese manufacturers in many different industries (Yoshino 1976, p. 28). Continental European multinationals are also more diversified than their American counterparts, and more diversified in their foreign production than they are at home (Franko 1976, p. 21). The high degree of diversification of Japanese and European firms thus limits their opportunities for rationalization of production and explains their lower aversion to joint ventures.

Complete control of subsidiaries is also sought by firms that differentiate their products by advertising. Few European and Japanese multinationals are spending as much on advertising as their American rivals. There are few continental European multinationals selling consumer products like processed foods, cosmetics, soap, and drugs, which are typically heavily advertised and for which coordinated international advertising sometimes yields substantial economies of scale (Franko 1976, p. 123). Yoshino notes that only a handful of Japanese firms produce goods that can be differentiated by advertising. Most of the firms that do, however, sell their products in the United States under the brand name of American manufacturers and mass merchandisers, and, consequently, have not felt the need to establish wholly owned subsidiaries (Yoshino 1976, p. 82). The few Japanese producers of consumer durables that have chosen to sell under their own brand names have insisted on 100 percent ownership of their subsidiaries (Yoshino 1976, p. 153).

The strong orientation of European and Japanese subsidiaries toward local markets has also influenced their greater use of joint ventures. Historically, most of the subsidiaries of continental European firms have been established in other European countries in order to jump tariff and nontariff barriers and to take advantage of government contracts and subsidies to local production. As of 1971, more than half of the subsidiaries of European-based multinationals (with the exception of Italy) were located in Europe (Franko 1976, table 4-2, p. 80). The output of most of these subsidiaries was mainly destined to local markets.[10] In contrast to American subsidiaries, subsidiaries of continental European firms are very rarely specialized by product and are minimally involved in international trade (Franko 1976, p. 224). That lack of international perspective is partly a result of the persistence of significant nontariff barriers to intra-European trade. But much of that national orientation can be attributed to noncompetitive environments. Given the lack of competitive pressure in European markets, continental European firms have not felt the same pressure as their American rivals to rationalize production and to standardize the marketing efforts of their foreign subsidiaries (Franko 1976, p. 225).

The lack of global perspective on the part of continental European firms is also evident in their Third World operations. European multinationals are not using their Third World subsidiaries as platforms for exports to the same extent as American firms. As of the early 1970s, only about 3 percent of the subsidiaries of European enterprises in less-developed countries were exporting more than half of their production (Franko 1976, p. 126). There are, unfortunately, no strictly comparable data for American companies. Some studies, however, show that American multinationals have established a much larger number of export-oriented subsidiaries in less-developed countries than European firms. Chang (1971, pp. 17–20) surveyed the subsidiaries of multinational firms located in Southeast Asia, Mexico, and the Caribbean that produced electronic components for export. There were over thirty subsidiaries of American firms, but only three, much smaller, European subsidiaries operating in these countries. In Southeast Asia, the majority of American plants, but none of the three European factories, were exporting over 50 percent of their production. Since, as we have seen, export subsidiaries are generally wholly owned, the small number of European export-

oriented subsidiaries explains the greater tolerance of European producers for joint ventures.

The lower degree of integration and specialization in continental European firms, as compared to their American and British
rivals, is reflected in their respective organizational charts. Until
1971, most continental European multinationals were organized according to the mother-daughter form of organization, under which
the foreign subsidiary president reported to the parent president.
Franko notes that

> the greatest contrast between the mother-daughter structure and alter-
> native structures . . . lies in the fact that none of the managers in the
> "mother-daughter" form of organization has strictly supranational re-
> sponsibilities, whereas there is an implicit recognition of cross-border
> responsibility, co-ordination and communication in all the alternatives
> to the mother-daughter relationship. [1976, p. 193]

American firms have used mother-daughter structures in the early
stages of their foreign manufacturing experience, but by 1970 they
had all abandoned such structures in favor of other organizational
forms (Franko 1976, p. 188). Dutch and British multinationals had
also largely followed the American lead. The continued reliance of
other European multinationals on mother-daughter structures is a
tangible sign that, as of the early 1970s, they had not yet developed
an integrated strategy and that their subsidiaries were pursuing independent policies (Franko 1976, p. 202). Not surprisingly, the firms
that had moved away from mother-daughter structures had done so
at the urging of their American subsidiaries (Franko 1976, pp. 198–
99).

Japanese affiliates are also mainly oriented to local markets. As
shown in table 22, a significant share of Japanese foreign direct
investments was, as of 1974, located outside Europe and North
America. About one fourth of the total capital stock was in manufacturing subsidiaries in Asia, the Middle East, Africa, and Oce-
ania. As shown in table 23, few of these subsidiaries were majority-
owned: the greater part were joint ventures of Japanese trading
companies, Japanese suppliers and their client firms, and local distributors. Many of these joint ventures had been established by
Japanese trading companies when faced by trade barriers and local
competitors. To avoid losing their export markets, trading companies had persuaded their suppliers to substitute local production for
exports (Yoshino 1976, p. 70; Tsurumi, 1976, p. 75). The bulk of
Japanese manufacturing investment was therefore geared to local

TABLE 22   Japanese Stock of Foreign Direct Investment Abroad by Area and Industry, 1974 (in million U.S. dollars)

	Europe and North America		All Other		All Countries	
Resource-oriented investments[a]	557	(5.6%)	2,819	(28.4%)	3,376	(34.0%)
Manufacturing	522	(5.3%)	2,370	(23.8%)	2,892	(29.1%)
Sales subsidiaries	967	(9.7%)	230	(2.3%)	1,197	(12.1%)
Other[b]	1,562	(15.7%)	894	(9.0%)	2,456	(24.7%)
Total	3,608	(36.4%)	6,313	(63.6%)	9,921	(100.0%)

Source: Tsurumi 1976, table 1-5, p. 34. Reprinted with permission from *The Japanese Are Coming,* Copyright 1976, Ballinger Publishing Company.
a. Agriculture, forestry, fisheries, and mining
b. Construction, banking and insurance, tourism, and real estate

TABLE 23   Percentage of Majority-Owned Japanese Subsidiaries, by Area (end of 1972)

Area	Number of Subsidiaries	Percentage Majority-Owned
Asia	1,339	41%
North America	614	87
Europe	275	74
Latin America	267	68
Middle East and Africa	108	41
British Dominions and Oceania	146	58
All areas	2,749	58

Source: Tsurumi 1976, p. 202. Reprinted with permission from *The Japanese Are Coming,* Copyright 1976, Ballinger Publishing Company.

production. Less than 19 percent of the sales of 661 manufacturing subsidiaries surveyed in 1972 by Japan's Ministry of International Trade and Industry went to outside markets, and less than 5 percent went back to Japan (Yoshino 1976, p. 75).[11] As in the European and American cases, the few Japanese subsidiaries that had been set up in these countries to export their output to other markets were wholly owned (Yoshino 1976, p. 145; Tsurumi 1976, p. 208). Japan's stake in Europe and North America was smaller, but over two-thirds of the Japanese subsidiaries established there were sales subsidiaries (Tsurumi 1976, p. 201). As our model would predict, and as table 23 shows, a high proportion of these subsidiaries were wholly owned.

The type of products introduced by continental European and

by Japanese firms help also to account for their greater use of joint ventures. As we have seen in chapter 3, the need for complete control of foreign subsidiaries is especially strong whenever technical and marketing information is being continually transferred between parent and subsidiary. Such is the case if the subsidiary is introducing new products into the local economy. In that case, the customer of the new product will require a considerable amount of information on the function of the product, its applications, its reliability, and the availability of repair services. Information feedback to the parent is also crucial because the product has often to be adapted to the customer's tastes and potential problems must be quickly identified and corrected. Whereas American firms have specialized early in the development of new consumer products geared to affluent customers, the firms located in continental European countries have concentrated mostly on ersatz material and on new material-saving processes for the manufacture of old products (Franko 1976, chap. 2; Vernon 1977, p. 42).[12] The international transfer of such innovations does not require the same level of continuous cross-border communication. Once the subsidiary has been given the technical information to start new plants incorporating the new processes and/or producing the new synthetics, no further exchange of information is needed. The buyers of ersatz products are usually manufacturers, and they are likely to require much less information and after-sales service than the buyers of new consumer products. There are few French, German, Belgian, and Italian multinationals in which there is a continuous exchange of information between parent and subsidiaries. These firms have therefore felt less need to minimize the cost of transferring information within the firm by having full control of their subsidiaries.

Japanese multinationals are also heavily concentrated in mature industries.[13] Japanese firms have been good imitators, but their innovative performance cannot be compared to that of the United States (Yoshino 1976, p. 90). Sony Corporation is among the few Japanese firms that have generated a continuous stream of new products. That firm has established 100 percent-owned manufacturing and sales subsidiaries (Yoshino 1976, p. 154).

The particular characteristics of continental European and Japanese multinationals help therefore to account for their greater tolerance for joint ventures. An analysis of recent changes in the ownership policies of these firms produces further evidence that the logic of the multinational firm calls for clear control of subsidiaries. There are some indications that the pressures of international competition are forcing European firms toward more unified strategies that will, in turn, lead to tighter control of their subsidiaries. Thus, by 1974, forty-seven of the sixty continental European companies that were organized under mother-daughter structures had adopted other forms of organization (Franko 1976, p. 209). The same processes seem to have been at work with Japanese firms. According to Vernon, Japanese-based multinationals have, since 1970, increasingly chosen wholly owned subsidiaries over joint ventures. Vernon attributes this change in strategy to a shift by Japanese firms toward an increasingly sophisticated product mix, from standardized textiles and food products toward electronic consumer goods and industrial equipment. These new products require greater control over the quality of their manufacture and over their distribution channels. Furthermore, Japanese multinationals are spreading from the insulated markets of Asia toward the larger, more interrelated European and North American markets. The resulting greater interdependence between their new subsidiaries has in turn increased their need for tighter control from the center (Vernon 1977, p. 36). As time goes on, American and non-American-based multinationals may therefore exhibit considerably more similitude in their preference for wholly owned subsidiaries.

Some of the characteristic features of the behavior of multinational firms, such as their ability to outbid purely domestic firms when buying out local enterprises, their predilection for acquiring unprofitable concerns, or their reluctance to issue share capital in their subsidiaries, are thus fully consistent with our model. Furthermore, we have shown that the theory also explains the presence of interfirm differences in their tolerance for joint ventures. Lastly, we have argued that the greater preference of American multinationals for wholly owned subsidiaries can be understood in terms of our model.

Conclusion

The main purpose of this chapter has been to test the ability of the model to account for the historical and geographical patterns of foreign direct investment. The failure of most British firms to establish foreign subsidiaries in the nineteenth century should be somewhat surprising to those that espouse the product cycle hypothesis, since it is directly contrary to the implications of Vernon's model. Our approach, however, predicts that if internal organization costs are relatively higher than market transaction costs, even if the latter are substantial, foreign direct investment will not take place. An examination of the size of firms and of the state of managerial and legal techniques in nineteenth-century England suggests that internal organization costs were so high relative to market transaction costs that they limited firms to rather small equilibrium sizes and made foreign direct investment an unprofitable alternative to other transfer modes.

The same line of reasoning explains the greater propensity of American firms to exploit their advantages through foreign direct investments. We argue that there are significant differences between the level of internal organization costs experienced, at a given firm size, by American firms and by their Western European rivals. These differences bias the choice of European firms toward licensing in those cases when American firms would choose subsidiary production. If our premises are valid, then a closing of the "managerial gap" between the United States and Europe would be accompanied by a rise in overseas investments by Western European firms. Although the evidence we have offered in support of our hypothesis is limited, our analysis would seem to warrant further research.

Finally, the model explains the otherwise puzzling preference of multinational firms for wholly owned subsidiaries. Multinational corporations are chosen to coordinate transnational interdependences whenever centralized coordination through managerial directives is more efficient than decentralized adjustment to market prices. The logic of the multinational firm pushes management to maximize the profits of the firm as a whole. Sharing the ownership of its subsidiaries discourages the multinational firm from following this strategy, and thus tends to reduce its overall profitability. One can therefore predict that an increase in the degree of international competition will lead non-American firms to opt increasingly for wholly owned subsidiaries.

CHAPTER 6

A Summary of the Model and Policy Implications

At this point, it may be worthwhile to retrace our steps. Our principal theme has been that the essence of the foreign direct investment phenomenon is not the international transfer of capital, technological know-how, goodwill, or marketing skills; exchange of goods (or bads) between countries is a necessary condition for the establishment of foreign operations, but it is not a sufficient one. For foreign direct investment to take place, it is necessary that these exchanges be more efficiently organized within firms than across markets. Our thesis can be seen as an attempt to determine the conditions under which managerial coordination (foreign direct investment) will be preferred to exchange through spot prices or long-term contracts, and to test the predictions of the model against some of the known features of international operations.

In chapter 1, we reviewed the existing literature on multinational corporations and foreign direct investment. We saw that the traditional view of foreign direct investment as capital movements is inadequate as (1) the majority of foreign direct investments is not directed toward countries poorly endowed with financial capital, (2) there is often a two-way flow of foreign direct investment between developed countries, and (3) a large percentage of the capital expenditures of foreign subsidiaries is financed from local sources. The modern theory of capital movements, based on the Markowitz-Tobin model of portfolio choice, is also inconsistent with the empirical characteristics of foreign direct investment: the tight integration of subsidiaries to their parent and the preference of the latter for majority control does not suggest that subsidiaries are held for diversification purposes. We therefore concluded that capital theories do not help us understand the foreign direct investment phenomenon.

Turning to other explanations of foreign direct investment, we examined briefly "imperialistic theories." These theories do not explain multinational firms per se, since they are consistent with both direct and portfolio investment. Trade theory offers another approach to our subject. The main body of literature follows Raymond Vernon's product cycle hypothesis. For Vernon, foreign direct investment originates from the desire of firms to exploit abroad firm-specific knowledge. Our contention was that this is not a sufficient condition for foreign direct investment, as evidenced by the failure of nineteenth-century British firms to exploit abroad their advantage through overseas subsidiaries. Richard Caves proposes a third theory. He argues that for foreign direct investment to take place, the firm must have an asset that is complementary to local sales, which cannot be readily imitated, and for which licensing is a less profitable alternative. This asset is the knowledge of serving a market, a knowledge acquired by successful product differentiation in the home country. Caves does not conclusively show, however, how product differentiation in one market confers advantages in another market, nor does his model account for the observed differences in the propensity of firms of various countries to exploit their advantages through foreign subsidiaries. Our brief survey thus demonstrated the need for a new approach to foreign direct investment.

Chapter 2 presents a model of the institutional choice between firms and markets that is similar to that first set out by John McManus (1972). The starting point is the realization that firms and markets are two institutions that organize economic activities. In the real world, there are costs associated with such a task. These costs will prevent both institutions from perfectly constraining all interdependencies and thus from internalizing all externalities. But because markets and firms differ in the methods they use to coordinate and constrain behavior, they experience, in organizing the same set of activities, different levels of organization costs, and consequently, divergent levels of external effects. The choice between firm and market organization will hinge on the cost of organizing cooperation through prices (market transaction costs) relative to the cost of doing it by managerial directives (internal organization costs) or, conversely, on the level of external costs that will arise in both types of organization. These costs will vary according to the nature of the activities to be coordinated and each institution will therefore specialize in handling a specific type of exchange. Thus markets will tend to be relatively more efficient than firms in handling transactions between a large number of buyers and sellers and involving homogeneous products or services. Markets will be at a comparative disadvantage when transactions are subject to a high degree of uncertainty and when they consist of long-term exchanges of complex and heterogeneous products between a comparatively small number of traders. In these cases, prices will not adequately reflect costs and benefits to the group. The firm will then be at an advantage because it does not rely on prices to reward parties to the exchange and because it economizes on the cost of providing them with all the relevant information. Instead the central party synthesizes the necessary information and sends directives to the parties for execution.

These very features, however, subject firms to another type of costs. The relaxation of the immediate connection between market-measured output and income, and the distortion problems inherent in the centralization of information, provide opportunities for misallocation and shirking. These costs rise with the overall size of the enterprise. At some point the internal organization costs associated with an additional transaction will exceed the corresponding market transaction costs. This point will set the boundary between firms and markets. Over time, the technological and organizational innovations that reduce market transaction costs and internal organization costs will affect the respective roles of firms and markets in organizing economic activity. In the latter part of the chapter, we demonstrated how improvements in legal forms, organizational structures, and labor management techniques have lowered the relative cost of firm organization.

In chapters 3, 4, and 5, we used our model of the comparative advantage of firms and markets to explain the main features of the foreign direct investment phenomenon. Chapters 3 and 4 were devoted to an explanation of the industrial structure of foreign direct investment, whereas in chapter 5 we dealt with its historical and geographical pattern and the ownership policies of multinational firms.

In chapters 3 and 4 we indicated how the two types of direct investments, vertical and horizontal, could be explained in terms of our model. Chapter 3 concentrated on vertical investments. Backward international integration was shown to arise from three conditions: the high costs of coordinating successive production stages by market prices when there are few parties to the exchange; the extension of trade over a considerable amount of time; and a high degree of uncertainty. The ownership by home country firms of foreign distribution facilities (forward vertical integration into sales) was ascribed to the existence of interdependencies between manufacturers and distributors, and to the high cost, in some cases, of constraining that interdependence through market prices or market contracts.

Chapter 4 analyzed horizontal investments and classified them into two types: those motivated by the high cost of exchanging goodwill through market processes, and those arising from high market transaction costs in knowledge. We showed that it is sometimes costly to prevent by contract firms sharing a trademark from free riding on the goodwill capital of the brand. Unpatented knowledge, we argued, is endowed with certain characteristics that make its market exchange costlier than its intrafirm transfer. Since the introduction abroad of new products and processes often involves the combination of many types of specialized but unpatentable know-how over extended periods of time and under conditions of uncertainty, the innovating firm will find it sometimes relatively more efficient to acquire foreign manufacturing facilities than to rent the know-how to foreign producers.

In chapter 5 we employed our theoretical framework to explain the historical and the geographical patterns of foreign direct investment and the ownership policies of multinational firms. We interpreted the recent development of multinational firms as caused by a decline of internal organization costs relative to market transaction costs. Because of the progress made in the recent period in managerial techniques, today's firms experience much lower internal organization costs than their nineteenth-century counterparts. They are therefore able to exploit their advantage overseas through the creation of subsidiaries, whereas high internal organization costs had prevented their predecessors from following the same strategy. We supported our argument by an analysis of the international transfer of knowledge in the first half of the nineteenth century, in which we demonstrated that the failure of British firms to exploit their technological advantages through foreign direct investment was due to the high internal organization costs they experienced.

The same line of reasoning was taken to explain the systematic differences in the method used by American and European firms to exploit abroad their advantages whenever the balance of net delivered costs and other factors favor local production. Whereas American corporations use mainly foreign subsidiaries, European firms seem to rely relatively more on licensing. We attributed this difference in behavior to the fact that European firms have experienced higher internal organization costs than their American rivals. In support of our hypothesis, we presented evidence as to the presence of a managerial gap between the United States and Europe, and of its gradual narrowing in the recent period. We concluded that the rather impressive growth experienced by European and Japanese enterprises and their accession to multinational status could be explained by their assimilation of American managerial techniques.

Finally, we examined the ownership policies of multinational firms. Their preference for wholly owned subsidiaries was shown to be fully consistent with our model. If, as we argued, the multinational firm's raison d'être is the coordination of internationally interdependent activities through hierarchical methods, then we would expect its managers not to maximize the parent's and subsidiaries' separate profits, but to maximize their joint profits. A claim to a share of the profit of the whole firm will therefore be worth more than a claim to a share of the profit of either the parent or the subsidiary. As a result, multinational firms will often be reluctant to sell—and local residents unwilling to buy—shares of the multinational's subsidiaries. Moreover, we would expect the strength of the incitation for joint profit maximization (and thus for full ownership of the subsidiaries) to vary with the degree of nonmarket mediated interdependence between the units of the corporate system. Differences in that level of interdependence would thus explain interfirm (and international) variations in ownership policies. We showed that there is a considerable amount of evidence that supports this hypothesis, and that interfirm and international differences in ownership patterns can be explained in terms of our model.

The foregoing analysis differs both in its approach and in its implications from other current theories of foreign direct investment. Vernon's product cycle hypothesis sees the establishment of foreign subsidiaries as the principal method used by firms to capitalize on the valuable firm-specific technological or marketing knowledge they possess. According to our model, exploitation abroad of firm-specific knowledge will only lead to foreign direct investment if intrafirm transfer is more efficient than market sale. Know-how, furthermore, is only one of the advantages whose possession is conducive to foreign direct investment. There are other goods or bads that are exchanged more efficiently within firms than across markets. Our model is thus a great deal more general than that of Vernon, and it has the additional merit of focusing on the essence of the phenomenon, rather than on one of the particular forms it has taken. We are thus able to identify the efficiency gains that derive from the institutional existence of multinational firms. These firms are efficient because they internalize some of the effects left external by international markets. Since these effects are, by and large, nonpecuniary, our model establishes a prima facie case for the multinational corporation as an institutional form.

From a cosmopolitan point of view, it is clear that the multinational corporation is a powerful vehicle of economic growth. Multinational firms owe their existence to the fact that they organize some interdependences more efficiently than markets. The creation of a multinational firm thus permits the realization of trades that would not otherwise take place. Multinational firms bring to the world the familiar gains of trade and specialization: economic goods (or bads) are now better allocated internationally, and economic tasks are to a larger extent assigned to those countries that are more efficient in performing them. Because multinationals experience lower organization costs than markets, they will find it desirable to introduce to some countries products or processes that could not be profitably licensed to local producers. The larger market they enjoy for their products will incite them to undertake more research and development and to bring about a greater international division of labor than a system of national firms.[1]

Note that we do not argue that international firms experience zero organization costs. On the contrary, we would expect intrafirm coordination to lead to some inefficiencies. But as long as parties in both countries are free to choose the system of organization that will best constrain their actions, we must presume that whenever they form an international firm the advantages inherent in this form of organization make up for its defects.

This view of the multinational corporation as internalizing nonpecuniary externalities has important implications for the type of policies followed by host-country governments. Some countries force foreign direct investors to share the ownership of their subsidiaries with local citizens. Others have attempted to "unbundle" the package of resources typically provided by a foreign direct investor and to restrict his investment to a particular element of the package. As we will show, both of these policies stem from an erroneous view of the nature of the multinational firm, and they often result in a net loss for all parties.

Sharing Ownership with Local Interests

We have seen that multinational firms have entered foreign markets through majority-owned (and often wholly owned) subsidiaries. These firms have secured complete control of their foreign operations because overall profit maximization required that their subsidiaries be tightly subordinated to the parents. Hence, a state that accepts majority-owned subsidiaries grants to foreigners the power to make decisions in matters of importance to the host country or its citizens. The possibility of foreign control that is implicit in majority-owned subsidiaries has proved to be very disquieting to some host-country governments. In a few countries, public authorities have introduced laws that restrict foreign ownership to a maximum of 50 percent. In many other states, governments have applied considerable pressure on foreign firms to persuade them to sell at least a portion of their equity to local capitalists.

The goal of such policies has been to create conflicts of interests within the multinational firm, and thus to force the parent to run the subsidiary as a separate enterprise. This was clearly stated in Watkins's report, *Foreign Ownership and the Structure of Canadian Industry* (1968, p. 344):

> The existence of minority shareholding . . . can be expected to facilitate the decentralization of decision-making within the multinational enterprise and increase Canadian representation on boards of directors. In both respects, this facilitates the expression of private Canadian points of view through the presence of Canadian citizens as managers, directors and shareholders and may provide additional channels for the Canadian government for the exercise of its power.

Host-country governments thus expect that the presence of minority shareholders will prevent parents from carrying out policies that are detrimental to the subsidiary.

Even if this expectation is realized, our analysis of the multinational firms suggests that such policies may be very costly to host countries. If, as we have argued, a share of the firm as a whole is worth more to host-country investors than a share of the subsidiary, selling equity in the subsidiary will be costly to the international firm. The firm will have to sell claims to its profit stream for a price lower than its opportunity value. One would therefore expect considerable resistance by multinational firms to such policies.

Not surprisingly, whenever host governments have relied on voluntary compliance, they have not been able to achieve their goals: both multinational firms and local investors have usually found such schemes unattractive, and host countries have ended up with the same percentage of wholly owned subsidiaries as that found in countries that have not insisted on minority ownership (Stopford and Wells 1972, p. 151).

When local participation has been made a condition for the establishment of foreign subsidiaries, the multinational companies that insist on wholly owned subsidiaries have generally declined to invest (Stopford and Wells 1972, p. 153). When required to give local shareholders majority ownership in their subsidiaries, some multinational firms have preferred to pull out. Thus International

Business Machines and Coca-Cola Company refused in 1978 to sell 60 percent of the equity of their Indian affiliates to local shareholders and chose instead to liquidate their subsidiaries.

The firms that have resisted joint ventures have often been those whose potential contribution to the local economy seemed to be the largest (Stopford and Wells 1972, p. 154). This is exactly what we would expect. The benefits derived by local factors of production from their association with the foreign firm are a direct function of the degree of interaction between the parent and its subsidiary. Since multinational firms organize those interdependences that are poorly handled by markets, the greater the level of interaction, the larger the potential gain to all parties from their membership in an international firm. As we have argued earlier, the insistence of multinational firms on complete ownership is also a function of the degree of interaction within the firm. Policies that require multinationals to accept local shareholders, besides reducing the profitability of the investing firm by preventing it from running the firm as an integrated concern, tend also to bar from investing those firms that have the most to contribute to the local economy.

Unbundling the Technology Package

Multinational firms, when they establish subsidiaries in a foreign country, usually transfer to that country a complex package of financial capital, expert manpower, patented and unpatented know-how, managerial skills, market information, and goodwill. Indeed, this is often thought to be the distinctive feature of foreign direct investment. As we have argued, this is its main advantage. Some economists, however, see in the coalescing of all these factors into one bundle the major source of the multinational firm's monopoly power. They argue that by conditioning the sale of one element to the purchase of the whole package, the multinational firm eliminates many of its smaller rivals that are unable to supply all components. They suggest that a country might acquire technology at better terms if it bought all of the elements of the package separately, in other words, if it bought plants through turnkey agreements, managerial know-how by management contracts, financial capital on the international capital market, etc. (Moxon 1976, p. 45). If we are right in arguing that the integration of all of the elements of the technology package within the international firm is the consequence of the comparative advantage of firms over markets in organizing complex interactions of that type, then government intervention to "unbundle" the package would seem ill advised. If the elements of the package were reasonably standardized, if their coordination was subject to a limited amount of uncertainty, and if the number of potential suppliers was large, then one would expect local firms (or governments) to buy the required factor bundle in disaggregated form. Conversely, the foreign firm would find it advantageous to specialize in the function it can do best, and to subcontract some or all of the other tasks to other specialized firms. Thus, even if there are alternative sellers for some parts of the package, the substitution of market processes for managerial methods in organizing production will usually result in higher organization costs. Government intervention to unbundle the technology package when economic agents have decided to transfer it in packaged form would thus seem inefficient.

Some Policy Proposals

What then should host countries do? Careful elaboration of policy proposals is beyond the scope of our work, yet the model we have developed points to some interesting possibilities. We have seen that multinational firms owe their existence to market imperfections. Although many of those imperfections are due to factors beyond government control, many others result from deliberate governmental policies. If many of these obstacles to the smooth functioning of international markets were lifted, multinational firms would become a less desirable method of organization. Just as rent control legislation leads to homeownership and discourages renting, restrictions imposed by host countries on licensing contracts between independent parties increase the desirability of foreign direct investment.

Unfortunately, nationalism is likely to hinder efforts to improve the functioning of international markets; national governments have often refused to make unilateral moves to facilitate international trade, while international agreements to that end have been plagued by bargaining and free-rider problems. It is therefore safe to predict that multinational firms will remain for a long time the most efficient institution to further trade and specialization.

Appendix:
Structure of American Foreign Sales and Labor Intensity

The goal of our analysis is to determine whether the choice between exports and foreign direct investment as ways of serving foreign markets is determined by the labor intensity of the production process. Testing this proposition is made difficult by the available data. First, figures on sales by American foreign affiliates usually include goods and services manufactured in the United States and exported to the subsidiary for resale and goods manufactured overseas for the American market. Second, exports are usually recorded on a product basis, whereas sales of American foreign affiliates are on an industry basis.

Local Production by American Foreign Affiliates

We obtained unpublished figures for the 1966 sales of all foreign affiliates of American firms in which one or more American firms held at least a 25 percent ownership interest (allied affiliates). No data were available for the exports to the United States of those affiliates, nor for their sales of goods imported from the corporate parents. We had figures, however, for the exports of majority-owned affiliates to the United States and for their sales of parent's products. We therefore subtracted these two sets of figures from the sales of allied affiliates to obtain the value of their local production. Since the overwhelming majority of allied affiliates are majority-owned, subtracting exports to the United States (and resale of goods produced by corporate parents) of majority-owned— rather than of allied—foreign affiliates should not seriously bias our results.

175

Exports

American exports for 1966 by Standard Industrial Trade Classification (SITC) category were obtained from United States, Department of Commerce, Bureau of the Census, *U.S. Exports, Schedule B Commodity Groupings* (FT 450) (Washington, D.C.: Government Printing Office, 1967). The conversion from SITC to SIC was done according to United States, Department of Commerce, Bureau of the Census, *U.S. Foreign Trade Statistics: Classification and Cross-Classification* (Washington, D.C.: Government Printing Office, 1970).

Labor Intensity Ratio

The labor intensity ratio series is the ratio of payroll to value-added by manufacturing in 1968. That ratio is calculated by R. A. Cornell in "Trade of Multinational Firms and Nations' Comparative Advantage," a paper presented at the Conference on Multinational Corporations and Governments, at the University of California at Los Angeles, November 14–17, 1973. The ratio was computed from United States, Department of Commerce, Bureau of the Census, *Industry Profiles* M70(AS)-10 (Washington, D.C.: Government Printing Office, 1968). Where necessary, aggregation was accomplished by using simple means.

Notes

Chapter 1

1. For example, it is not immediately obvious to foreigners that to reach maximum readership newspaper ads in France must appear on Tuesdays and Fridays, or that Germans and Dutch do not exchange gifts at Christmas, but on December 6. For some other examples of the pitfalls for foreign investors, see "Radio Shack's Rough Trip," *Business Week,* May 30, 1977, p. 55; and "The Fast Food Stars: Three Strategies for Fast Growth," *Business Week,* July 11, 1977, p. 65.
2. See Kwack 1972.
3. This point was brought to my attention by Craig West.
4. More precisely, total portfolio risk is equal to the variance of all assets contained in the portfolio. This in turn is equal to the weighted sum of the individual variances of all assets plus twice the weighted sum of the covariances of all pairs of assets, the elements of the portfolio being used as weights.
5. Ragazzi notes that the market value of stocks quoted in New York in 1970 was nine times the value of stocks quoted in London, which was itself almost equal to the aggregate value of stocks quoted in all other European markets.
6. Solnik (1973) reaches the same conclusion from an analysis of serial correlation between returns on securities quoted in European markets and in the New York Stock Exchange.
7. This fact was brought to my attention by Craig West.
8. The standard anecdote here is the attempt by Colgate-Palmolive Company to sell its "Cue" detergent in France, obviously unaware that "Cue" is phonetically similar to an obscene French word.

Chapter 2

1. In the course of our discussion, the terms "boss," "central party," "central monitor," and "peak coordinator" will all be used interchangeably.
2. However, since there may be no way of escaping these costs, some solutions may be Pareto-efficient in a comparative-institutional sense. See Demsetz 1969.
3. Cheung's article was brought to my attention by John McManus.

4. The validity of the model is thus limited to those countries in which economic agents can freely choose between organization modes.
5. It can be shown that the contingent price of a good is a function of the spot price for the good, of the rate of interest at which the future value of the good must be discounted to obtain its present value, and of the insurance premium to be paid to insure against a particular contingency (Meade 1970, p. 20).
6. This is a highly simplified view of the information transfer within firms. A more detailed treatment of the issue is reported on pp. 50–56.
7. I owe this reference to John McManus.

Chapter 3

1. As Olson notes (1964, p. 14) it is highly significant that, although large firms are free to enter these sectors, few have found it advantageous to do so. In agriculture, the big "bonanza farms" of the turn of the century and, more recently, the large Soviet agricultural enterprises, have all been failures.
2. All figures are in current dollars. The same data expressed in national currencies can be found in table 11. Examination of the table shows that these adjustments do not significantly affect the previously noted trends.
3. These figures are for the 8,621 subsidiaries for which ownership is known. American data are provisional as of 1975. Non-American data are final as of 1970.
4. For example, the consortia of steel firms that developed the iron ore mines in northwest Australia invested more than $600 million in the mine and its ancillary infrastructure (Scherer 1970, p. 87).
5. Following Lancaster (1966), we see products as having multiple attributes of value to the customer, such as styling, reliability, financing, availability of servicing, etc.
6. Such is the case with the retailing of gasoline. Efforts to differentiate gasoline have never been very successful: in the eyes of the consumers, one brand is as good as any other. The refiner's differentiation strategy has been to stress the quality of service at the point of sale ("I can be very friendly") and the appearance of the service station. Differentiation has therefore required the collaboration of the retailer. Hence the refiner's incentive for franchising and/or owning service stations.
7. The same considerations apply if the product moves through wholesalers. In this case the manufacturer will find it desirable to persuade the wholesaler to explain the features of the product to retailers and to convince them to stock it. Exclusive distributorships or integration into wholesaling will be two strategies that will be followed to achieve that goal.
8. In a comparison of two sets of franchises, one operated by franchisees, the other run temporarily by experienced managers motivated by bonuses that could reach 33 percent of their salaries, Shelton (1967, p.

1252–58) found that owner-managers (franchisees) earned higher net returns. When company employees followed franchisees, sales fell on average by 7.3 percent, whereas when franchisees followed employees, sales rose on average by 19.1 percent. Shelton also reports that the net revenue/sales ratio was 1.8 percent for company-run outlets and 9.5 percent for owner-managed ones. Eleven of the twenty-four establishments managed by employees made losses, versus two out of the twenty-nine managed by franchisees.
9. Mira Wilkins provided me with this reference.

Chapter 4

1. As late as 1972, 70 percent of Hertz's European business was tourist related ("Hertz Turns Around in Europe," *Business Week,* September 6, 1976).
2. Affiliates include subsidiaries, affiliates, foreign branches, and representative offices.
3. In automobile rental, the pattern is mixed; the larger outlets are company owned, the others are licensed. Hertz, for example, operates in Europe 600 company-owned offices and licenses 435 rental counters ("Hertz Turns Around in Europe," *Business Week,* September 6, 1976, p. 83).
4. An alternative explanation would be that successful managers convert to the Presbyterian and Episcopalian churches. But, given the unlikelihood of persons raised in the Catholic or the Jewish faith joining a Protestant congregation, this explanation cannot account for the observed differences. The homogeneity of French and Japanese managers is even higher. See Granick (1972, p. 188) and Yoshino (1976, p. 162).
5. This is why licensing of know-how involves patent rights. A recent study of licensing shows that thirty-seven of forty-five licensing agreements examined relied on the exchange of patent rights and only eight on trade secrets (Hall 1977, p. 14).
6. Jewkes, Sawers, and Stillerman (1959) have documented the frequent long lag between patentable invention and commercial use.
7. For an argumentation along the same lines see Magee 1977.
8. The nature of these requirements is sometimes far from clear. Edmund Kitch (1977, p. 281) writes that, in the United States, "numerous inventions that were not easily and immediately obvious either to their inventors or to others have been held invalid by the courts."
9. Since royalties and fees received from affiliates do not result from arm's length transactions, they do not necessarily reflect the market value of the knowledge transferred. Empirical studies show, however, no clear bias in the policies of multinational firms concerning the valuation of such transfers: parent firms are as likely to undercharge as to overcharge their subsidiaries (Nieckels 1976; Robbins and Stobaugh 1973). Note also that some market transactions, such as cross-licensing, do not generate payments of royalties and fees. Overall, these data provide us

with rough estimates of the relative importance of arm's length versus intrafirm technology transfers.

10. Royalties and fees include payments for the use of rights or intangible property (patents, techniques, processes, formulas, designs, trademarks, copyrights, franchises, manufacturing rights) and management fees. Excluded are payments for training, marketing, management and economic consulting, and engineering services. Some of these payments are included in the management fees received from affiliates, but transactions of this type with unaffiliated foreigners are not reported. On the other hand, some parents do not always charge their subsidiaries for their use of patents, processes, or trademarks, even if they receive royalties on the same assets from unaffiliated customers.

Chapter 5

1. In a letter to the author, John McManus suggested another reason why British firms in the nineteenth century did not directly invest in foreign countries. According to McManus, taxes of all kinds will bias the choice of institution toward firms. The imposition of individual income taxes, for example, leads individuals to increase their demand for nonpecuniary goods and to decrease their demand for pecuniary goods; an employee will therefore be willing to join a firm for a lower pecuniary salary, thus decreasing the relative cost of hierarchical versus market coordination. On the other hand, the corporation income tax tends to work in the opposite direction, but McManus discounts its importance on the grounds that it only impinges on net income. Although no extensive testing of this alternative hypothesis is possible here, it is interesting to note that the income tax was introduced in England as early as 1842, but not until 1913 in the United States. Yet by the beginning of the twentieth century, the large English firm was of a much smaller absolute size, controlled a smaller share of its market, and had integrated a much more limited range of manufacturing and mining activities than its American counterpart (Payne 1967, pp. 519–20).

2. Even twenty-five years after adoption of the Company Act, limited liability companies made up less than 10 percent of the total number of large British firms (Payne 1967, p. 520).

3. Royalties and fees consist here of payments for the sale or use of intangible property, of management fees, service charges, film and television tape rentals, and other rentals for tangible property.

4. Local subsidiaries of foreign firms are excluded in these figures. American subsidiaries in England, France, and Germany were the first to adopt multidivisional structures. Diversified firms are firms in which no product contributes more than 70 percent of total corporate sales.

5. Of course, the degree to which joint operation is more profitable than separate profit maximization will vary in each case. Some subsidiaries are run like quasi-independent concerns, and the relationship between parent and subsidiary is then very close to a market exchange.

6. When Ford of England offered to buy back the shares of its minority shareholders at 145 shillings a share, the market quotation was in the low 90s. The local shareholders that owned 40 percent of the stock thus made a capital gain of better than 50 percent (Kindleberger 1969, p. 30).

7. In Stopford and Wells's study, joint ventures with other foreign competitors and those with a large number of small local shareholders were excluded from the analysis. Subsidiaries in countries that severely limit ownership choices (Japan, Spain, Ceylon, India, Mexico, and Pakistan) were excluded. Wholly owned subsidiaries are subsidiaries in which the parent owns 95 to 100 percent of the equity, majority-owned are those in which the parent owns 51 to 94 percent, and minority-owned those in which the parent owns more than 5 percent but less than 50 percent of the subsidiary's equity (Stopford and Wells 1972, p. 100).

8. Thus Queensland Alumina Ltd., a company engaged in extracting bauxite in Australia, is jointly owned by American, Canadian, French, and British vertically integrated aluminum producers (Mikdashi 1974, p. 184). Swedish, Italian, Belgian, and American steelmakers had joined forces for an iron ore venture in Liberia (Stopford and Wells 1972, p. 117). Other joint ventures of the same type were active in crude oil, nonferrous metals, and paper.

9. Setting up all subsidiaries as independent units and letting markets coordinate their activities would solve this particular problem, as competition between subsidiaries would force them to specialize in products in which they have a comparative advantage and would eliminate the least efficient plants. However, in the type of firms we are considering, the output of each plant is specialized to the firm's other plants. As shown in chapter 3, market exchange between the units of the system would thus result in high bargaining costs and poor long-term coordination.

10. In 1973, for example, 57.6 percent of the exports of American subsidiaries and branches in the United Kingdom went to their parents or to other members of the parent system. The figure for other direct investors in the United Kingdom was 40.5 percent (Dunning 1976, p. 101).

11. In 1974, majority-owned manufacturing affiliates of American firms were exporting 37 percent of their production (Chung 1976, p. 28).

12. That difference in innovative performance is attributed by Franko and Vernon to differences in home market environments and in relative factor costs. High per capita incomes have led American firms to specialize in convenience products that save labor and are geared to high incomes, while the persistently higher cost of raw materials and land, relative to labor, in most European countries, and especially in France, Germany, Belgium and Italy, has biased the development effort of multinationals based in these countries toward ersatz products and raw-material-saving processes. In resource-rich Sweden and in free-trading Switzerland and Britain, the ratio of raw materials to labor costs was closer to that of the United States (Franko 1976, pp. 41–43).

13. Tsurumi (1976, p. 73) thus lists the principal product lines of the largest seventy-nine Japanese manufacturing subsidiaries abroad in 1972:

Product	Number of Subsidiaries
Electric and electronic appliances (electric fans and transistor radios)	25
Apparels, textile yarns, weaving and dyeing	19
Galvanized iron sheets, wire drawing and pipes	13
Knock-down assembly of trucks and passenger cars	9
Pulp, lumber, plywood	4
Nonferrous and iron ores pelletizing	3
Cement and sheet glass	2
Sewing machine assembly	1
Polyvinyl chloride	1
Aluminum fabrication	1
Vegetable oil	1

Tsurumi notes that the two most technology-intensive manufacturers of electric and electronic appliances—Sony Corporation and Sharp Corporation—did not have foreign manufacturing subsidiaries in January, 1971, and that neither did Fujitsu Limited, Japan's main computer firm (Tsurumi 1976, p. 73). Since then, all three companies seem to have committed themselves to foreign production: Sony Corporation has opened two wholly owned manufacturing subsidiaries in the United States and one in the United Kingdom. Fujitsu has acquired a minority ownership in two American companies and is planning a manufacturing plant in San Diego. Sharp is also planning a joint venture with Thorn-EMI in England and a plant in Malaysia.

Chapter 6

1. Mansfield (1981, p. 7) notes, for example, that American multinational firms would reduce their research and development expenditures by 20 percent if they were denied access to foreign markets, and by 12 to 15 percent if they had to exploit their innovations through licensing, export, and joint-ventures, instead of through their majority-owned foreign subsidiaries.

Selected References

Alchian, A. 1969. "Corporate Management and Property Rights." In *Economic Policy and the Regulation of Corporate Securities*, edited by Henri Manne. Washington, D.C.: American Enterprise Institute for Public Policy Research.

Alchian, A., and Allen, W. 1969. *Exchange and Production: Theory in Use*. Belmont, Calif.: Wadsworth Publishing Co.

Alchian, A., and Demsetz, H. 1972. "Production, Information Costs and Economic Organization." *American Economic Review* 62:777–95.

Aliber, R. 1970. "A Theory of Foreign Direct Investment." In *The International Corporation*, edited by C. Kindleberger. Cambridge, Mass.: MIT Press.

Allen, G. C. 1929. *The Industrial Development of Birmingham and the Black Country: 1860–1927*. London: Allen and Unwin.

Allen, T. 1964. *The Utilization of Information During R and D Proposal Preparation*. MIT Sloan School of Management Working Paper, no. 97-64. Cambridge, Mass.: MIT Sloan School of Management.

———. 1969. "The Differential Performance of Information Channels in the Transfer of Technology." In *Factors in the Transfer of Technology*, edited by William Gruber and Donald Marquis. Cambridge, Mass.: MIT Press.

Armour, H., and Teece, D. 1978. "Organizational Structure and Economic Performance: A Test of the Multidivisional Hypothesis." *Bell Journal of Economics*, Spring, pp. 106–22.

Arrow, K. 1962. "Economic Welfare and the Allocation of Resources for Invention." In *The Rate and Direction of Inventive Activity*, edited by Kenneth Arrow. Princeton: Princeton University Press.

———. 1969. "Classificatory Notes in the Production and Transmission of Economic Knowledge." *American Economic Review* 59:29–49.

———. 1974. *The Limits of Organization*. New York: W. W. Norton.

Ashton, T. S., and Sykes, J. 1929. *The Coal Industry in the Eighteenth Century*. University of Manchester Economic History Series. Manchester: Manchester University Press.

Baranson, J. 1969. *Industrial Technologies for Developing Economies*. New York: Praeger.

———. 1970. "Technology Transfer through the International Firm." *American Economic Review* 60:435–40.

183

Barlow, E. R., and Wender, I. T. 1955. *Foreign Investment and Taxation*. Englewood Cliffs, N.J.: Prentice Hall.

Bartlett, F. C. 1932. *Remembering*. Cambridge: At the University Press.

Bator, F. 1958. "The Anatomy of Market Failure." *Quarterly Journal of Economics* 72:351–79.

Belli, D.; Allnutt, S.; and Murad, H. 1973. "Property, Plant and Equipment Expenditures by Majority-Owned Foreign Affiliates of U.S. Companies." *Survey of Current Business* 53:19–32.

Belli, D., and Maley, L. 1974. "Sales by Majority-Owned Foreign Affiliates of U.S. Companies, 1966–1972." *Survey of Current Business* 54:25–40.

Berle, A., and Means, G. 1932. *The Modern Corporation and Private Property*. New York: Commerce Clearing House.

Berthoff, R. T. 1953. *British Immigrants in Industrial America, 1790–1900*. Cambridge, Mass.: Harvard University Press.

Bohlen, J., et al. 1961. *Adopters of New Farm Ideas*. North Central Regional Extension Publication, no. 13.

Boulding, K. 1966. "The Economics of Knowledge and the Knowledge of Economics." *American Economic Review* 58:1–13.

Brash, D. 1966. *American Investments in Australian Industry*. Cambridge: At the University Press.

———. 1972. "United States Investment in Australia, Canada and New Zealand." In *Direct Foreign Investment in Asia and the Pacific*, edited by Peter Drysdale. Toronto: University of Toronto Press.

Brooke, M., and Remmers, H. 1970. *The Strategy of Multinational Enterprise*. New York: American Elsevier Publishers.

Buchanan, J., and Tullock, G. 1962. *The Calculus of Consent*. Ann Arbor: University of Michigan Press.

Buckley, P., and Casson, M. 1976. *The Future of Multinational Enterprise*. London: Macmillan & Co.

Burck, C. 1976. "A Group Profile of the Fortune 500 Chief Executives." *Fortune* 94:173.

Buzzell, R. 1968. "Can You Standardize Multinational Marketing?" *Harvard Business Review* 46:102–13.

Canadian Department of Industry, Trade and Commerce. 1974. *Foreign Owned Subsidiaries in Canada*. Ottawa: Information Canada.

Casson, M. 1979. *Alternatives to the Multinational Enterprise*. London: Macmillan & Co.

Caves, R. E. 1971. "International Corporations: The Industrial Economics of Foreign Investment." *Economica* 38:1–27.

———. 1974. "Causes of Direct Investment: Foreign Firms' Shares in Canadian and United Kingdom Manufacturing Industries." *Review of Economic and Statistics* 61:279–93.

Caves, R. E., and Murphy, W. 1976. "Franchising: Firms, Markets and Intangible Assets." *Southern Economic Journal* 42:572–86.

Chandler, A. 1961. *Strategy and Structure*. New York: Doubleday & Co.

Chang, Y. S. 1971. *The Transfer of Technology: Economics of Offshore Assembly, the Case of the Semiconductor Industry.* New York: United Nations Institute for Training and Research.

Channon, D. F. 1973. *The Strategy and Structure of British Enterprise.* Boston: Division of Research, Harvard Business School.

Cheung, S. 1969. "Transaction Costs, Risk Aversion, and the Choice of Contractual Arrangements." *Journal of Law and Economics* 12:23–42.

———. 1973. "The Fable of the Bees: An Economic Investigation." *Journal of Law and Economics* 16:11–33.

Chung, W. K. 1976. "Sales of Majority-Owned Foreign Affiliates of U.S. Companies in 1974." *Survey of Current Business* 56:25–34.

———. 1979. "Capital Expenditures by Majority-Owned Affiliates of U.S. Companies in 1979." *Survey of Current Business* 59:32–37.

Chung, W. K., and Fouch, G. G. 1980. "Foreign Direct Investment in the United States in 1979." *Survey of Current Business* 60:38–51.

Coase, R. 1937. "The Nature of the Firm." *Economica* 5:386–405.

———. 1960. "The Problem of Social Cost." *Journal of Law and Economics* 3:1–44.

———. 1974. "The Lighthouse in Economics." *Journal of Law and Economics* 17:357–76.

Cohen, B. I. 1975. *Multinational Firms and Asian Exports.* New Haven and London: Yale University Press.

Coleman, D. C. 1958. *The British Paper Industry: 1495–1850.* Oxford: Clarendon Press.

Curhan, J.; Davidson, W.; and Suri, R., 1977. *Tracing the Multinationals.* Cambridge, Mass.: Ballinger Publishing.

De Alessi, L. 1980. "The Economics of Property Rights: A Review of the Evidence." In *Research in Law and Economics,* edited by R. Zerbe, vol. 2. Greenwich, Conn.: JAI Press.

Deane, R. 1970. *Foreign Investment in New Zealand Manufacturing.* London: Sweet and Maxwell.

Delapierre, M., and Michalet, C. A. 1976. *Les Implantations Etrangères en France.* Paris: Calmann-Levy.

Demsetz, H. 1964. "The Exchange and Enforcement of Property Rights." *Journal of Law and Economics* 7:11–26.

———. 1966. "Some Aspects of Property Rights." *Journal of Law and Economics* 9:61–70.

———. 1967. "Towards a Theory of Property Rights." *American Economic Review.* 57:347–59.

———. 1969. "Information and Efficiency." *Journal of Law and Economics* 12:1–22.

Diebold, J. 1968. "Is the Gap Technological?" *Foreign Affairs* 10:276–91.

Dubin, R. L. 1970. "Management in Britain-Impressions of a Visiting Professor." *Journal of Management Studies,* May, pp. 183–98.

Dunning, J. H. 1966. "U.S. Subsidiaries and their U.K. Competitors." *Business Ratios* 1

————. 1970. *Studies in International Investment.* London: Allen and Unwin.

————. 1971. "United States Foreign Investment and the Technological Gap." In *North American and Western Economic Policies,* edited by C. P. Kindleberger and A. Shonfield. London: Macmillan & Co.

————. 1973 "The Determinants of International Production." *Oxford Economic Papers* 25:289–336.

————. 1976. *United States Industry in Britain.* Economist Advisory Group Research Study. London: Wilton House.

Dyas, G., and Thanheiser, H. 1976. *The Emerging European Enterprise.* London: Macmillan & Co.

Eastman, H. C., and Stykolt, S. 1967. *The Tariff and Competition in Canada.* Toronto: Macmillan of Canada.

Enos, J. 1962. "Invention and Innovation in the Petroleum Refining Industry." In *The Rate and Direction of Inventive Activity,* edited by Kenneth Arrow. Princeton: Princeton University Press.

"Europe's Rich Market for Advice: American Preferred." 1969. *Fortune* 87:128.

Fama, E. 1980. "Agency Problems and the Theory of the Firm." *Journal of Political Economy* 88:288–307.

"Fast Food Franchisors Squeeze Out the Little Guy." *Business Week,* May 31, 1976, p. 47.

"The Fast Food Stars: Three Strategies for Fast Growth." *Business Week,* July 11, 1977, pp. 56–68.

Franko, L. G. 1974. "The Move Toward a Multidivisional Structure in European Organizations." *Administrative Science Quarterly* 19:493–506.

————. 1976. *The European Multinationals.* Stamford, Conn.: Greylock Publishers.

Freidlin, J. N., and Lupo, L. A. 1974. "U. S. Direct Investment Abroad in 1973." *Survey of Current Business* 54:10–24.

Furubotn, E., and Pejovich, S. 1972. "Property Rights and Economic Theory: A Survey of the Recent Literature." *Journal of Economic Literature* 10:1137–62.

————. 1974. *The Economics of Property Rights.* Cambridge, Mass.: Ballinger Publishing.

Granick, D. 1972. *Managerial Comparisons of Four Developed Countries: France, Britain, United States and Russia.* Cambridge, Mass.: MIT Press.

"The Graying of the Soft Drink Industry." *Business Week,* May 23, 1977, p. 70.

Gruber, W.; Mehta, D.; and Vernon, R. 1967. "The R&D Factor in International Trade and International Investment of United States Industries." *Journal of Political Economy* 75:20–37.

Hall, C. 1977. "Selling Ideas." MS.

Hamberg, D. 1963. "Invention in the Industrial Laboratory," *Journal of Political Economy* 71:95–116.

Hayek, F. 1945. "The Use of Knowledge in Society." *American Economic Review* 35:519–30.

Henderson, W. 1965. *Britain and Industrial Europe 1750–1870.* Leicester: Leicester University Press.

"Hertz Turns Around in Europe." *Business Week,* September 6, 1976, p. 83.

Hicks, J. 1969. *A Theory of Economic History.* Oxford: Oxford University Press.

Hood, N., and Young, S. 1979. *The Economics of Multinational Enterprise.* London: Longman Group.

Horst, T. 1972*a.* "The Industrial Composition of U.S. Exports and Subsidiary Sales to the Canadian Market." *American Economic Review* 62:37–45.

———. 1972*b.* "Firm and Industry Determinants of the Decision to Invest Abroad: An Empirical Study." *Review of Economics and Statistics* 54:258–66.

Hughes, J. R. T. 1970. *Industrialization and Economic History.* New York: McGraw-Hill.

Hymer, S. 1970. "The Efficiency (Contradictions) of Multinational Corporations." *American Economic Review* 60:441–48.

———. 1972. "United States Investment Abroad." In *Direct Foreign Investment in Asia and the Pacific,* edited by Peter Drysdale. Toronto: University of Toronto Press.

———. 1976. *The International Operations of National Firms: A Study of Direct Investment.* Cambridge, Mass.: MIT Press.

Hymer, S., and Rowthorn, R. 1970. "Multinational Corporations and International Oligopoly: The Non-American Challenge." In *The International Corporation,* edited by Charles Kindleberger. Cambridge, Mass.: MIT Press.

Jack, A. 1957. "The Channels of Distribution for an Innovation: The Sewing Machine Industry in America, 1860–1865." *Explorations in Entrepreneurial History* 10:113–41.

Jacquillat, B., and Solnik, B. 1978. "Multinationals Are Poor Tools for Diversification." *Journal of Portfolio Management 4* (Winter):8–12.

Jensen, H., and Meckling, W. 1976. "Theory of the Firm: Managerial Behavior, Agency Costs and Ownership Structure." *Journal of Financial Economics* 3:305–60.

Jewkes, J.; Sawers, D.; and Stillerman, R. 1959. *The Sources of Invention.* New York: St. Martin's Press.

Johnson, H. G. 1970. "The Efficiency and Welfare Implications of the Multinational Corporation." In *The International Corporation,* edited by Charles Kindleberger. Cambridge, Mass.: MIT Press.

Kindleberger, C. 1969. *American Business Abroad.* New Haven, Conn.: Yale University Press.

Kitch, E. 1977. "The Nature and Function of the Patent System." *Journal of Law and Economics* 20:265–90.

Knickerbocker, F. 1976. *Market Structure and Market Power Consequences of Foreign Direct Investment by Multinational Corporations.* Washington, D.C.: Center for Multinational Studies.

Koslow, R.; Rutter, T.; and Walker, P. "U.S. Direct Investment Abroad in 1977." *Survey of Current Business* 58:16–22.

Koszul, J. P. 1970. "American Banks in Europe." In *The International Corporation,* edited by Charles Kindleberger. Cambridge, Mass.: MIT Press.

Kwack, S. Y. 1972. "A Model of U.S. Direct Investment Abroad: a Neoclassical Approach." *Western Economic Journal* 10:376–83.

Lancaster, K. 1966. "A New Approach to Consumer Theory." *Journal of Political Economy* 75:132–57.

Landes, D. 1969. *The Unbound Prometheus.* Cambridge: At the University Press.

Langrish, J.; Gibbons, M.; Evans, W. G.; and Jevons, F. R. 1972. *Wealth from Knowledge.* London: Macmillan & Co.

Leftwich, R. 1974. "Foreign Direct Investment in the United States in 1973." *Survey of Current Business* 54:7–9.

Leibenstein, H. 1966. "Allocative Efficiency vs. 'X-Efficiency'." *American Economic Review* 56:392–415.

Levitt, T. 1968. "The Gap Is not Technological." *Public Interest* 12:119–29.

———. 1976. "Management and the Post-Industrial Society." *Public Interest* 43:69–103.

Levy, H., and Sarnat, M. 1970. "International Diversification of Investment Portfolios." *American Economic Review* 60:668–75.

Lowe, J. H. 1981. "Capital Expenditures by Majority-Owned Affiliates of U.S. Companies." *Survey of Current Business* 61:34–39.

McManus, J. C. 1972. "The Theory of the International Firm." In *The Multinational Firm and the Nation State,* edited by Gilles Paquet. Don Mills, Ont.: Collier Macmillan Canada.

———. 1975. "The Cost of Alternative Economic Organizations." *Canadian Journal of Economics* 75:334–50.

McNulty, N. 1975. "European Management Education Comes of Age." *Conference Board Record* 21:38–43.

Magee, S. 1977. "Information and the Multinational Corporation: An Appropriability Theory of Foreign Direct Investment." In *The New International Economic Order,* edited by J. Bhagwati. Cambridge, Mass.: MIT Press.

Malmgren, H. B. 1961. "Information, Expectations and the Theory of the Firm." *Quarterly Journal of Economics* 75:399–421.

Mansfield, E. 1968. *The Economics of Technological Change.* New York: W. W. Norton.

———. 1981. "International Technology Transfer: Rates, Benefits, Costs, and Public Policy." Paper presented at the annual convention of the American Economic Association, December 28–30, Washington D.C.

Mansfield, E.; Rapoport, J.; Schnee, J.; Wagner, S.; and Hamburger, M.

1971. *Research and Innovation in the Modern Corporation.* New York: W. W. Norton.

Mantel, I. M. 1975. "Sources and Uses of Funds for a Sample of Majority-Owned Foreign Affiliates of U.S. Companies, 1966–72." *Survey of Current Business* 55:29–52.

March, J. G., and Simon, H. A. 1958. *Organizations.* New York: John Wiley and Sons.

Markowitz, H. 1959. *Portfolio Selection: Efficient Diversification of Investment.* New York: John Wiley and Sons.

Marris, R. 1967. *The Economic Theory of "Managerial" Capitalism.* London: Macmillan & Co.

Meade, J. E. 1970. *The Theory of Indicative Planning.* Manchester: Manchester University Press.

Meier, G. 1970. *Leading Issues in Economic Development.* 2d ed. Oxford: Oxford University Press.

Mellors, J. 1973. "International Tax Differentials and the Location of Overseas Direct Investment: A Pilot Study." University of Reading Research Paper on International Investment and Business, number 4. Reading: University of Reading.

Mikdashi, Z. 1974. "Aluminum." In *Big Business and the State: Changing Relations in Western Europe,* edited by Raymond Vernon. Cambridge, Mass.: Harvard University Press.

Moore, R. 1969. "The Role of Extrazonally Controlled Multinational Corporations in the Process of Establishing a Latin American Automobile Industry: a Case Study of Brazil." Ph.D. dissertation, Fletcher School of Law and Diplomacy, Tufts University.

Moxon, R. W. 1976. "The Cost, Conditions, and Adaptation of MNC Technology in Developing Countries." Paper presented at the Conference on Economic Issues of Multinational Firms, November 4–5, 1976, at New York University. Mimeographed.

Mueller, W. 1962. "The Origins of the Basic Inventions Underlying du Pont's Major Product and Process Innovations, 1920 to 1950." In *The Rate and Direction of Inventive Activity,* edited by Kenneth Arrow. Princeton: Princeton University Press.

Myers, S. 1968. "Industrial Innovations and the Utilization of Research Output." National Planning Association. Quoted in Edwin Mansfield, *The Economics of Technological Change,* p. 127. New York: W. W. Norton.

National Science Foundation. 1974. *Research and Development in Industry.* Washington, D.C.: National Science Foundation.

———. 1976. *Research and Development Industry–1974.* Washington, D.C.: National Science Foundation.

Nicholas, S. Forthcoming. "British Multinational Investment before 1939." *Journal of European Economic History.*

Nieckels, L. 1976. *Transfer Pricing in Multinational Firms.* New York: John Wiley and Sons.

North, D., and Thomas, R. 1973. *The Rise of the Western World.* Cambridge: At the University Press.

Olson, M., Jr. 1964. "Economic Growth and Structural Change." Paper delivered at the Annual Meeting of the Midwestern Economic Association, April 17, 1964, in Chicago. Mimeographed.

———. 1965. "Some Social and Political Implications of Economic Development." *World Politics* 17:526–54.

Parker, H. 1967. "Can British Management Close the Gap?" *McKinsey Quarterly,* Summer, pp. 38–44.

———. 1968. "Government Regulation: Tampering with the Mainspring." *McKinsey Quarterly,* Winter, pp. 10–13.

Parker, J. E. S. 1974. *The Economics of Innovation.* London: Longman Group.

Pavitt, K. 1971*a*. "The Multinational Enterprise and the Transfer of Technology." In *The Multinational Enterprise,* edited by John Dunning. New York: Praeger Publishers.

———. 1971*b*. *The Conditions for Success in Technological Innovations.* Paris: Organization for Economic Cooperation and Development.

Payne, P. L. 1967. "The Emergence of the Large Scale Company in Great Britain, 1870–1914." *Economic History Review* 37:519–42.

Pejovich, S. 1971. "Towards a General Theory of Property Rights." *Zeitschrift fuer Nationaloekonomie* 31:141–55.

Pelz, D., and Andrews, F. 1966. *Scientists in Organizations: Productive Climates for Research and Development.* New York: John Wiley and Sons.

Pizer, S., and Cutler, F. 1962. "Expansion in U.S. Investments Abroad." *Survey of Current Business* 42:18–25.

Pollard, S. 1965. *The Genesis of Modern Management.* Cambridge, Mass.: Harvard University Press.

Porter, M. 1974. "Consumer Behavior, Retailer Power and Market Performance in Consumer Goods Industries." *Review of Economics and Statistics* 54:419–36.

Prachowny, M. J. 1972. "Direct Investment and the Balance of Payments of the U.S.: A Portfolio Approach." In *International Mobility and Movement of Capital,* edited by F. Machlup, W. Salant, and L. Tarshis. New York: National Bureau of Economic Research.

Price, W., and Bass, L. 1969. "Scientific Research and the Innovation Process." *Science* 164:802–6.

"Radio Shack's Rough Trip." *Business Week,* May 30, 1977, p. 55.

Ragazzi, G. 1973. "Theories of the Determinants of Direct Foreign Investment." *International Monetary Fund Staff Papers* 20:471–98.

Reuber, G., and Roseman, F. 1969. *The Takeover of Canadian Firms, 1945–61: An Empirical Analysis.* Ottawa: Queens Printer.

Robbins, S., and Stobaugh, R. 1973. *Money in the Multinational Enterprise.* New York: Basic Books.

Rogers, E. M., and Shoemaker, F. 1971. *Communication of Innovations: A Cross Cultural Approach.* New York: Free Press.

Rowthorn, R. 1971. *International Big Business, 1957–1967.* Cambridge: At the University Press.

Safarian, A. E. 1966. *Foreign Ownership of Canadian Industry.* Toronto: McGraw-Hill.

Schelling, T. 1971. "On the Ecology of Micromotives." *Public Interest* 25:61–98.

Scherer, F. M. 1970. *Industrial Market Structure and Economic Performance.* Chicago: Rand McNally.

Schmookler, J. 1957. "Inventors Past and Present." *Review of Economics and Statistics* 39:321–33.

Scholl, R. B. 1972. "The International Investment Position of the United States: Developments in 1971." *Survey of Current Business* 52:18–23.

———. 1975. "The International Investment Position of the United States: Development in 1974." *Survey of Current Business* 55:30–35.

Schon, D. A. 1967. *Technology and Change.* New York: Delacorte Press.

Science Policy Research Unit. 1971. *On the Shelf: A Survey of Industrial R and D Projects Abandoned for Non-Technical Reasons.* Brighton: University of Sussex, Centre for the Study of Industrial Innovation.

———. 1972. *Success and Failure in Industrial Innovation: Report on Project SAPPHO.* Brighton: University of Sussex, Centre for the Study of Industrial Innovation.

Scitovski, T. 1954. "Two Concepts of External Economies." *Journal of Political Economy* 17:143–51.

Seiler, R. 1965. *Improving the Effectiveness of Research and Development.* New York: McGraw-Hill.

Servan-Schreiber, J-J. 1968. *The American Challenge.* London: Hamish Hamilton.

Shelton, J. 1967. "Allocative Efficiency vs. 'X-Efficiency': Comment." *American Economic Review* 57:1252–58.

Shilling, C. W., and Bernard, J. 1964. *Informal Communication Among Bioscientists.* George Washington University Biological Sciences Communication Project Report, number 16A. Washington, D.C.: George Washington University.

Solnik, B. 1973. "Note on the Validity of the Random Walk for European Stock Prices." *Journal of Finance* 28:1151–59.

Steuer, M. D.; Abell, Peter; Gennard, John; Perlman, Morris; Rees, Raymond; Scott, Barry; and Wallis, Ken. 1973. *The Impact of Foreign Direct Investment on the United Kingdom.* London: Her Majesty's Stationery Office.

Stevens, G. V. G. 1969. "Fixed Investment Expenditures of Foreign Manufacturing Affiliates of U.S. Firms: Theoretical Models and Empirical Evidence." *Yale Economic Essays* 9:137–98.

Stigler, G. 1951. "The Division of Labor Is Limited by the Extent of the Market." *Journal of Political Economy* 51:185–93.

———. 1961. "The Economics of Information." *Journal of Political Economy* 61:213–25.

Stonehill, A. I. 1965. *Foreign Ownership of Norwegian Enterprise.* Oslo: Central Bureau of Statistics.

Stopford, J. M., and Wells, L. T., Jr. 1972. *Managing the Multinational Enterprise.* New York: Basic Books.

Strassman, W. P. 1968. *Technological Change and Economic Development.* Ithaca, N.Y.: Cornell University Press.

Svennilson, I. 1965. "The Transfer of Industrial Know-how to Non-industrialized Countries." In *Economic Development with Special Reference to East Asia,* edited by K. Berrill. London: Macmillan & Co.

Swedenborg, B. 1979. *The Multinational Operations of Swedish Firms.* Stockholm: Almqvist and Wicksell.

Taylor, A. J. 1960. "The Subcontract System in the British Coal Industry." In *Studies in the Industrial Revolution: Essays Presented to T. S. Ashton,* edited by L. S. Pressnell. London: Athlone Press.

Teplin, M. F. 1973. "U.S. International Transactions in Royalties and Fees: Their Relationship to the Transfer of Technology." *Survey of Current Business* 53:14–18.

Thompson, D. 1971. *Franchise Operations and Antitrust.* Lexington, Mass.: D. C. Heath and Co.

Tobin, J. 1958. "Liquidity Preference as Behavior Towards Risk." *Review of Economic and Statistics* 25:65–86.

Tsurumi, Y. 1976. *The Japanese Are Coming.* Cambridge, Mass.: Ballinger Publishing.

Tugendhat, C. 1972. *The Multinationals.* New York: Random House. United Kingdom Board of Trade. 1968. *Board of Trade Journal,* August 16.

United Nations, Department of Economic and Social Affairs. 1973. *Multinational Corporations in World Development* (ST/ECA/190). New York: United Nations.

———. 1978. *Transnational Corporations in World Development: A Reexamination* (E/C. 10/38.) New York: United Nations.

United Nations Conference on Trade and Development. 1974. *Restrictive Business Practices in Relation to the Trade and Development of Developing Countries.* (TD/B/C.2/119/Rev. 1). New York: United Nations.

———. 1975. *The Role of the Patent System in the Transfer of Technology to Developing Countries* (70/B/AC. 11/19/Rev. 1). New York: United Nations.

U.S., Department of Commerce, Bureau of the Census. 1963. *U.S. Census of Population, 1960: Occupation by Industry.* Washington, D.C.: Government Printing Office.

———. 1972. *Enterprise Statistics: 1967, Part I.* Washington, D.C.: Government Printing Office.

U.S., Department of Commerce, Bureau of Economic Analysis. 1975 *U.S. Investment Abroad, 1966, Final Data.* Washington, D.C.: Government Printing Office.

———. 1976a. *Foreign Direct Investment in the United States.* 9 vols. Washington, D.C.: Government Printing Office.

―――. 1976*b*. Data on international payment and receipts of royalties and fees. Mimeographed.

U.S., Department of the Interior, Bureau of Mines. 1975. *Minerals Yearbook—1973,* vol. 1. Washington, D.C.: Government Printing Office.

U.S., Tariff Commission. 1973. *Implications of Multinational Firms for World Trade and Investment and for U.S. Trade and Labor.* Washington, D.C.: Government Printing Office.

Utton, M. A. 1977. "Large Firm Diversification in British Manufacturing Industry." *Economic Journal* 87:96–113.

Uyterhoeven, H. 1963. "Foreign Entry and Joint Ventures." Ph.D. dissertation, Harvard University.

Vaupel J. 1971. "Characteristics and Motivations of the U.S. Corporations which Manufacture Abroad." Paper presented to a meeting of the Atlantic Institute, June, 1964, in Paris.

Vaupel, L., and Curhan, J. 1973. *The World's Multinational Enterprises: A Sourcebook of Tables.* Boston: Division of Research, Harvard Business School.

Vernon, R. 1966. "International Investment and International Trade in the Product Cycle." *Quarterly Journal of Economics* 80:190–207.

―――. 1971. *Sovereignty at Bay.* New York: Basic Books.

―――. 1977. *Storm Over the Multinationals.* Cambridge, Mass.: Harvard University Press.

Vernon, R., ed. 1974. *Big Business and the State: Changing Relations in Western Europe.* Cambridge, Mass.: Harvard University Press.

Ward, J. 1973. "Product and Promotion Adaptation by Foreign Firms in the United States." *Journal of International Business Studies* 3:25–26.

Watkins, M. 1968. *Foreign Ownership and the Structure of Canadian Industry.* Ottawa: Queens Printer.

Whichard, O. G. 1979. "U.S. Direct Investment Abroad in 1978." *Survey of Current Business* 59:15–37. (pt 1.)

―――. 1980. "U.S. Direct Investment Abroad in 1979." *Survey of Current Business* 60:16–37.

―――. 1981*a*. "Trends in U.S. Direct Investment Position Abroad, 1950–1979." *Survey of Current Business* 61:30–56.

―――. 1981*b*. "U.S. Direct Investment Abroad in 1980." *Survey of Current Business* 61:20–37.

Whichard, O. G., and Freidlin, J. N. 1976. "U.S. Direct Investment Abroad in 1975." *Survey of Current Business* 56:40–60.

Wilkins, M. 1970. *The Emergence of Multinational Enterprise.* Cambridge, Mass.: Harvard University Press.

―――. 1974. *The Maturing of Multinational Enterprise.* Cambridge, Mass.: Harvard University Press.

―――. 1977. "Modern European Economic History and the Multinationals." *Journal of European Economic History* 6:575–95.

Williamson, O. E. 1970. *Corporate Control and Business Behavior.* Englewood Cliffs, N.J.: Prentice-Hall.

————. 1975. *Markets and Hierarchies: Analysis and Antitrust Implications.* New York: Free Press.

Wood, A. 1971. "Diversification, Mergers and Research Expenditures: A Review of Empirical Studies." In *The Corporate Economy,* edited by Robin Marris and Adrian Wood. Cambridge, Mass.: Harvard University Press.

World Bank. 1978. *World Bank Atlas.* Washington, D.C.: World Bank.

Yoshino, M. Y. 1976. *Japan's Multinational Enterprises.* Cambridge, Mass.: Harvard University Press.

Index

costs, 134–40; main features, 69; as portfolio diversification, 6–17, 166; product cycle theory of, 131–34, 167, 170; and product differentiation, 167; and sales maximization, 63–69; source countries, 20, 70, 130, 133; and technology transfer, 3–4; in the U.S., 20, 118–21. *See also* Multinational enterprise

Foreignness, cost of, 1–2, 24, 62, 97, 177n

Foreign Ownership and the Structure of Canadian Industry (Watkins), 172

France, 18, 74, 144–47, 158

Franchising: automobile rental, 179n; in distribution, 84–86, 178n; efficiency of, 179n; fast-food restaurants, 59, 85, 92; and goodwill, 90–92; international, 24, 90–92. *See also* Contracts; Licensing; Royalties

Franko, L., 147, 161, 181n

Fujitsu, Ltd., 78, 182n

Functional structure. *See* Unitary structure

General Electric Company, 68

General Motors Corporation, 55, 85

Germany, West: foreign direct investments, 18, 20, 133; management in, 145–48; ownership of subsidiaries, 74; royalty and fee receipts, 138–40

Gibbons, M., 96

Goodwill, 8, 76, 80–83, 90–92

Gort, M., 66

Granick, D., 143–45

Gruber, W., 76, 116

Hamberg, D., 116

Harvard Multinational Enterprise Project, 13, 69–70

Hayek, F., 44

Hertz, 179n

Hicks, J., 48

Hierarchies. *See* Firms

Holdings, 145

Holiday Inns, Inc., 24

Horizontal expansion: and goodwill, 89–93; and knowledge, 93–121

Horst, T. 76

Hymer, S., 5, 23, 76–79, 151–52

Imperialism and foreign direct investment, 18–19

India, 172–73, 181n

Information transfer: in firms, 31, 41–42, 44–45, 51–56; in markets, 30. *See also* Control of loss

Innovation: adoption of, 98; in Europe and Japan, 163, 181n; lag between invention and, 104; legal, 46–50, 58, 129, 180n; organizational, 46, 141; process of, 94–97; in the U.S., 19–20, 131. *See also* Knowledge transfer; Multidivisional structure; Patent system; Product cycle; Research and development

Internalization: of customs duties, 62–63; in firms and markets, 28–61; of goodwill spillovers, 89–93; of knowledge, 93–122, 151, 171, 182n; McManus's theory of, 25–27; and ownership of subsidiaries, 150–65, 171–73; of pecuniary and nonpecuniary externalities, 77–79; and vertical integration, 79–89

Internal organization costs, 31, 46, 167–68; changes in, 168–69; and geographical dispersion, 44, 66, 84–85, 91, 178n; international differences in, 140–50; and observation of behavior, 44. *See also* Control of loss; Firm size; Management; Shirking

International Business Machines, 172–73